T0245539

THE SHRINE THIEF

THE SHRINE THIEF

Finding Wisdom
in a Life of Music

A MEMOIR

W. A. Mathieu

Terra Nova Press
NEWARK   CALLICOON   MATSALU

2024

Library of Congress Control Number: 2023931791

ISBN: 978-1-949597-29-5

published by:

Terra Nova Press
NEWARK   CALLICOON   MATSALU

Publisher: David Rothenberg
Editor-in-Chief: Evan Eisenberg
Proofreader: Tyran Grillo
Book design: Martin Pedanik
Set in Marion and Gotham

Printed by Tallinn Book Printers, Tallinn, Estonia

First Printing

www.terranovapress.com

Distributed by the MIT Press, Cambridge, Massachusetts
and London, England

You think you are the teacher and find you are the taught.
You think you are the seeker and find you are the sought.

— Murshid Sam Lewis

Table of Contents

Preface
A Visit to the Shrine

I live with my wife, Devi, an hour north of San Francisco on a country road, a gently curving two-lane blacktop that runs along the floor of a valley in hilly land. The road is lined with overarching oak, willow, buckeye, and eucalyptus trees mixed with clustered stands of California bay laurel, known a few hundred miles north as Oregon myrtle. Except for a brief rush hour, barely twenty cars pass through the valley every hour. Cows graze in the pastures. A few of the houses survive from the late 1800s; most were built early and mid-19th century—ours in 1950. Some are old and worn. Others are country modern. By county law, no parcel may be less than five acres; most are quite large, and there are a few ranches of a hundred acres or more. There are long, white stretches of fencing that remind me of Kentucky horse farms.

I take a walk along this road every day I can. Sometimes with Devi, often alone, I walk a mile west and a mile back. When I was younger, I'd go on a ways to climb the steep 600-foot hill that crests as a plateau from which you can glimpse the Pacific Ocean five miles farther west, glimmering through the trees. Not for me these days—a mile out and a mile back is pushing it a bit. I've done some version of this for forty years and counting.

It's all I can do to balance myself on the sometimes-narrow shoulder, crossing and recrossing the road to avoid the precipitous drop-offs or perilous ditches, facing traffic when possible, and listening like an owl so as to avoid an untimely death. I've learned the weave of this. It is *my* road.

About a quarter-mile west of my house, one comes to a steep rise that would have been a lot steeper if a road cut had not been fashioned there, exposing about four vertical feet of rock on either side. This is a spot where the beautiful white-board fences line the road and gently follow its contour on both sides. The road narrows here, but on the right one can walk up a slender, rocky path that rises, fence and all, well above the road. At its high point, there is a little plateau beside a stripling oak where Devi and I often hang out before moving on. When we were young partners forty-five years ago, we'd climb like kids onto the fence's bottom board and lean out toward the forest sloping down to the creek, invisible far below. After five years of living and loving together, often mentioning marriage, I said, one bright November day as we were leaning out looking at the green, "Let's get married." Instantly, she replied, "When?" which I took to be an affirmative. So we set an April date and, at this writing, are going on thirty-five years of ascent into the golden years. Since the spot by the fence beside the young oak felt so special, it deserved a special name: Marital Heights. But then Devi, to include the myrtle trees, suggested Myrital Heights, and such has the name remained ever after.

In 1968, years before I met Devi, I met a Sufi holy man who would swerve me toward a more meaningful inner and outer life. This was Sam Lewis, known now generally as Sufi Sam, although we all called him simply Murshid, a Persian word meaning high teacher. He was a short, bearded mystic, world traveler, initiate of several spiritual lineages, and scholar of many more. He was energetically intelligent and had equal capacity for righteous anger and all-encompassing love. He was the first adult to truly recognize me, to acknowledge both my spiritual youth and my mature artistic gifts. With his blessing, I gathered together the more musical of the singers around him and, with their enthusiastic collaboration, wrote a library of choral settings of sacred texts and poetry—music of suffering, joy, gratitude, and praise. We thrived, recorded many albums, played gigs on both coasts, and illumined the hearts of our listeners. Five years previously I'd been a well-trained atonal composer struggling to render academic cant into meaningful emotional narratives. Murshid saw what I needed well before I did, and guided me onward. Many dozens of his followers can tell their own version of this story and still, over fifty years after his death, through his teachings and successors, so can many thousands more. He died in early 1971. Once I got over my fury at his dying on us, I constantly sought to realize in my outer life the guidance I had internalized while he was alive.

The long white boards of the fencing along my road are hammered onto 3½" square posts set about eight feet apart. One day, quite near the summit of Myrital Heights, I found under my feet a huge lump of white quartz. When I picked it up, it fit perfectly into my hand, and when I lifted its concave side to my forehead, its coolness was a stone's gift. Instantly I planted the quartz atop the summit fence post. It balanced perfectly. It seemed to me to honor Murshid Sam, my private little shrine to his living presence.

I love rocks to the point of obsession. I visited many a rock shop when they used to dot the roadsides of the western landscape. Out here in our valley, I discovered that every spring, the rains churned the creeks in such a way that magic stones would appear on the shallow bottoms. I would pick up as many as I could carry home and arrange them all over our gardens and grounds. On my way home, I might balance one of the smaller ones up against the top edge of one of the three fence boards of the shrine, wedging them against the summit post. Soon there arose a lovely design of colorful creek rocks, lateral white boards, and a stout post, all topped with a quartz forehead-stone: a proper earthly shrine for an honored teacher of the spirit.

On my walks, I would check out the shrine stones, rescue the windblown or rainswept ones, rearrange and adjust, always a little differently. Maybe I'd replace a rock or two with a new treasure. I made certain to ask permission of the property owners, an architect and his artist wife. They gave their blessing. One day, I noticed that someone had left some flowers there, artfully arranged. Another day, a new rock; once, a small bundle of long-stemmed oat grass woven through the design. Someone had discovered my secret! Maybe several people. It made me glad.

And occasionally I would climb the path and press the quartz coolness to my forehead, and an image of Murshid would appear, floating in an ethereal space. Sometimes he would be dancing his Krishna dance whilst playing a mimed flute; sometimes he would be dressed in beautiful rust-red robes, arms outstretched, spinning a dervish spin, intoning the syllable *Hu*. I'm not a mantra person, but this one is personal. Its meaning, if it has one, represents the sound of the universe itself, the Ur sound, the sound of all sound. It is made by pushing the lips forward as if to whistle, and slowly blowing out the refined *ooo* phoneme on the breath. It is one of the few practices that has sustained me through my life, and right this moment, there spins Murshid modeling it for me.

At other times I would just hear Murshid's rough voice, saying *watch your breath* or *do the sun-walk*. Other times he would just sort of appear and disappear. I knew these cool quartz apparitions were not some woo-woo message from the dead. I don't do woo-woo. I did know they were aspects of Murshid's guidance, aspects I was allowing my intuition to show me in figurative form. And they were comforting. After twenty seconds or so, something said *enough*, and I would replace my vision-stone securely back on its perch and do my best to navigate down the rocky path so as not to propel my freshly illumined bod onto the roadbed.

About six years ago, I went through a period of dark grief and flaming fury. The pain of loss was so acute that I felt I was losing control of my mind. I could still teach, and music was still pouring out as it always has, but I could scarcely sleep. Alone during the day, I wept and screamed in exhausting alternation. As a beggar for guidance, I visited Murshid's shrine often, and he appeared palpably on demand, sanctifying my grieving space by his mere presence. Usually he would give me a practice: *there is only this breath*, or *feel the hollow warmth of your chest*, or *stand tall*. After three years, I was getting clear of the murk, and my world had changed. I began to see my life as a gift to share for the benefit of others. I began to own my talents and abilities and give them willingly, to give Devi the pure love she deserved for supporting me through this terrible time. And I began to think seriously about prying my life away from my musical works sufficiently to write the book—this very book—that I knew I had to write.

As I began to feel stronger and lighter than I ever had, Murshid began to play hide-and-seek. I would wonder why he wouldn't show up at my quartz prompt. Was there a lesson in this? Next time he showed up, he said, "Leave me be. You don't need me anymore." I had to ponder this. Yes, it was true; many initiates of Murshid were becoming Murshids in their own right. I am not big on titles or degrees of initiation—everyone is to be honored for what they have— but I do know that age and experience matter.

Murshid did return in vision a few times and gave me more guidance, but in a form more and more veiled: a faceless whirling robe, a heart-field with only feeling for content, a moment of deep peace. Okay, I'd think as I put the quartz back on its post, maybe it's time to look seriously at this, to accept without pride whatever mastery I had developed. That's not so easy to do.

Meanwhile, this book, maybe my last, was coming more and more into daily life. The problem was that I wanted to put everything in it—pages and pages of unpublished writing, journal entries, a life of letters exchanged with my father (who was also a writer), a sheaf of poems, essays about music, about being alive through music, about being alive. I had long lists of titles—standalone titles begging to be essays—and profiles of the teachers who have shaped my life and work. At the same time, I wanted to toss most of it forever. But I didn't know how to do that, how to fashion a memoir of a musical life into a book anyone would want to read. I am a member of the group Virginia Woolf called "the authentically obscure," those whose obscurity is hard-won. Who would choose to read that?

On my daily walks, Murshid began predictably to not appear. When he did show up, he presented as totally neutral. Then, for a while, nothing, and I'd be an old man standing by a roadside fence holding a stone to his head. Slowly I did begin to own the responsibilities of being a master teacher. My teaching took a leap, and so did my enjoyment of it. I taught music, but lessons became more and more about self-knowing and realization in the world. Zen master Nyogen Senzaki said that wisdom is like drizzle: At first, you hardly notice it's raining until you realize you are soaked through. It is okay to acknowledge such a development without fear. It is necessary. There were many months of testing this, of accepting the trajectory of my life toward mastery without self-inflation.

One bright day, nostalgic with Murshid-love, I approached the shrine thinking whatever happens is fine by me. Something did happen: All the rocks were gone! Gone! The fence shrine was a bare fence, bright white in the sun. I thought the stones had fallen, or someone had brushed them away. I looked all over the ground. Not there. Were they tossed into the woods beyond the fence? No trace. Across the road? Someone had carried off my precious creek rocks, undone my shrine. Who would do such a thing? Who could? What was the lesson here? The mystery of it made me stand quite still. Then suddenly I was very happy, a rush of light from inside out. I was weightless, empty. In the next beat, my book—this book—fell into place with an audible click. I could see the entire scheme, the rubric under which all the material would organize itself, and whatever did not belong would toss itself away. The shrine thief had given me the greatest gift I could receive: I was free of the shrine. This shrine or any other one, free from any symbol of realization, wholly in the present where no sign is needed, no affirming names or forms are necessary, no x marking the spot, only the streaming present. All homage to the Shrine Thief of Myrital Heights, whoever you may be! Lift high your stones! Long live the Shrine Thief!

As far as this book was concerned, I now had the title and the confidence that things would take shape as I went along. The theme would be the nature of transmission—how wisdom passes through transparent beings, how we recognize it, where it goes, and what it does. Teachers and teaching would be a narrative thread, from parents to grave, and music itself shown to be a chalice for the lessons I've learned and passed on. For a wild moment, I thought I would build a shrine to the Shrine Thief, but then I realized no, it was time to begin.

PART ONE

1

The Expanding Present

I

I am standing by myself on a newly cut lawn in the early morning sun. The refracted rainbows of the dew fill my senses, radiating light from every cell of my two-year-old boy body. I am the dewdrops and the sun that shines through them. I am the light itself. I am Dew God.

This is my earliest memory. It comes to mind frequently, and when it does, I can experience the effulgence from the inside while simultaneously, from the outside, witnessing the boy who is experiencing his lit self. Before that morning, I seem to have no memories—I draw a blank. After it, my life unscrolls turn by turn. I am living that life now and witnessing it, too, subject and object at once.

The Dew God lives outside of time. There is no need for past or future. My sister Sue was six at the time, and we were close, but I didn't see her as a model of someone older than me. There was no future me. And aside from expectations arising from daily patterns, there was no past me, either. As I'm writing now, I'm at the far end of my allotment of years trying to imagine how it could be that when I'm well gone, the world will still be aborning. And like millions of other gaping-brained mystics, I'm wondering the same thing about the worlds before this world, an unknowable no-thing—glitter down the deepest well. Before this extant universe, there is an unknowable no-thing, followed by fourteen billion years of existential history in which we abide, followed by an unknowable no-thing. That balances itself against my singular life: an unknowable no-thing, then my allotted decades of self-awareness plus some imagined personal future, followed by an unknowable no-thing. Yet somehow these strangely parallel time frames at widely different scales—the universe's and ours as individuals—do not seem unbalanced. To me, they seem balanced, and fair.

As I've grown, the sense of past and future has gradually expanded from Dew God's eternal present into time measurable by a clock. The joke: the longer I live the more the two ends of this string—the eternal and the momentary—curl toward each other into the lit globe of an expanded present. Dew God is not illusion, but prophesy. Time is no longer some constant thing I walk through; it is my sense of the eternal present. Given the unfathomable vastness of the world beyond my knowing and its inconceivable minuteness, I suspect this is as clear a view as I can have. And it is a magnificent view, just what I've traveled so far to gaze at.

I turned five in 1942, the year World War II was at its most perilous. Millions had already died violently, and the headlines were filled with daily body counts. Even if the world's suffering was scarcely comprehensible to our relatively safe adults, a profound anxiety was in the air. Yet America seemed to protect its youngest from the fears of war. I was very much in the world at age five, but a sense of the reality of death, including my own, was yet to come. The same was true of my sense of history. I knew I had three living grandparents, not four—my paternal grandfather died when Dad was seventeen—but I didn't feel any loss. And I knew that there were cowboys and Indians, but those were in movies.

As I turned seven, an ancient rifle with a long bayonet was brought down from the attic. Stood upright on its butt, it reached high above my head. Family history recounts that it had belonged to the father of my dad's mother, Clara. In 1847, Abraham Wormser was born in a log cabin at the site of what is now Fountain Square, Cincinnati's main downtown shopping center, replete with angular buildings of commerce looming tall over his ghost. In 1864, at age sixteen, he was conscripted as a drummer boy for the fighting Union Army. After a few months, riflemen were needed far more than drummer boys, so my great-grandfather was issued a captured Confederate rifle, which he kept throughout his life. As an old man, he lived with his daughter, my Grandma Clara, and her young son, my dad Aron. The Civil War had ended only forty-five years before; Clara insisted that the gun be kept out of sight. But when I was ten, the Civil War was nearly a century in the past, and Grandma Clara wanted her grandson to own the rifle proudly as a rite of passage. Its daily presence in my room fascinated and repelled me. According to family legend, there still were traces of blood on the bayonet, Yankee and Dixie both. I checked it out with a magnifying glass—maybe so, maybe not. The cock and trigger still worked fine. The dreadful object was so heavy I could barely lift it to aim at eye level, but I lived with it for years, sometimes displaying it high on the wall. Now I was living with nearly a full century of past time.

On D-Day in the spring of 1945, our family went to the best restaurant in Cincinnati, a tasteful, smoothly run room on the eighth floor of the premier hotel. Down in the street below, there had already been joyous chaos for hours, and the auto horns never stopped. There were hoarse screams, whoops of ecstatic relief, drunken songs, and firecrackers near and far. I had a headache. I wasn't hungry, and I wanted everyone to stop the noise and, peevishly, I said so. My father became stern and lectured me on why it was necessary to celebrate the end of such a frightening slaughter. He talked about how democracy and morality and et cetera had won out. Now I was really distressed, but over the next few days the war became real enough to me so that when we obliterated two Japanese cities a few months later, my sense of a meaningful past with present consequences sprang psychologically and emotionally to life.

When I was ten, my maternal grandfather, Moritz Feher, died: my first family death. I didn't feel it much—I hardly knew him, and he lived far away—but I suddenly found myself interested in genealogy. Moritz was born in 1876 in Beregszász, Hungary. As a kid, he would often take his violin to a nearby Roma camp and learn to play their songs. I heard him play once, and the music sounded discordant and shrill to me, although I heard just enough of the inside of the sound for his life history to become more real for me. My embodied past now stretched back sixty years to the Hungarian countryside of the 1880s. In that same year, 1945, Sue was pubescent, and I was able to imagine her as an adult with children—like someone I might become. At least for a moment, my expanded future felt like solid ground.

Shortly thereafter, I learned that my *paternal* great-grandfather was born in Paris in 1830. During the revolutionary chaos of 1848, his impoverished family was reduced to eating rats, so my dad's grandpa was packed off to America. Eating rats hit home, maybe even more than bayonet blood. My lived-in past now stretched back to 1830, and stimulated an interest in the tumult of French history.

In contrast, my sense of future time was slower to expand, any possible prescience veiled by my intense experience of rapid blooming, the long in-breath of youth. That gradually changed in my mid-twenties: back pain, persistent migraines, an uneasy sense of instability, lots of cannabis, and an increasing search for inner meaning that could not be spoken. But immediately upon the arrival of Lucy Amadea, my first-born, when I was turning thirty, the living future became real. Suddenly, almost violently, I was newly a part of the natural world of life and death, of the generations unending. The infinite possibilities of stardust had materialized into a life form—*mine*—and will disintegrate into infinite possibility. Now, as I plow my eighties, the nature of nature continues to reveal itself, sometimes in lurches, like a brainstorm in the shower or a beatific vision out of the blue. There is also an increasing sense of connectivity with humankind, and with the lushly orchestrated flora and fauna surrounding our house. And there are always the beautiful little rocks that well up after the rains. The most striking of these I gather up and arrange for shrines I build and, sometimes, sweep away in a single gesture.

Three Themes

Three principal themes braid through this book. They can be hidden, or announced fortissimo. They merge and reemerge. They mix it up with many variations, major and minor. As they play themselves out, they define the narrative.

First, this is an autobiography seen through the lens of a lifelong musician with an eye on the inner life. It is about one single life only—mine, of course—but my life's longing reaches out to all lives, yours in this moment, which is why God made books.

The second theme asks a question: What is the difference between mere experience and experience that proves useful to others? What is there to distill, to pass on, and what is trivial detail that should fall away? What is to become of my deceased mom's business letters and old bank statements? Or my daily email chatter? And how important is it that you know details of my romantic lives that ought to stay between no more than two people? These are ongoing concerns for everyone, but especially for teachers, and particularly persistent concerns for autobiographical writers.

The third theme is the transmission and recognition of wisdom. How does experience, from the most wounding to the most rapturous, refine into wisdom? More broadly, how does *subjective* experience—from a vast past accrued into a single life—become *objective* wisdom, and how does it pass through us into the lives of others, and into future lives? More specifically, how does wisdom transform negative transmission, like bullying and abuse, into the positive transmission of a balanced, easeful, and praising life?

Let's begin with language. *Transmission* comes directly from the Latin *transmittere*, to send across, to let go, or to cause to pass. Notice the mixture of active and passive, especially in "cause to pass," joined with wisdom. So, wisdom transmission could mean *discernment allowed to pass*. The Oxford English Dictionary adds "conveyance or passage through a medium." Webster's Ninth Edition gives "to cause or allow to spread, to permit passage." Again, notice the suggestive mixture of active and passive. Note as well the consistency, across many centuries and many languages, in the sense of both words.

Recognition comes from the Latin *cognoscere*, to know, to learn about. The prefix *co-* means together, and *re-* means again. The sense I make of this: the realization of something already known but with new clarity and scope.

What does *wisdom* mean? The word comes from two related sources: the Sanskrit *veda*, I see, I know, especially inner, or sacred knowing, hence the Vedas (an ancient sacred text); and the Middle Latin *vidēre*, to see (hence video). Later, it appears in Old English as *witan*, knowledgeable, sagacious (hence wit); in Old Saxon as *wīs*, shrewd, discerning; in Middle High German as *wīse*, learned, experienced; in German as *weise*, and in Middle English as *wizard*, very shrewd and wise, especially in magic. The modern definition is given in the Oxford English Dictionary as "prudence, practicality...the combination of experience and knowledge with the ability to apply them judiciously." Webster's Ninth Edition adds "the accumulated ability to discern inner qualities and relationships...sane mental soundness."

The Spark

I believe there was no identifiable *me* before I was born, nor will there be after I die. The view that the self is entirely atomized at death is closely analogous to a drop of water evaporating from the ocean and then falling back into the ocean. All pronouns disappear before life and after death: no *I*, no *it*, and no expansive surrogates like *ghost* or *soul*. The soul of the drop becomes the ocean of Being itself, not a separable entity. Of course, I am interested in the life history of my teachers—Bach, for instance. I do have a vivid sense of him as an actual guy, a product of his time, unimaginably smart, socially myopic. His joy was music, his devotion was to Christ. But when I am deep into the wisdom of his music, there is no Bach.

The Civil War Rifle

I want to internalize the magnificent vibrational organization of a fugue that has captured me; everything else is beside the point. What remains of a person is not that person, but what we have drawn from that person to keep alive in ourselves. This may yield a useful working definition of wisdom transmission: guidance for judicious and compassionate conduct that has transcended the person-ness of the one who has modeled it. *The person goes away.*

What is that, I want to know, and how does it happen?

Whatever it is, in *The Shrine Thief* I am looking directly at it. Am I, in trying to discover the dynamics of wisdom transmission, like Einstein's blind man who investigates the shape of a snowflake with his finger, only to melt it with his touch? Perhaps so. Let's find out. Many would say, with a shrug and finger pointing up to the blue, "God's work." The operative expression for me is "the nature of nature." When I look directly at the nature of nature, I realize that I myself am part of what I'm looking at. This realization recurs and refines over the arc of a life's experience until *I* am indistinguishable from *it*, and I simply point up to the pretty blue air and go on with my work.

Wailing Wisdom

Can wisdom be taught? And who are our teachers? When I was in my mid-forties, on a coach flight from Chicago to San Francisco, two rows in back of me, a young baby on its mother's lap was crying incessantly, from expressive whimpers to fitful shrieks to long sirens of despair. The young mother was heroic in comforting her child, and the lady directly in back of me turned around, kneeling on her seat, to help in any way she could.

Many of the passengers had their headphones plugged into music. Most everyone seemed forbearing enough. I have a low tolerance for loud sounds; I couldn't stomach listening to music with baby wails mixed in, and I was going nuts. For several hours.

Poor child!

Poor me!

By the time we landed, the baby was in a fitful sleep. We all climbed out of our seats, hauled down our luggage, and stood waiting to exit. Just behind me, I noticed a woman I hadn't seen before, maybe in her early thirties, calm, self-contained, with unusually beautiful and refined features. Deftly I stripped us both naked, we had perfect sex right then and there, after which, in reality, nodding toward the baby, I said with a smug smirk, "Aren't you glad she's not ours?" With natural grace, she lifted her head, looked directly into my eyes, and, holding our gaze steady, said evenly: "She belongs to all of us." The effect of these words, spoken so soon after my aggressive pan-insult by the woman whose body and soul I had just imagined possessing, was a sharply felt slap. I shrank to a dot, an empty not-thing clinging to a carry-on surrounded by humans.

By the time I was headed toward my town on the airport bus, I'd had a little time to digest the lesson I'd been given. Sinking into my seat, I *recognized* that the woman with the clear gaze had given me an understanding of universal compassion I had often mouthed but rarely lived up to. After I'd debased her in fantasy, she modeled compassion in reality. She raised me up, and enabled me to feel a little more ready to be an honest man. In a long life of reading holy writ and listening to holy men talk, she remains one of my most important guides.

Our wisdom teachers are all around us. Ultimately, everyone and all of experience become our wisdom guidance when we learn to recognize it. It took the reply of a stranger on a plane—her truly kind reply—to lift me up from smug entitlement. But we do mellow. Recognition of wisdom is the ongoing reward my life offers me, which I hope these stories and reflections will offer you.

Whatever wisdom is, I now know that I've been given the opportunity to live my days within it. My elder self is increasingly aware that an inheritance of fourteen billion years, including the rats of Paris and the blood of lingering wars, passes through me, through the wide circle of humans I know and have known, and through my music, my books, my students, and their students' students into the flickering, fiery future.

And this tastes indescribably delicious. It makes my life comprehensible. It makes birth and death the only way. It makes you and me having a lovely time in this secluded corner of our favorite bistro the absolutely perfect place to be right now. Is this my last meal ever? That's okay. Same time tomorrow night? That's okay, too.

#98

Memories are like sides of beef
hanging row upon row in the locked cooler,
drained of their lives,
softening as they age.

The only way to revive their vitality
is to eat them;
as food they are reborn
as yourself in present time.

That is why we write memoirs—
memories are revitalized as pages
and take the form of *reading material*,
something a distant hungry someone may be wanting
to digest.

Your memories will then live
but not as yourself,
just as the well-aged filet you so enjoyed
for dinner last night is no longer steer #98,
nicknamed Soul Eyes.

Dots

The euphoria is so very good. That rosy light again! Time completes itself. Sue and I are lying on our backs on Dad's bed, me nested under his right arm, Sue under his left, and our Dad is loving us. We are playing word games, telling stories. We are laughing, love-jelly-wonderstruck in the circumscribed globe of childhood. I am Glow God.

Such beatific scenes I recall only as brief moments, bright screens on the walls of memory. Conversely, the traumas are little movies of endured suffering I am given to watch again and again, short stories about dying without surcease—not death, but dying, then more dying, the pain of separation, rage in the boy gut of the world.

As a young three-year-old, I've outgrown my crib. I am standing up on my nursery bed, which fits snug in a corner, headboard against the wall. From that position, I can closely examine the intricacies of the wallpaper filled with duckies of all kinds in lovely pastels, a few wavy light blue waves, and the pleasing rough fiber of the off-white paper between them. I love to trace the outline of the ducks with one finger, petting each in turn. On this day, I take a pencil and draw designs connecting the duckies in the secret alphabet of childhood. The artist then stands back a step to see that he has now merged himself with the duckies' world, and their world with his.

Mom and Dad Kissing

Mom soon comes in, sees this, and is horrified but temperate. She explains that walls are not to be written on, but I think she merely hasn't understood duckie-boy union—a child's version of Kant's Categorical Imperative—and she erases the wall clean as she can. A few days later, I try out a new alphabet, a tad darker and broader. Although the duckies seem less happy, I know Mom will be pleased. Five minutes later, she is not.

Loudly she says she is going to tell my father as soon as he comes home. He, in turn, explains the Territorial Autonomy of Walls and gives me an art gum eraser to restore the lovely off-white of the fiber—hopeless in so many ways. I am left alone. Ten minutes later, Mom comes in, does her best with the art gum, and says, "Don't write on the wall."

About a week later, during my afternoon nap, the right answer comes to me: dots. Yes, dots, precisely drawn. The dots will connect us all, and we will connect the dots into a Perfect Duckie-Dot Family. I am very careful and gentle. It is a masterpiece! When my mother sees this, she is angry and says, "I'm going to tell your father as soon as he gets home." A scared hour passes. The moment Dad returns, Mom calls to him from the nursery. As he appears, she announces: "He did it again!"

In 1940, my father has recently begun publishing a new magazine, *Modern Photography*, and it is struggling. The situation in Europe late that year is extremely disturbing, and the US is divided about entering the war or standing aside. Tensions are high and money is tight. Dad must have had a particularly rough day. He comes into the nursery, glances at my dots, sits down on my bed, takes me up, turns me over onto his knees, swipes down my pajama pants, and spanks me with his open palm. The spanks keep coming, and between gasps, I am wailing. Through my tears, I glimpse the streaked figure of my mother, hands wrung, pleading, "Aron, don't!" He gives me a final wallop, pulls up my pants, lays me down, and says to the heap of his son, whom he loves as much if not more than anyone, "D-d-d-on't. Wr-wr-. W-Wr-wr-write on w-w-. W-W-*Walls!*" He follows my mother out of the nursery, closes the door behind.

I don't remember the pain of the spanks. What I do remember is that neither parent understood the Perfect Duckie-Dot Family. Isn't everyone supposed to be happy, dancing and singing in a circle? But instead everyone is angry, and I am all alone.

This movie takes only ten seconds to play out in the theater of my memory. In real time, from the first ducky tracings shot to the final credits, it takes about ten days, and it has taken a lifetime to unpack. It seems impossible in normal, everyday consciousness to re-experience the heavens and hells of childhood. Half-buried pleasures and pains are like unimpeded inside weather—the bluest of skies and the blackest of storms passing through a closed-up house.

I'd thought the Ducky-Dots story was all about my dad. But sixty years after I got spanked for my duckie art, I recognized how my mother passed on the responsibility of disciplining me to her husband, thus casting Dad as the bad guy. She pleads with him to stop, thus preserving the precious bond of the nurturing mother with her son. When he goes too far, it's too late for her to stop him, and the result is a vivid memory of my Dad, intact and perpetually returning.

I'm not sure how accurate or useful that insight proved to be, but twenty years after *that*, while writing these pages about merging with my duckies, another piece has fallen into place. Dad's father, Will Mathieu, was a stern, withdrawn man who believed only in teaching his son about the hard work that results in a living wage. He wanted his son to be disciplined and educated, and little else mattered—few if any good times, no love bond, an almost impenetrable vacuum between father and son. As their only child was learning to read, the father's alienation began to express in the son as a stubborn stutter that increased through Aron's puberty. But at age forty-seven, Will died suddenly, and Dad, now seventeen and freed from constant criticism and reprimand, developed quickly into his gifted writer-editor self. His affliction subsided except for rare moments of extreme anger; then Dad's old stutter would return and, lock-jawed, red-necked, and embarrassed, he would hastily retreat.

When Sue was born, Dad was happy, but he longed for the son he could love as he himself had never been loved. I came along when Mom and Dad had been married for a full decade, and Dad was ecstatic for over a year. I was the world's most perfect child. The father-son love he had longed for was found, reciprocal at last. But the glow gradually dimmed as the realities of raising a two-year-old boy sank in. His own childhood rage against his dad began to surface and, dangerously, mirror as anger directed at me. During such episodes, he identified with his own father's incapacities and frustrations. Thus he became simultaneously Will the father raging at Bill the victim son, and Aron the victim son as well. In this fluidity of identities, Dad would be simultaneously enraged and victimized, and the old stutter would return full force.

These insights about the parental triangle, however scrambled or incomplete, have proved useful for understanding my parents simply as a couple in their young thirties, diligently working through the tangled mysteries of their lives. Human beings being human.

Of course, such insights didn't help me then, a shy boy-child slung over his papa's knees. Do children often get caught in their parents' crossfire? *If you think you had a happy childhood, you didn't* goes the therapist's refrain. I'd always thought I had a happy childhood, and more often than not, I did. But it was a childhood with fear as a distant ostinato. Later, the intuitive wisdom of my inner therapist (if you please) allowed me to recognize this, and I can now more easily release my parents from story and judgment. I can love them unconditionally for being exactly who they were, for protecting and nourishing me until I was fledged.

As for the dots? They are the drawing talent I never could seem to develop, although for decades I did get a secret thrill whenever I wrote on walls. Still do. And my lovely duckies? I love them still, they still love me, and they've let me sing in their choir.

2

Human Family: Dad

His Ashes

Of all my teachers, the most influential, closest to the bone, easiest to attach to and hardest to shake has been my father. Most of my earliest memories of him are sweet, admiring, even adulatory. As I grew through childhood and adolescence, he took care to imprint upon me a template of social and aesthetic values that became my primary point of view. For the remainder of my life, it was my job to unbraid myself from his worldview and fashion my own, a job that is still being done.

Dad died a quarter-century ago when he was eighty-nine and I was fifty-nine. A few weeks later, Mom received a cardboard box in silver wrapping paper, nine inches long, five inches wide, and five inches deep, with Dad's ashes inside. She kept them, unopened, on a high shelf. A few years later, she offered the ashes to me. "I don't want them," she said. I brought them home, intending to scatter them on our land, but I couldn't bring myself to do it. I put the box in a large salad bowl—a piece of Mexican pottery much favored by Dad—on a high shelf. Maybe when this book is finished, Devi and I will do the deed. Stay tuned.

A New Word

Sue is eight, I am four. We have a private evening ritual. Around six o'clock we begin growling at each other, saying *Ogr-r-r*, clawing the air, and laughing conspiratorially. *Ogr-r-r* stands for Ogre, Sue's new spelling word, and the ogre is Dad. As his car pulls into the driveway, the growls intensify, but then we joyously run to meet him, he hugs us and picks us up in turn. We are really happy to greet our loving, kind, attentive, and brilliant father. We never tell him our secret.

The Gun

I am six. Mom has been complaining about some cheap merchandise she's bought from the five-and-dime up the street. "They gipped me," she says, distressed.

Nobody cheats my Mom and gets away with it. After school I walk home the long way, toward the five-and-dime, and saunter in. I case the joint. At first, I carefully examine the gum and the penny candies. Then I spot the gun: a 49-cent black plastic pistol with a whistle instead of the eye sight. It fits snugly into the left pocket of my winter wool coat. I choose three cents' worth of candy, take it to the cashier, and dole out three pennies.

"Is that all, son?"

"Yes."

"Are you sure?"

"Yes."

"What's in your pocket?"

I squeeze my left arm over the gun: "Nothing."

"I see something," she says, waving over to the manager at the end of her aisle.

He walks quickly toward me and takes the gun out of my pocket.

"Wait here," he commands.

Three minutes later, a cop comes through the door, takes me to his car, sits me in the front passenger seat, drives me home, but *past* my house.

"Take a last look, son."

Now I'm afraid.

"Where are we going?"

"The orphanage."

Panic. I am making very loud sounds now.

He drives about a mile to the next cross street, turns left, drives another half-mile, and slows to a stop.

"I'll let you see your parents one last time," he says, turning the car around. Now I'm merely sobbing. When we get home, he knocks on the back door.

It is Grandma's day to be with us, and my parents aren't home yet.

Alarmed, she answers the door. I rush inside and get immediately behind the kitchen table, my back to the wall. Then my legs give out; I must have fainted. Grandma moves the table out, sets me upright.

"He stole a toy gun," says the cop. "His parents should speak to him."

He tips his cap and leaves.

I don't remember waiting for Mom and Dad to arrive, but when they do, all is tearfully explained. Dad takes me gently down to the cool privacy of the basement, lays me down on an old chaise lounge, sits opposite me on an ancient chair, and calmly begins to speak. By this time, I can actually listen. He explains the morality of the case: If everyone stole whatever they wanted whenever they wanted to, there could be no ordered society. Everyone would be afraid, and so in order not to be always afraid, we have laws and punishments, and so on. Then, after a pause, he says, "Think this over, Bill, and when you think you understand it, come up and have dinner with us."

I was old enough, and scared enough, to hear this. I remember lying there considering what he said, picturing an ordered world as opposed to a chaotic one, side by side. In my mind, that was convincing. But in my heart, something was missing. After a while, I went up to dinner. No more was said, then or ever after, but for the next few decades, I became a ten-cent kleptomaniac, copping gum, candy bars, pencils, little stuff, without ever being caught. It was only in my mid-fifties that I came to realize what my father did *not* say. So, as my father, I had to learn to tell my six-year-old self, "Bill, that was no way to deal with your feelings about your mother." It was not only about moralities and societies but more about Mom and me, about the authentic sympathy I felt for her. The wisdom of the episode was latent until I had that recognition on my own, and when I did, my petty theft stopped for good. What *didn't* happen, what *wasn't* said or done, is an example of what I call negative transmission. Even though it sometimes takes many years and much experience for the recognition of such guidance to appear, it can become one's highest guidance.

Doing the Math

I am seven. Fifteen minutes before our dinner guests will sit down to a sumptuous meal prepared by our "colored" cook and served by our "colored" maid, Dad says, "The answer is eleven, can you remember that?" Head down, I nod. About a half-hour into the lively dinner conversation, Dad finds an opening to boast about his son's exceptional mental ability.

"You ready, Bill? We'll start with seven," and proceeds slowly enough through a series of math problems for the guests to follow.

I "guess" the answer: "Eleven."

After a moment of awe and praise from all sides, Dad deftly changes the subject before anyone can get a malodorous whiff. I was a fake star and felt used, as though I had been forced to deceive. Over my mother's objections, this occurred at many dinner parties. He couldn't resist. What I knew every time: Faking an answer is like stealing a toy gun. Immediate kid-wisdom. But it took a long time to have the courage to request a surcease to the sham, which Dad did grudgingly grant.

Click

I am eight. It is 1945, and Dad has been editing his creation, *Modern Photography*, since I was born. He's selling enough advertising of photography products and services to turn a sustainable profit while consistently improving the tone and look of the magazine. The circulation numbers are rising, and the budget allows him to publish pictures and commentary from some of the greatest photographers alive, especially those who have fled Europe during the war. They are hungry, even those working for *Life* or *Look*. He is in touch with Henri Cartier-Bresson, Berenice Abbott, Alfred Eisenstaedt, Ansel Adams, Stanley Kubrick, Alfred Stieglitz, Edward Weston, masters all.

Dad lays out this month's submissions on the living room floor and says, "What should I publish, Bill?"

I choose two.

"Why those?"

"That's a pretty lady in that picture, and I like the horses in that one. Those people in those other pictures look sad."

He then gives me a tutorial on what makes a good photograph, a subject he does indeed have a refined understanding of.

I really listen. He buys me a good camera, a twin-lens Argoflex.

"Take two good pictures out of a roll of twelve, and I'll have our carpenter build you a darkroom."

He has my rolls of film developed at his plant. After six months, I succeed. Now I have a darkroom on the second floor with a contact printer, a good enlarger, all the chemicals I need, trays, darkroom light bulbs, and I fall into the fascination of making clean, well-balanced enlargements. I take my camera to grade school, then college,

My New Argoflex

and make pictures in the dorm darkroom. I take my camera on the road with Stan Kenton and make a library of photos of that year. At age forty I move to the country and make a darkroom out of a storage space in the garage, producing two hundred stellar 11x14 enlargements, mostly of Sufi friends. After several years of this, I have to make up my mind about whether to be a photographer or a composer. Of course, I choose the latter. So, for years more, I shoot movies with a camcorder. When iPhones come out with acceptable digital editing, I take thousands of pictures. I try to make "good photographs" in digital format, a bit of an oxymoron, but what we have.

During the dozen years Dad was the editor of *Modern Photography*, he set aside about a hundred prints, some from submissions that were never returned, some by permission, some simply forgotten. A few became immensely valuable. Dad resisted his impulse to sell them, instead willing them to Mom, who willed them to me. Through the Michael Shapiro Gallery, I sold some of the treasures for high sums—now a big chunk of my retirement fund. So, from my Dad, this was a pure transmission of expertise, aesthetic sensibility, and shrewd practicality.

Naming Me

Until my first pubic hair appeared, my father was most often kind and generous, especially when we were alone together. He loved to spirit me away from Mom and Sue. Every other Sunday, he made the hour drive from our house in Silverton to the hundred-acre farm in Maud he had convinced his company to buy during the war as an escape from possible German blitzing of Cincinnati's crucial machine-tool industry. After the war, it became a working farm replete with a succession of tenant farmers. Often he took his two kids, but when Sue was elsewhere he delighted in being alone with his son. During these drives over the verdant southwestern Ohio countryside, with its hills and valleys and vistas and Burma-Shave signs, he would talk, always teaching, always showing the salient point, defining a new word, expounding on his business strategies, or showing me the difference between Guernsey, Black Angus, Hereford, and Holstein cattle as we rolled past them at our leisure over the two-lane black tops.

One evening, driving home over a high plateau, farm fields stretched out in the valley below us, there appeared a deeply orange setting sun, enormous and dusky behind the haze on the western horizon. I reported to Dad that I could count four sunspots visible at the same time. Dad slowed to a stop and peered out the passenger window. Sure enough, there they were.

"You are very observant," he said. "Do you know what that means?"

I wasn't sure.

"It means that you notice things other people might miss. O-b-s-e-r-v-a-n-t."

I spelled it back.

"That's right," he said, and from that day onward, *observant* became a core component of my self-image.

I am an observant person.

The next morning, a rare occurrence of four simultaneously visible sunspots was reported on the front page of the *Cincinnati Enquirer*.

Your Very Eyes

My father's project with his son was twofold. He wanted to maintain the father-son bond for life; his continual impulse was to mold me into my generation's version of himself. He taught me endlessly about the publishing business, profit and loss, postwar global politics, the family finances, coupon bonds and annuities, all of which I found truly boring, even repugnant, although I did my best to pay attention. He also recognized my uniqueness, my talent as a musician, and my intellectual potential. He actively encouraged my music but discouraged my reliance on it for my livelihood, warning me darkly of its pitfalls. He enlisted professional jazz musicians to advise me to keep my nose clean. He himself was musically naïve; he really didn't know how to listen. The only style he seemed to respond to was boogie-woogie, very popular in the '20s and '30s but still alive with master players in the '50s. He often requested me to play him some riffs that I was practicing and would dance around the living room like a four-year-old kid, flinging his arms, stepping in crazy circles, and grinning the while. I wonder if he could have made any sense of the gorgeous displays of athletic grace and communal spirit among the dancers at the Apollo in Harlem.

The legacy of my father that was the toughest for me to deal with was his skein of values. Like it or not, they were imprinted upon my character, and they left me the task of smoothing the wax, of clearing his imprint so my own guidance could emerge. Despite his endless creative energy, Dad had a cynical eye. It was get or be gotten, and protect—at all costs protect—what you have. He was a very white liberal, a do-good racist, though he would be shocked to hear himself called that: "All they'd have to do is get themselves an education, and their problems would be solved. But they prefer being maids and garbagemen." Clueless, you say, but that was the zeitgeist among liberal whites of southern Ohio at the time. Just across the river, Kentucky was proud Dixie territory. In Cincinnati, segregation was often rigid, even extreme. In my college-prep high school, one of the best rated in the US, Black kids weren't allowed to swim with the white kids. And they changed out the water after "Negro swim days." Socially, the Black kids were isolated, invisible to white kids. I made good friends with a gifted Black singer in my class, a deeply rewarding friendship for me, but that was singular in my tony school. It wasn't until I moved to California that the reality of the unconscious racism my father had impressed upon me began to dawn. Fifty years later, it's still dawning.

Aside from race issues, Dad was a classic type-A man-spreader, upwardly mobile within an immigrant Jewish culture. He had the capacity to walk in another's shoes, but only to get something he wanted. It was his joy to teach me such values through verbal instruction, but it was his living example that I inherited directly. I admired him, and feared him, and watched him operate, and had no idea how deeply his values had become my own. I'm finding out now and, Gentle Reader, your very eyes are helping me along.

Value and Beauty

When I am ten Dad and I become philatelists. Dad buys the two of us a Christmas present: *The Modern Postage Stamp Album*, with pictures of stamps from the United States stamps and from all the other countries of the *whole world*. The pictures for each country are arranged chronologically, and you may collect as many as you want or can afford. If you buy an inexpensive canceled stamp, you attach it to its proper place on the page with a special gummed hinge. If the stamp is uncanceled, you first place it in a protective glassine square, then you gum the glassine square to the page.

The game is to balance beauty with value. Some of the early American stamps were not beautiful but seemed like perfect investments. Stamp collecting was, at the time, one of the most appreciated hobbies, and prices for rare stamps were high and rising. We bought several. I even paid for some out of my allowance, a big sacrifice for some distant future. Stamps vendors sent stamps by mail "on approval." Dad and I would sit together, considering stamp after stamp: This one is going to be worth really a lot, this one isn't worth much but it's gorgeous.

I would send away for a packet of two hundred mixed stamps for seventy-five cents. I could afford that. When they arrived, they were mostly canceled, but a few foreign uncanceled ones slipped through, and some were really beautiful, well worth the price. Now, seventy-five years later, the winner for value? There are none. Stamp collecting is no longer the rage, and prices have tanked. The winner for beauty: a block of four 1926 Air Post stamps from Greece, pencil sketches filled with softly glowing watercolors. I have them still. I'm

Dad the Friend

looking at them now. Those were sweet times. This was not music, this was not the publishing business, this was a meeting in some pleasant valley of acceptance.

Out On The Town

Most memorably, when I was thirteen Dad surprised me after dinner one Saturday night by saying, "Get your coat. We're going out."

"Where?"

"You'll see."

In his head, he had a night on the town all planned out. In the car he drove quietly, not holding forth but allowing the evening to unfold on its own. The first stop was a favorite bakery of ours.

They were closed, but, as if expecting us, they let us in and gave us a tour, a loaf of fresh bread, and a bag of the day's unsold cookies. Good beginning.

The next stop surprised me. We drove to the Emergency Room of Cincinnati's General Hospital and sat on a long bench in the back of the waiting room. The room was half-full of folks in various states of extremis toughing it out, trying to stay upright on their benches or their folding chairs. There was a strong odor of disinfectant. The shootings and knifings came in on gurneys and were whisked away to surgery. The less wounded were bleeding into fresh bandages. Pain and anxiety, tempered perforce with patience, were punctuated with groans and quiet weeping. The staff behind the desk and the nurses shunting people back and forth were calm and efficient. We watched and listened, sitting very still for about a half-hour. Back in the car, I was full of questions about violence and poverty. Dad answered quietly, "This is what it is, son, and it never stops."

At the time of this evening's adventure, Dad had made friends with an ally of Buddy Hiles, my new Black jazz teacher. The man's name was Babe Baker, owner of Babe's, a private Black bar about a mile uphill from the inner city, in an area that was home to relatively affluent Blacks. We were welcomed in and led to Babe himself, who greeted us warmly. Babe parked me in a far corner of the bar with a 7-Up and a perfect side view of a Hammond B3 electric organ being played by the most astonishing musician I'd ever heard. His hands on the keyboard and feet on the pedals were everywhere at once. I felt dizzy with a new musical energy I could hardly contain. The bartender kept his eye on me, refilling my glass with 7-Up. I don't think I blinked for a half-hour. Dad was in back learning about the bar business from Babe, who was looking for white money, which I think Dad modestly supplied (in exchange for Babe's watchful eye over me, I do believe). When the organist took an intermission, Babe introduced me around, and we left. On the way home, I was speechless, no questions, not wanting to talk. The evening was a generous, thoughtful, loving gift from my father that altered my life's course more than any teaching talk ever could. Dad let the evening play itself out as transformative, direct experience: the pleasure of fresh bread kneaded and baked by honest hands, the suffering of those whose privation was beyond despair, and an ecstatic music that wove opposites together into a new vision of a wider, wilder world.

Eye To Eye

Because I often had doctors' appointments or some particular errand after school, and so could catch a ride home from downtown with Dad, I was a frequent visitor to the fifth floor of 22 E. 12th Street, where Dad was the boss of an entire factory floor of typists and secretaries—rows and rows of them—plus advertising personnel, accountants, and junior editors. Around the two window sides of the building, four senior editors and Dad had glass-enclosed office cubicles. My presence was always informal. Folks would wave hello, I would wave back and make my way to Dad's office, where I would sit and watch him—tie loosened, coat off, sleeves rolled up—complete the day's work. He would be handing letters he had signed back to his personal secretary with instructions: "Be sure this arrives by Monday," "Send a note confirming the deadline," "This goes Special Delivery." I watched with a certain detachment but also in awe of how much authority he projected and how much detailed information was streaming through him. He was responsible to his bosses, who owned the printing company for his four publications: *Modern Photography*, *Farm Quarterly*, *Writer's Digest* (plus its correspondence courses), and *Writer's Yearbook*. No profits, no magazines.

One day, when I am fourteen, Dad decides it is time for me, as the boss's son, to be more formally introduced. He wants me to take interest in everyone's job, ask what each does. He shepherds me through the first two ladies, then asks me to go around on my own.

Being asked to pose as the boss's son learning the business, I am deeply embarrassed. I try to feign interest, but I'm not interested. What I *am* interested in is who these people actually are, as opposed to the roles they are being forced to play. I am both sexually aroused by and deeply sad for these women in high heels, short skirts, and perfectly cosmeticized faces, especially those at the lower end of the work chain, the mere typists. This one, Judi Lee, is so painted over in every octave that I feel her heart is buried at 22 E. 12th St. At the next desk, Mary Lou, same story. I try to connect with her eyes, and for a moment, Mary Lou is a brave woman, and we do connect eye to eye, and I see so much I feel like crying. Desk after desk, I feel the trap under their show of enthusiasm until I get to the managers and the editors, but even then, it's only the boss behind his glass who is exempt. His tie is loose, his sleeves are rolled, and he's moving a mile a minute.

The innate, unconscious template of class privilege protected behind glass runs through the whole. I didn't have the perspective then, or the language, to articulate this to myself. Dad's sense of privilege has accumulated through his steady rise to success, and acts as a protective sealant against the shadow of his early life. There is scant way for privilege thus earned to be recognized as the great danger of being cut off from the humanity of others, and from one's own humanity. For me, the imprint of privilege worked fine. It elevated me from any suggestion of insecurity. Although I did have the liberal's normal empathy for privation and suffering, when push came to shove I'd keep my first-class ticket. It's taken a lifetime to understand that the sense of oneness with all humans can be hard work, that guidance is called for, and that at a certain point you yourself are called to be the guide. My dad's transmission to me of class privilege (and white privilege as well) is a fine example of negative transmission. Only to the extent that I've been able to lift myself out of my Dad's molding and shaping has my own guidance appeared. Along the way, I've had many guides to help me look directly at my interior self. Sometimes this is how the gradual call of guidance works: the shadow is lifted imperceptibly through the endless seasons, until one day, there is a speck of new blue in the sky.

I Win A Bet

When I was sixteen and a junior in high school, my father was forty-six and in the prime of his creative life. I was having a hard adolescence, both behind and ahead of my classmates at Walnut Hills. I was socially young and physically awkward, but at the same time absorbed in music, poetry, and philosophical, even mystical, issues. My big sister Sue had already left home for the University of Chicago, and my teenage rebellions were beginning to wear down Dad, who was anticipating the serenity of a child-free nest.

One morning, Dad said, almost offhandedly, "Instead of spending your senior year at Walnut Hills, how would you like to go to the University of Chicago next year as an early entrant?"

He explained that the University was experimenting with a program allowing certain students to skip one or two years of high school and plunge into a college liberal arts program.

"I'll never be accepted," I lamented. "I'm a B-minus student, and I fall asleep after lunch."

I knew it was hopeless to even think about it. But he convinced me to try, at least, and during that January weekend I filled out my application, wrote my essay, and waited dolorously for the expected rejection, which arrived late in March. I hadn't been rejected out of hand, however. In his letter, the admissions officer suggested that I reapply the following year after "one more year of high-school experience."

My dad had a good nose for opportunity, and he smelled one here.

"I'll bet you can talk your way in," he said.

I recognize a winning bet when I see it. I thought, "At least I'll get something out of this," and heard myself asking, "How much?"

"Ten dollars," he replied, and we shook hands instantly, before I could realize what he had done.

"You'll be on a plane tomorrow morning," he said as he disappeared into the den, where he spent an hour on the phone.

Sure enough, the next morning, I was on a Chicago-bound plane at 9:00, and at 1:00 that afternoon, I was sitting opposite the very admissions officer who had written the letter.

"Tell me why you want to come to the University of Chicago," he said.

The truth is, I was stoked up. I really *did* want to go to the University, not only to escape the halls of high school but also to discover peers who were as aesthetically committed and as socially weird as I was. My father understood my desire very well. It was he who had given me my taste for what is creative and original in thought and art, he who set a living example in his professional career and in daily life with his family. He had always drawn me on artistically and intellectually, and at this moment, pleading before a stranger, I realized how passionate I was about what I truly wanted and how I needed to speak my passion. And I did. Although I felt the force of my father's eloquence behind my words, I was speaking for myself.

"We'll let you know," said the admissions officer, and I flew home.

"How'd you do?" asked Dad.

"Okay, I guess," I said.

Two weeks later, the letter of acceptance arrived, and of course I was elated. When Dad came home from the office, I ran to greet him like I had when I was a six-year-old boy, but instead of responding to my exuberance, he shook my hand and said, "You owe me ten dollars."

I was crestfallen at his response, and besides, I didn't have ten dollars (remember, these were 1954 dollars). But I saved some and earned some and borrowed the rest. The next week, I went to a bank and exchanged ten crumpled old dollars for an uncirculated shiny ten-dollar bill. That evening, with some dignity, I presented it to Dad, who, in a single gesture, received it from my hand and tore it neatly in half.

"Where's your wallet?" he asked.

I hauled it out of my pocket. He handed me my half of the ten.

"Keep this on your person forever," he said. "Whenever things seem impossible, take out your wallet and look at your half of the ten. Maybe then things won't seem so impossible. I'll keep my half in here," and he showed me the place in between two pages of a precious book—our stamp collection, our old hobby, our rallying point.

Eight years later, I was a hungry musician in Chicago. Although my half of the ten had survived through several new wallets, I hadn't thought much about it since Dad and I made the bet. In those days, you could redeem damaged bills, and one day, standing in line at a bank, I noticed the bill in my wallet and, with a shrug of guilt, unloaded it for four dollars and eighty-nine cents. My first thought was that I was a few bucks up on my dad. But then, more and more, I began to regret cashing it in. I noticed, during ensuing episodes of difficulty, bad luck, or self-doubt, that my memory of the bill was clear and present and supported me through critical moments. I gradually realized that, thanks to my father's wisdom, I had actually won the bet. Twenty-five years later, Dad handed me the stamp album, which had long been lying untouched in his dresser drawer.

"It's yours now," he said. "Take it home to California with you."

Guess what I found between Egypt and Estonia?

So, I won my bet with Dad not once but twice. And, if you count my pleasure in telling you this, three times.

My Mother's Words

Here is one final story before I escape for good into University and lay claim to my own life. In the summer quarter between my freshman and sophomore years at U of C, I am living at home in Cincinnati for the last time. At my father's insistence, I am working every day on the fifth floor of 22 E. 12th St., *learning the publishing business from the ground up*, just like he did, just like Ed Rosenthal the founder did, as did his sons, and his sons' sons. Meanwhile, Dad has been under increasing pressure to maximize the profit of his magazines, and he is hard to live with, especially for Mom. Recently I heard her exclaim, "You bastard, you're just being mean. You really *are* a bastard!" I am shocked; this talk is over the top for Mom. I agree my father is a total drag much of the time, but really? Face to face? That's harsh.

A few days later, I make arrangements to meet with Connie, my fiancée, at her friend Leona's apartment up in the Avondale hills to spend the day alone—the plan is for me to lose my virginity at long last, and I've procured two rubbers (prophylactics, remember?) from a musician friend. Quality time alone has not presented itself until now. Look, I tell myself, Dad's a guy. He lived this very same story with Mom thirty years ago. I *know* he'll understand and excuse me from one lousy day of work.

But I'm afraid to broach the subject, keep putting it off. On the appointed morning, when we are driving near the friend's apartment, I plead my case. *It's a very big day for me, please let me take a rain check from the office for a day, Connie's waiting for me, I'll make it up, this really really means a lot to me, please, you've got to understand.* Dad summarily refuses. The more I plead, the more he moralizes about my responsibilities to the work ethic. The exchange becomes more and more heated, but guess who's driving.

Dad turns down from the hills toward Columbia Boulevard, a wide swath of level road cut from the cliffs that reach from the heights all the way down to the Ohio River—a most scenic route. Dad keeps driving, and I know that there are no side streets for several miles. I begin to despair. Connie, naked in her friend's bed, is waiting for me.

Dad begins to get really angry. Me too. Not much premeditation here.

"You really *are* a bastard," I spout.

Safety aside, Dad pulls over, stops, commands, "G-g-g-get out! N-n-now!"

I slam the door hard as I can. Off drives Dad.

I am on a narrow pedestrian walkway. Every quarter-mile, there is a break in the high retaining wall with steep steps leading up to the next roadway carved from the slopes. About five of these long climbs bring me to a busy street that might have a bus. I am already hopelessly late. I'll bet Connie has given up and gotten dressed by now. No phone booth anywhere. I'm lost. I begin to walk. I walk until I come to a street name I recognize, far away from everything. I'm hungry, thirsty, and barely have bus fare. Now it's 2:45, Connie's surely gone home, and that's what I do, too. I find a bus that takes me more or less in the right direction, ride to the end of the line, and call Mom, who drives five miles to fetch me. We get home just before Dad. I have one nickel in my pocket.

Nothing is said.

Had I not been away at school already for a year, the bastard incident would have lingered in the air between Dad and me. But since I was in the process of escaping for good, it didn't need to linger, it was done. In the act of writing this story, however, I've had a little lightning bolt of realization—the kind I've learned to be suspicious of, but here it is. I used *Mom's* words to make Dad the bad guy. Wasn't that a nice little flip from the Duckie-Dot incident when Mom used *my* dots to make Dad the bad guy? In each case, the perp (Mom first, then me) got hers/his. Mom had regret because Dad went too far; I suffered a dreadful day that still haunts me in recurring dreams of finding my way home.

Two weeks later, Connie is visiting us. Mom and Dad invite us to go out to lunch. We decline, they leave, and we instantly go to bed, hunkering down in the same room where I'd drawn the Duckie-Dots sixteen years earlier. With considerable anxiety and awkwardness the act is accomplished. My virginity vanishes into the ethers forever. We hurriedly get dressed. Connie brushes my hair and squares my shoulders. She is six years my senior, six years more experienced, and seriously patient with her subdued, grateful groom-to-be.

Coda

These stories are a scrapbook of the early learning from my father, my primary teacher. Looking back, I can sense patterns of conscious knowing (the sham of the math game, the desperation in Mary Lou's eyes) and unconscious acceptance (being served by servants, being the boss's son, the power of position). As my life goes on, these internalizations transform and have real consequences for others. That is the plot, with its dust and its clarity, with its knowing and unknowing, that we are following.

Later in the book, in "The End Game," the narrative of my father and me will resume thirty years on. I will then be in my early fifties, and Dad will be at the beginning of his decline into dementia.

3

Human Family:
Mom, Grandma Clara, Sister Sue,
and Uncle Milton

THREE MOM STORIES
Octaves

One day, when I was nine, I was practicing a Mozart sonata. It began with a major triad arpeggiated in octaves, the left hand playing the lower octave, the right hand playing the upper octave. My teacher had warned me about sloppy playing the week before. As I started to practice the piece, I must have tried twenty times to get those simultaneously sounding octaves accurate, but a mistake occurred in each iteration, always in a different place. Try as I might, the simple passage would not come clean. I had not been given the mental tools for clean playing, only an admonition against sloppiness. I couldn't find the frame of mind to listen to the music while simultaneously feeling my hands playing. Unsurprisingly, the sloppiness would not go away. In a crisis of frustration, I banged both fists on the keys and threw myself onto my knees with my head on the piano bench. My mother suddenly appeared, sat in the big comfortable chair near the piano, and beckoned me to sit in her lap. She held me as if I were a three-year-old, which at that moment, I was. She explained patiently how one has to work through one's difficulties and that troubling times come and go. She was telling me in her way, between pats on the head and snuggles on the neck, that life was cyclical and that I should not give up, not this time, not ever.

This was maternal transmission unadorned, without a veil, a direct hit. After a few minutes, I didn't want to be three years old sitting on my mother's lap anymore. I sat down on the piano bench once again, a little taller this time, doped out the technical difficulty on my own, played the passage quite well, moved on through the rest of the sonata, and from there onward through the remainder of my musical life. There is no special story here, just the pure experience of generations, just the reason God made mothers and sons.

How Hollow Was It?

I don't remember the reason for my sudden disenchantment with family life but, almost certainly bristling against some reasonable request or newly imposed discipline, I decide, at age eleven, to run away from home. It is late afternoon. Dad is having dinner with Sue downtown. Waiting until Mom is distracted, I nonchalantly walk out the kitchen door straight for the woods in front of me, a few acres of beautifully diverse trees, bushes, tangles of brambles, and ancient fallen timber. As I walk through my old haunts, I remember a hollow log I used to crawl into many years before when I was much smaller. Would I still fit? After a short search, there it is, its full five-foot length lying sleepily on a bed of rotting leaves and loose soil. I get down on my knees and peer through the larger end. It's still open at both ends. Squirming on my stomach, I venture inside, all caution.

The interior is full of unimaginable life forms, but seems friendly: *You will be safe here.* I crawl farther, get almost all the way in, and slowly turn over onto my side. This is precisely what I want. I am totally free, master of my aloneness, king of my dark dampness, sole proprietor of my life. I spend the late afternoon half-awake in the carnival of animated images that can stream through an unencumbered eleven-year-old boy's newly liberated mind. If left alone, that is, if left alone.

It must be around six o'clock that I get hungry. I'm hungry and getting hungrier. I squirm out of the log, brush myself off, and head back to where I used to live. When I climb the steps to the back porch, I'm surprised to find the back door locked. I knock. Although the curtain to the door's window has been drawn closed, Mom must be home because her car is in the driveway. More knocking. Maybe my mother is upstairs and can't hear? I knock impatiently, *fortississimo*, hurting my knuckles. After a spell, the curtain is drawn back to reveal my mother's eye. She speaks sweetly but very, very far away through the glass.

"Who is it?"

"Your son!"

"Yes?"

"It's me, Bill," I explain.

"What can I do for you, Bill?"

"*MOM!!*"

"Didn't you leave?"

"Please let me in."

Mother disappears, there is a pause, I knock politely. Mother reappears. I'm downright pleading now:

"Mom, I'm *home*, and I'm really *hungry.*"

The door is unlocking. I slink into the kitchen. Mother points to some covered dishes on the stove.

"You may take your dinner up to your room tonight. I've already had mine."

I do what she says.

It is one of the loneliest meals I've ever eaten.

And, for that matter, one of the most illuminating lessons in gratitude I have ever eaten.

The Broom Handle

I turned thirteen in July 1950 and, a few weeks afterward, made my initial discovery of sexual ejaculation. The premiere was an experience marked more by curiosity and wonder than pleasure. What is this stuff? Is it made of me? Why should this substance, under certain conditions, quite suddenly appear? Rigorous scientific empiricism ensued, a hands-on laboratory course in the color, taste, and viscosity of this strange new seed from my once-familiar body. The initial reality was self-contained, but subsequent experiments were accompanied by thoughts of females and thus by ever-increasing pleasures. The fascination was polymorphously projected onto exudations of every nature—all were part of my singular, miraculous body wanting to know itself, to experience its new physical and psychological world. Such was the solipsistic bubble around this research that there could be no outside world, no witness.

But one lay-abed Saturday morning, while I was deeply involved in a new laboratory experiment, my mother pierced the bubble by insisting that I get up out of my smelly bed *right now*, change my filthy sheets, and open the windows to freshen the room. "It stinks in here," is the way she put it. But I lay there finishing my lab work. A half-hour later, Mom appeared again: "This is your last warning." But I lay there somewhere between a glow and a stupor. Yet once more, Mom appeared, quite stern now: "I'm going to count to ten." She counted; I lay still. "I mean it this time, Bill." She disappeared and returned immediately holding a broom in her hand.

Mom and the Mail

My Mom had never struck me—a potch or two on the rear perhaps, but never anything close to a blow. Now I was facing a woman resolutely holding a broom near its base and waving the long stick of its handle. A new phase of maturity evidently was facing an escalation of weaponry. To be sure, it was a thin stick, but it was a fast-moving stick. "Get up *now*."

The arc of the broom handle began behind Mother's head and swung down hard up on me, but my reflexes were quick. I raised my arm to catch the blow, which hit the tip of my elbow and was surprisingly painless. With a satisfying crack, the broom handle splintered in two. Just as in baseball, half of it went skittering across the infield. A high-pitched laugh of delight cascaded out of me. It came from a stranger, a fresh young face in the ongoing generational battle. Mom, her half of the broom pointing upward, turned her back and left the room. As the sound of her footsteps receded down the stairs, I lay motionless, my manic laugh hanging brittle in the air.

Clearly I had won, but won what? The right to stink up my room with bodily effluent? That didn't seem to be a totally classy victory. I realized I had taken my mother as far as she cared to go. It's one thing, I reasoned, to wallow in your own smells, quite another to be fair to your mother. Supine, I pondered. Then I was up, washed, dressed, and as industrious as any other young soldier making his room tidy and fresh before breakfast. I wasn't doing this for myself, you understand, but for Mom, my good-old Mom who couldn't hurt a fly, broom handle or no.

These are engaging memories for me, each with a kernel of wisdom that was mine to internalize. From my infancy, the ongoing narrative between Mom and me was not very dramatic but was one of mutually modulated, ever-present support and familial love. We never got too close. There were few ups and downs. Mom always showed up when I needed her, and the reciprocal was true: on the occasions she called for my support, I was there. There was no clinging, and a true friendship evolved over time.

When I went away to college, did she miss me more than I missed her? Yes, because she was my mother. But the reason that such a functional distance maintained itself over seven decades is that we were both workaholics, committed at least as much to what we considered our work as we were to our circle of family and community.

Mother was fascinated by the use of herbs in cooking. When she was in her early thirties, she began serious writing and teaching about herbs. By the time I was thirteen Mom had a thriving herbal business. Her book, *The Herb Grower's Complete Kit and Guide*, was reviewed by Clementine Paddleford in the *New York Times*, and was selling very well by mail order. She became a maven of this subject, an early American prophet.

When I got home in the late afternoons from junior high, there were often four or five neighbor women-of-a-certain-age sitting at a long table on the second floor, reading mail, taking orders, sorting seeds, filling sachet packets, and packaging complete *Kit and Guides*. Mother herself spent many hours experimenting with essential oils mixed with dried leaves and blossoms (and additional proprietorial ingredients), making potpourri, some of which, fifty years later, is still fragrant. She was possessed with the fragrances of sachets and potpourri, but the fragrances themselves were not confined to the product. They got into our clothes, our furniture, our nostrils, and the nostrils of our friends. Once, at the school cafeteria, I snuck up behind a friend, put my hands over his eyes, and said, "Guess who."

"Bill," he stated.

"How could you tell?"

"Sachet smell."

I found this disturbing, but Dad found it personally and professionally appalling, an ever-present source of gall. The two never stopped bickering about it, but Dad didn't have a leg to stand on since much of the success of Mom's business was due to Dad's marketing savvy and his public relations expertise. Because he knew so many people in journalism, he garnered for Mom enviable publicity exposure, locally as well as nationally, for the product and the personality of the Herb Lady. The truth is, Dad loved that his sales skills were enabling his wife more than he hated the smell. The orders poured in, and the ladies kept filling them, thus permeating the house with ever more fragrance of ground seeds, freshly harvested leaves, and essential oils. Meanwhile I was writing music like a demon, Susan was away at college, Dad was away at the office, and Mom and I maintained our supportive, if preoccupied, distance.

Threaded through this was the competitive relationship between my parents. Dad, an only child of poor, hardworking folk, had fought his way upward through the social classes to professional success and societal admiration. Mom, the eldest of six children afforded a flourishing middle-class Hungarian upbringing, had, by her thirties, become her own woman in her own house, a matron of her self-made circle. Mom and Dad did often display a domestic intimacy with each other, going through the necessary list of household issues with calm discipline. And often they exchanged love pats, coos, and smiles. But just as often they were bickering, or arguing outright, sometimes quite angrily. Compared to most families, we had it easy, but the angry part did disturb me a lot. I knew where Dad's temper could lead him, and my mother's disappointment and resentment grew over the years.

The real story between Mom and me develops much later. When she was ninety-five, I was sixty-four, and Devi was fifty-one. Both Dad and Sue had died. We moved Mom from Cincinnati to a nearby assisted-living residence so we could be near her. During the seven years left to us being together, a true friendship developed. It meant a serious seeking of the other, some level gazing—real work on all sides.

This became simultaneously arduous—she was really old—and dearly precious—she was really old—and I will tell you all about it with pleasure when we get there. In the meantime just try to go to sleep. We'll be home before you know it.

SISTER SUE
Sue And I Hunt Down Our Baskets

Far from anything Christian, my parents nevertheless gave in to our insistence to hunt for candies on Easter Sunday. The usual routine was that candies and decorated hard-boiled eggs would be scattered about the house, especially in our rooms, mine more obviously since I was younger. But when I was six and Sue was ten, our parents decided to save themselves some trouble by simply hiding a fully decked-out Easter basket in each of our upstairs bedroom closets.

At dawn on that Easter morning Sue and I, both still in pajamas, reported downstairs to the living room as usual. The rule was: finders keepers. We rummaged through drawers and under cushions—no candy anywhere in the living room. We ransacked the kitchen—no candy. Sue and I consulted: she took Mom's closet, I took Dad's. No candy, not even eggs. The parents, at first amused, were becoming restless, then annoyed.

"Just go get dressed," they suggested.

No way—not until we'd found some nourishment, some special prize. Dad's bureau drawers, for sure!

"Off limits. Why don't you just get *dressed* first?"

"We want candy!"

Mom and Dad in unison now: "*Just go get dressed.*"

Sue caught on first and raced up the stairs. But she did not race for her own bedroom closet, which was at the far end of the house from the stairs. She ducked into my bedroom, first door on the right, found the basket mixed in with my shoes, and claimed its festive hulk for her own.

"Dibs!" she declared as she rushed past her forlorn brother, beating me to her own closet by three paces. "Dibs on both!" she crowed, her face more radiant in that moment than perhaps it had been in the six years of a childhood lived in her kid brother's shadow.

I went shrieking down the stairs two at a time straight into my mother's arms. Sue realized at this point she wasn't going to get away with it. Indeed, Mom took us both by our hands, brought us back up to Sue's room, and patiently explained to her how I wasn't yet as bright as she. Petulantly, Sue gave me my property, and we trudged back down to the living room. Within three minutes, all the eggs and candies were spread out on the carpet, and we were in the seasonal trading frenzy.

"Three greenies for a chocolate egg."

"Four!"

"But the eggs are teeny."

"Four!"

"Three cherries and a lemon."

"Okay, if you give me the littlest bunny for my turtle."

"Okay."

Although my specialness as the gifted male child was a thorn for Sue, there was also our silent but firm understanding that no matter how special I appeared, she would always have the jump on me. And she did. We were best friends and still are, even after her little brother has outlived her for a generation.

It Isn't Fair

At the least hint of favoritism, siblings can so easily claim *it isn't fair*, but from my early memories to her early death, Sue's heartfelt iterations of the phrase have slumbered restlessly in a dark nest of my heart. This is because she was so often right. Often it was indeed *not* fair and, sensing that, I would mock her to my Mom. Because Sue was the eldest and often enough did get the preference, I had my share of running to Mom. Maybe things evened out eventually, maybe not. Although such things passed quickly between Sue and me, her justified plaint sounds often in my ear.

When Sue, propped up in a hospital bed installed in her bedroom, had about one more day left to her life, I spent the afternoon by her bedside. Alone with her healthy, active sixty-two-year-old little brother, she, at sixty-six, had mere hours to live, none of them well. Sue was quiet, exhausted, without much to say. In her hand, she loosely held the automatic device that raised and lowered the bed. After a long pause in the conversations, she tried to make her head lower but couldn't get the device to work. Click, nothing. Click, click, higher, click, nothing. Click, her feet moved up. She threw the black *thing* into the bedclothes.

"It isn't fair," she pleaded, and it wasn't.

And it isn't.

And I'm crying now.

Unperturbed

Sue is fifteen, almost sweet sixteen. She is being wooed by the tennis coach at our local court, David Silver: lithe, demure, bright, eager for prey, and *in college*. In the late afternoons, he coaches her for free, then walks her home, and they sit through summer evenings on the cushioned furniture of our front porch, where his arms and hands are continually restless. On this particular Saturday afternoon, just before leaving for the courts, Sue is talking seriously to Mom. They are standing in the hall. They are talking about David Silver. I am not picking up on content, but my little-brother ears hear that it is about a protective strategy for Sue's overly affectionate, *older* new boyfriend. I am on my way to the kitchen for ice cream.

I am just twelve, socially childish, and I relish the role of pest. I stop, forming a momentary threesome. I hear enough to recognize that Sue is just now on the way to her tennis date with David.

In my most annoying voice, I pipe up, "Are you going to kiss him when it's fifteen-love?"

Without blinking, or apparently without even noticing, Sue rears her right arm back and slaps me open-palmed, full and hard on the left cheek. The blow is devastating, and for a moment, I black out—more from surprise, I think, than physical shock. The slap, a new watermark in sisterly attention, really throbs. But that's not why I remember this incident so well.

What happens next is the actual surprise. Mom and Sue keep on talking as if I had never appeared. Mom doesn't even turn her head to look at me. No word is dropped from the conversation. I am invisible to them, and then—and here is the moment of transmission—I am invisible to myself. I walk into the kitchen in an empty state. In one instant, Sue has shown me her true upper hand, and our matriarch, with the absence of any outward sign, has acknowledged that simple truth.

Such was the last off-color remark I ever made to Sue. After that, I tried sincerely to be a gentleman. Sue, of course, was never chastened for hauling off on her kid brother. And make no mistake, Gently Amused Reader: all afternoon, my cheek felt as if a bee had stung it, and that *was* fair.

The Keys

Dad is eighty-seven, about a year and a half away from a death locked deep inside dementia. For the Christmas holidays, Sue and I have flown to join Mom and Dad on Sarasota's Siesta Key. After being lost a few times while driving, and having survived a couple of near misses, Mom has forbidden Dad to drive. But he won't physically give up the car keys. He has hidden them. Mom can't find them. She has appealed to Sue and me. So after dinner on the second night of our visit, the children present a united front to the waning patriarch.

"It's time, Dad. Where do you hide your car keys?"

"They're on my person, and you can't have them."

He retreats to the screened-in porch of the lanai, reaches into the deep tennis ball pocket of his shorts, and claws out the keys. Now he cups them with both strong hands. They are the last crust of bread on the planet.

Asserting her prerogative as eldest born, Susan steps forward and puts out her hand.

"You need to let them go, Dad."

Dad puts his left hand behind his back. Now I step forward and gently take hold of his left wrist, lifting the whole arm with the keys tightly tucked in its palm. Dad is still a tall man, and I can't quite reach the fist at the end of his upstretched arm. Sue grabs his upper arm and forcefully brings it down. In turn, I grab a dangling key and twist, not entirely gently. With a look of vacant surprise, Dad realizes his hands are empty. He himself stands empty for a long moment.

"Ogr r r r," I think. our Ogre has been overcome.

In the late night, over red wine, as the parents are sleeping, there arises in the quiet conversation of siblings a delicious silence.

"Ogr-r-r-r," I growl.

Sue looks blankly at me, then throws her head back and laughs quietly, like a young girl.

"Ogr-r-r-r," she replies, showing her menacing claws.

Both Sue and Dad will be gone within two years. And, as I'm writing this, 25 years later, Sue is still honored by the large Jewish community she served with such grace. And our Ogre is currently still as he's in a box in a large bowl, high on a shelf.

It is true that I was the putatively gifted child. My talents as a musician and writer showed young and were proclaimed prodigious by my early twenties. But Sue had a talent I had never rightly heeded—she had the gift of family.

By the time we had won the Battle of the Siesta Keys, Sue had wonderfully raised three great kids, successfully navigated a complex marriage, and built a life of service within her Reform Jewish community. She was beloved by her children and grandchildren and was the go-to creative source of outreach in her community circle. She was a peacemaker, an empowerer. That night, on Siesta Key, I took a good look at her and abdicated my position as gifted sibling. My own life as husband and father had been far less serendipitous, less nourishing for all. Alimony and child support were my legacies.

Three marriages are not one marriage. Jovial family gatherings for Seder are not one-nighters in Des Moines. Suddenly my sister wasn't boring anymore. I listened carefully as she told of her grandson's latest triumph in kindergarten. Something of the historic composer softened; my bronze bust on some future mantle began to look blurry. A sudden impulse to play Monopoly, a childhood favorite, came over me, and if Sue were alive right now, I'd see to it, with all the great-grandchildren playing too.

"*Monopoly?*" they would ask, incredulous. "How about *Super Smash Brothers?*"

"Or *Ticket to Ride?*" the youngest would chime in.

Transmission between bonded siblings is like none other. It is the *sending across* the thinnest imaginable membrane separating self and other, a line so invisibly sewn into us that sometimes it's impossible to tell who's giving and taking what from whom. I got a teeny chocolate egg (my favorite) for three cherries and a lemon, all right, and for sure Sue got the littlest bunny for the turtle she didn't want anyway, but after a few minutes, on that long ago Easter morning, we just went halvsies on most everything.

Grandma Clara

I never really knew Grandma Clara when she was alive. She died at age eighty-six when I was twenty-six. At her funeral, Dad, to project the impression of boredom, invited me to play imaginary tic-tac-toe on his sleeve.

My father had fought so energetically and persistently to rise up from his working middle-class family to the status of an elitist creative businessman that he quickly grew ashamed of his mother, her plebeian manners, her stream-of-consciousness speech, and her imperfect English. In truth, he disparaged her at every turn. He phoned her rarely, but when he did, he put the phone on his shoulder and rolled his eyes, saying every so often into the mouthpiece, "Yes, mother." Even as a young boy, I understood this as cruelly dismissive, but his aversion seems to have imprinted itself onto me. For all of my youth, Grandma Clara was a non-person to me. Even as she patiently babysat us kids, even as she was loving her grandchildren with fullness of heart, it was easy to cut her off. All of her goodness and all of her kindness could not move me past my father's shame for his ignorant mother.

Grandma Clara had to sell fish at Fulton Market to put Dad through Ohio State. She would gladly walk two miles to save the nickel for a streetcar transfer. Everything in her town apartment, where I was fed on Sunday afternoons after Temple School, was

Clara at Twenty

old and quaint: old lace, cloth, and furniture from the turn of the century, lamp shades with colored bulbs from the twenties. She fed me liver and onions and saved string. The smell of mothballs and the tidy look of fastidious parsimony were everywhere.

Widowed at age forty-seven, Clara's emptiness never filled. When she was in her eighties, to divert her from lonesomeness, Dad suggested that she begin to write her autobiography. He sat with her and organized her memories into a chronological outline. She followed it as she wrote, and write she did. I found the manuscript among my files while researching this book and, to my amazement and delight, discovered my Grandma Clara's voice, at once vital and trivial, alive and habitual, full of longing and thankfulness, and very long on memory.

I have chosen some of her stories so the voice I could not hear when she was alive I can share with you now. I've found her lonesome, loving, self-eclipsed writing beautiful as old, crack-laced porcelain. Through her sentences, her person shines like a distant sun, and without reservation, I have invited her person into my own.

From Grandma Clara's 1963 memoir:

> As I sit here daydreaming on Thanksgiving Day I think of my dear parents, who lived to celebrate their golden wedding anniversary. I was one of four little girls, Lilly, Rachel, Bessie, and myself, Clara. I was born in February 1878. As my parents at that time had a little difficulty in finding a suitable apartment for us, my blessed grandmother arranged for Mama to share some of the many rooms of the Rockdale Avenue Temple Annex, so that is why it happened I was born there. I don't know if that made me religious or not, but during my life I tried to do right and be a good Jewess.
>
> Although we were never rich we always had a happy and contented family. My father became a cigar maker. Later, as I grew up, we owned a cigar store and there my father rolled his own cigars to sell. As he made the cigars, he rolled them around on his own saliva to hold them together. In those days, no one thought of germs as they do today. He had a helper who bought the tobacco, and we children used to strip it. It was fun. And I was quite proud that my father would allow me to weigh out the snuff for Old Man Bonti, a regular customer.
>
> We had a "Blue Sunday Law," so we used to close the store on Sunday, as did others, but people went around to the back and got what they wanted. It seemed as though there was never an officer about, and no one ever was arrested. Strange to relate, though, no matter if the finances were needed or not, no cigar maker would ever work on Monday.
>
> When I was fourteen, my father became the Assistant Sexton to the Judah Torah and United Jewish Cemeteries. When anyone passed away, he had to go to the courthouse, get the certificates signed, and also see that the person was all paid up for his dues to the temple before burial was permitted.

In 1884, when City Center was 100 years old, the Centennial exposition was held. I was about six years old. A canal was running through the city where Central Parkway is now. It was a beautiful sight—the canal was all lit up, and gondolas all decorated going up and down the canal holding passengers. There were glass blowers, too. They also had a cow made of papier-mâché. All the children crowded around the cow because for five cents a child would "milk" the cow and receive a large glass of milk.

Living cows and pigs that had to be delivered to the slaughterhouse were driven through the streets. Often cows would get scared, and men with very large sticks would beat them to get them in line. People used to run into stores or hallways to escape the wrath of these animals. It was very exciting, but it was not funny, you can take my word.

On many a Saturday afternoon we used to go to Middleton's Dime Museum on Sixth and Vine. For the sum of ten cents plus a nickel for peanuts we saw the fat man, the thin man, the bearded lady, the fire-eater, the giant, the midget, and a lady who sat in the swing with only half a body. We marveled and stared and stared and wondered. Later my father used to take us to the real circus—he never once missed taking us. We also went to the Burnett Woods concerts where we were delighted to hear Bellsted the cornetist. He was the best ever, such fine music. We also used to go to Music hall to hear the fine Sousa Band, and to Eden Park. We never rode, we always walked, and enjoyed it, too. And we went to the Art Museum. I never will forget the whole family—including Mama—all would go to Wyler's, which was a fine saloon. All the best people used to go there. Later, as we got older, we went to Hall's theater and our hearts used to almost stand still as the villain put the heroine on the railroad tracks, but our hero was always there on the spot to save her.

I was married right from our home on Army Avenue in 1903 under a large and magnificent bell, it was all white and really beautiful. I can still see the flowers. Our dining room set was given to us by my two uncles, Uncle Saul and Uncle Dan. After all these years, I still have the dining room table. How many times, in later years, our whole family used to sit around this table. Years go by, and one by one the dear ones pass away. But the mind's wonderful memory God gave us still lingers with us. I have thanked God many times for the memories of older days.

Even though I was reared in a strictly kosher home, one day, my dear husband Will said he would like bacon for breakfast. My heart stood still. What should I do? Well, on the third floor was a good, dear neighbor and a devout Catholic. I was a young bride and so was she. I asked her what I should do. Don't worry she said, and she went out and bought some bacon, prepared it

Clara at Seventy

in her apartment and, of course, used her own dishes (I would not and could not use mine). I brought the tray down to Will for his Sunday breakfast and prepared coffee for both of us. He ate all his breakfast in silence, and my Will never mentioned bacon ever to me again. He was a good sport and I, of course, never ever said a word either.

My dear baby was born on April the 23rd 1907, an unusually cold and rainy day for that time of year. Doctor Max Dreyfus called at our house at seven in the morning on the 22nd, Aron was not born until 11:00 am the next day, and I had serious trouble. He was a long thin baby and weighed 9 pounds. And yet today he is the finest and best son a mother could wish for. Believe me he is quite handsome. Not long ago I said to my Rosella, "Aron is certainly handsome," and her answer was, "Yes, mother, your son is handsome." And he is.

When Aron was eight, he was a pupil at Hoffman School. At that time, while he did stutter, he also talked very fast. I took him to the doctor and was told not to give him fried food. A private teacher taught Aron how to breathe and how to stand correctly, and to talk softly and clearly. She was a fine teacher and we made many trips to see her. When Aron was ten I started him in a class with Jamie Mannheim, a real elocution teacher. She taught him how to enunciate. One day she had her class meet at the old ladies home on Ashland and McMillan. My dear son recited a long piece and then had to recite it again after the applause. At the end he stood so straight and said, "I'm going to be president some day." Well he could be too. My son is the greatest and the best.

I sit here today, 85 years old writing all this. I wonder if Aron ever reads these pages, he will recall any of these things I have written about. Maybe he will and maybe he has forgotten, but I guess mothers never forget.

Uncle Milton: Off-Center Zen

He was my favorite uncle. I loved his vibe. During the war and into the late 1940s, Milton Feher, Rosella's kid brother, visited our Cincinnati home from New York yearly. Just out of college, he had been a Broadway dancer, sustained injuries, and refashioned himself as a healer. By the time he was in his early thirties, he had opened a studio, The Milton Feher School of Dance and Relaxation, at 200 W. 58th, where he lived and taught for almost sixty years. He was tall and lithe, perpendicular as a flagpole. When I was six he taught me to stand tall on his shoulders—no hands—while he walked around, simultaneously still and moving, on our lawn. When he was dancing his sweat smelled sweet and his skin glowed, a kind of Krishna presence, though I didn't know that name then. I didn't pay much attention to his message of balance and relaxation, just his bright love of teaching me.

Over time, his fame grew in New York. Here are excerpts from an article the *New York Times* ran about him on June 20, 1988:

> [I]t is reason enough to pay attention when a 75-year-old man glides about his studio with the ease of a gazelle and stands interminably on one leg in a storklike pose. Feher considers posture, which our mothers nagged us about, the foundation of all that he teaches and believes. The foundation of posture is the earth. "Feel yourself press into the earth," he instructs. "Feel the earth holding you up. The more you press against the earth, the more relaxed you become. . .. Relaxation depends on alignment. You don't relax from a feeling of being relaxed but from the knowledge that your body is straighter." . . . We live in an age of science. There must be a rational explanation for everything grounded in the reality of proven knowledge, but Milton Feher flies in the

face of this and his ideas take on an ethereal quality. His ideas can sound like so much humbug. . .. Still, after half an hour, one has learned to stand straighter, to be lighter on the feet. Is it the inherent truth behind the theory, or the persuasiveness of the theory's proponent? Never mind. You can stand storklike now.

Milton was sanguine in his praise for his allies and full of derision for those who did not respond positively to his views. He thought of himself as the world's teacher, yet he freely insulted multitudes, especially those closest to him. But if you sailed along with him he could change your life. He could relax you enough to feel your marriage with the ground, with gravity, the force that, according to Uncle Milton, gives life its vitality. But he could go too far, making powdery claims that pushed you past your tolerance for poetic metaphysics. In the same breath, he would insist that all your troubles come from not listening deeply enough to him. When I was grown and he would do this to me, I would try to maintain presence for my once-favorite uncle. I might have felt good in my body, but I felt cheated in my psyche because I had to totally buy into his panacea in order to benefit from his experiential wisdom. This is a wisdom transmission bought with false currency. Though you have the prize, you have to pay a great price—wisdom with an asterisk.

Uncle Milton was a grounded narcissist. His connection to Zen practice was clear: he understood the purity of mind that comes from sensate meditation. Although he helped a lot of folks in his world, I could never reconcile his wisdom teaching with his hungry ego, his need to be seen as a prophet in an impoverished land. Perhaps, from the perspective of inner realization, he was simply an unbalanced human, but from a psychological point of view I guess he had the symmetry he needed to get along. I think I wanted him to be as perfect as my childhood self saw him: so graciously could he leap! But perhaps his jeté was the only airborne time he was allotted.

Although my father followed Milton's exercise regimens, which no doubt kept him active as a tennis player until his mid-eighties, he never completely bought into Milton's inner work. Uncle Milton sensed the rejection, and when Dad died Milton remarked to Mom, "Aron died too soon because he didn't ever feel the ground."

On the other hand, my mother, Milton's beloved sister, his elder by six years, swore by his work and its inner meaning. Rosella and Milton were in loving and restorative communion their whole lives. She would listen by the hour to his "relaxation tapes," some of which he made especially for her. *The Relaxation Record* has been carried

Young Milton Leaps

by Smithsonian Folkways ever since he recorded it in 1962. The Smithsonian speaks of "Milton Feher's hypnotic voice," and goes on to say that fifty years after its release, *The Relaxation Record* remains a fine listening meditation.

When I'd moved to California and was well into my forties, Uncle Milton would phone me from time to time to make sure I was following his instructions. Unsurprisingly, some gems came from these conversations. A particularly definitive one I remember: *Every fucking thing clarifies through feeling the ground.* Another gem, more pragmatic to me as a pianist: *Any note widens the shoulders.* Gems aside, I felt the pressure of his need and resisted it.

"You are my uncle whom I love," I once said. "I already have a Sufi Murshid and a North Indian Guru. You are not my teacher, Uncle Milton. Please be my uncle."

For this, he berated me until I finally had to hang up on him, though during subsequent calls he became calmer, even loving.

Many years later, in a conversation during a period of grief over the passing of his wife, speaking his spontaneous prosody slowly in

Old Milton Sees

his resonant baritone, the poet in him declared: *Of the twenty-six bones of your feet, you don't know any of them enough to experience the full emptiness of your wife dying.*

Full of chaotic anger, Milton died in April 2011, when he was ninety-nine and an intolerable burden to those closest to him. I hope that the voices of his gods did tell him, finally, how to let go of himself.

Milton is long gone from us, so I can plunder his wisdom with impunity. When I'm practicing piano, *every note widens the shoulders* makes my fingers smarter, more fleet, and the more I remember to do it, the more I see how he's nailed it. Milton's teacherly compassion allows me, through my own hearing, to feel my body just as he wanted me to feel it. Uncle Krishna, glowing of skin, leaps to the rescue. The light around his body rests gently up and down my spine, and my skeleton rejoices. Could it be that I am fully feeling the ground now? Could it be that I am relaxing into the wholeness of the universe? Uncle Milton might be dead as a doornail, but Krishna is smiling his little blue smile.

4

A Young Voice:
Nine to Nineteen

My voice as a musician has developed continuously over a life devoted to music. When I make music I want its perfection to be heard, and that is the driver. My writer's voice, however, has developed catch-as-catch-can: sporadic journal writing, a poetic impulse here and there, out-of-the-blue projects, or snail-mail letters when there were such things. I've always been aware that there was some drive, some bossy tailwind that moved the pen, but I shrugged it off as an *accoutrement* from my literary family and artsy education, an unearned inheritance. To be sure, four published books have made me look inside the central nervous system of the craft. More importantly, they have made me quicken to the hearts of writer and reader beating together, and the roiling fields of language our minds are playing in. As I'm writing *The Shrine Thief*, my fifth and likely my last, I'm ever more curious about our connection in the moment of writing and reading—you and me right now, this felt presence that spurs my reluctant self to write.

The three chapters in this book devoted to my journals serve as a micro-autobiography told through the journalistic lens, an album of imaginary photographs, many stories woven into a single life story told by someone learning to tell it.

My sister Sue was thirteen when I was nine. Like most girls her age, she kept a diary, which she warned me to never-ever-*ever* touch or even *think* about reading. In little-brother retaliation, I placed "Five-Year Diary" at the top of my 1946 Christmas list, pushing my request for a photographic enlarger down to second place. Sure enough, under the tree on Christmas morning of my ninth year appeared *The Rumson Five Year Diary* bound in real leather. On the inside cover I wrote:

> IF LOSTED REURN TO ME...
> IF NOT LOSTED LEAVE ALONE!

And on the flyleaf I wrote:

> I got this for Christmas 1946. I had a very merry one. I got an enlarger. My first enlargement turned out to be very good.

Every day, I wrote a sentence or more. Here are a few entries. (Johnny, a year ahead of me, was my nextdoor neighbor).

> *Friday January 3, 1947*
> Got flu shots. Johnny had some cigarettes and we smoked them. It was fun. Got a splinter in my leg. Flu shots reacted.

> *Monday January 6, 1947*
> First day of school. Sue washed my face with snow. I had a piano lesson. Headline of *The Cincinnati Post* was "15° above zero." It's the coldest day of the year so far.

> *Monday February 3, 1947*
> I had a Music Lesson. I got Mozart Sonata K. 545 in C. It's a pretty hard piece and very beautiful.

> *Thursday February 27, 1947*
> Nothin' much

> *Sunday March 9, 1947*
> Didn't have to go to Sunday school. There wasn't any.

The daily discipline then ceased abruptly in favor of music practice, a portent of a lifelong jousting match between words and music.

The next year, I fell in love with my fifth-grade teacher, Miss Virginia Rhode, a tall blonde ranch woman from Colorado who, like my parents, was in her mid-forties. She was forthright, dear, a perfect teacher of children, and I was her special child. My mother invited her over for dinner, after which she posed by the fireplace mantel while I shot out a roll of Tri-X film. Next day, I developed the film and made prints. *Gosh, she's pretty*, I thought as I watched her images appear one after another in the developer. I gave her the two best prints. "*Aw-w-w,*" she said. A few weeks after that, as Miss Rhode was giving my class of ten-year-olds a grammar lesson, she sternly cautioned us never to begin a sentence with *And.* By that age, I had read some of my father's books. My hand shot up, but with a dismissive wave of her wrist, Miss Rhode said, "Oh, well not *you,* Bill," thus exonerating me forever from at least one needless, plebeian rule of grammar. Ms. Rhode's recognition allowed me to identify myself as a writer, as someone with permission to write with my own voice. Even though this was a vivid moment in my life, I was too preoccupied with learning music to write much of anything save obligatory letters to family members. But with a certain sense of superiority, I wore Miss Rhode's permission like a badge.

By spring 1950, the end of seventh grade, I was about to turn a fully pubescent thirteen and had a lot to say. I picked up the diary again, filling in the pages I'd left blank three years earlier. It begins with a memory from 1946.

Late May 1950 [age 12, remembering age 9]
In 1946, Johnny started a fire by accident. Mother decided to get rid of an old stump. She used gasoline, and the stump burned a long time as an ember. One day Johnny and I got the brainy inspiration to start small fires in the woods and then stomp them out, but the fires, fed on the dry leaves of the preceding autumn, kept spreading. The flames were low to the ground and they spread with incredible speed. Johnny ran up to a house not too far away. Some men came and put out the fire with shovels. Since I'd been elected to stay with the burning stump, my hair and eyebrows got outstandingly singed. When it was all over, Johnny managed to sneak into his house and procure a dull scissors with which he cut my hair and eyebrows by almost pulling them out. With said shave and haircut I went home where I was questioned for days about the strange appearance of my hair. Eventually I took the blame for playing with fire, but Mom took the blame for trying to let the stump burn itself out.

The following is written toward the end of an eight-week stay at Camp Roosevelt, a boy's camp on Lake Eerie, far from my Cincinnati home.

Late August 1950 [age 13]
A diary is a thing in which you record your notes, experiences, and feelings. For nearly two months I have recorded my experiences. Now I will try feelings, just as they come to mind.

Camp is supposed to be a place where you learn to have fun, apply discipline, and learn to get along with other boys. Well, to me camp is a burden. Why is it? I like to be alone to think. To share my own company. I like to play my own style of music different from any other I have ever heard. And I don't believe camp will teach me to get along with other boys because I know I won't return to Roosevelt and so care little about what people think of me or how they talk about me.

Last week I had a dream. Somehow I was home. I embraced everything, every piece of furniture, every person, every building. Who am I to say what dreams mean, but I know I've been away from home too long. I listen to the radio about 2½ hours a day— I'm listening as I write. Songs like *Tenderly* and *Slaughter on Tenth Avenue* thrill me no end. That alone is worth a lot to me.

My sense of isolation stoked my desire to write. There is a sense of relief in the act of writing down on flat paper in cogent sentences what was swirling around inside. I hear the nascent writing quality of a boy whose soprano voice is about to change to baritone. And indeed, by late September, I was immersed in school, parties, and the full flush of puberty, and my writing voice seems primarily hormonal.

Friday, September 29
We all gathered at Wise Temple and then rode up to Handle Bar Ranch in a hay wagon without any hay. Mary and Sylvia brought their ukes and we sang and sang and sang. When we got there we rode bikes and then ate dinner. After dinner we had the wildest time ever. There is a hill overlooking Handle Bar, and most of the kids climbed up there and literally just tackled everybody in sight. Some people tackled just for the sake of tackling. Another reason was so that the girls would fall on top of you. Then we danced, and came home in wagons with real hay.

January 17, 1951
The music world is a gaping hole waiting to envelop me. I am on the doorstep of this cave, waiting to plod into its depths, to obey its commands and accept its challenges. Its trials and tribulations. And its endless pleasures.

February 26, 1951
I should not consider myself such a high and mighty immortal. Conceit is all right if you have something to be conceited about. Happens that I don't. Today was a pretty bad day. I said something. Very bad. It was to Laura. She was opening her locker and I said, "What's that in there, your Kotex?" She slapped me really hard.

Alice was with her. Before I knew it, Sylvia knew, and said, "I would have done more than slapped." Then Sue knew, and she doesn't *respect boys like that* and Jane was an icicle. I apologized but in a meager, gruff way. I felt horrible about it because it could have cost me jobs for my band. And to top it off I was on damn bad terms with my parents. This was a bad day.

February 27, 1951
I recovered from yesterday, and the girls were nice enough to forgive and forget. I'll have to live right the second time around. My band got the Wise Temple dance job.

March 10, 1951
The primary reason for me starting a band is really in effect now—popularity. All the girls: Jane, but Sylvia especially. And Lynn and Mary. But it's just an introduction, a first step. I have to do the rest for myself.

March 14, 1951
Maybe I think too much about my popularity and that's why I'm not as popular as I could be—??

March 23, 1951
First you go to parties where children's games are played. Then parties where boys always throw food, then you play Wink, and Post Office, and then dance close. And then at last you go to parties where people can sit around and talk. We've reached that stage. The party broke early, but for two hours we entertained ourselves by telling or shouting amusing stories, anecdotes, jokes, clean and otherwise, impressions, and opinions. It was pleasing. I'd like to live it over again.

March 31, 1951
I remember at a certain dancing class I was acting very "feminine" around Jane. I think it was after that that we broke up. So then the striking blow came when Dad said that if you are, as I am, just a touch feminine, sometimes, and kiddingly, you act feminine, "it's a burlesque on yourself." Then Mom said I was really very masculine, so why do I do what I do? Well—of course that's the answer. I idolize Mary and Sylvia and some other girls who are popular and try to act like them. If I act like someone else—well, who wants to be a fake, anyway? So I tried acting like me last night on my date, and it really worked. I had a wonderful time and I know Janie did too.

April 27, 1951
Well, the impossible has happened—in dancing class I won the cup for best dancer. I was dancing with Jill, and right in front of Jane! We went into semi-finals, but we could have won only if we could do more than one step. So at the last minute I rigged up with Jill another step Mr. Goorian taught us.

Conversation went thus:

> "Let me lead.... Okay go straight...now (we do the new step)... straight...now...He's watching, OK, wait...OK, now...etc. Well, four couples left...3...2. It was torture. I was shaking all over and Jill was really scared, but we managed to keep rhythm. With only two couples remaining, Goorian was going to give cups to each couple, but the class booed it. After a lifetime of panging torture: "Well, it was really tough but here you are...." He handed Jill and I each our cup. I'm going to have mine engraved tomorrow at Richter's Jewelers. I think Goorian was mad that the best dancers in the class could only do two steps.

Although I did write up certain events that seemed important, the daily writing stopped while music, dating, and my band, The Musical Knights, took over my life. The last entry in my high school journal came in the middle of my sophomore year.

> *December 1, 1952* [age 14]
> Writing makes these thoughts drift in to less distance *from*, more in relation *to* one another. The goal is to sort them into a cobweb file. The Lord knew what He said when he uttered, "Know thyself"—if He really said it, which is debatable.

I abandoned my diary entirely at that point. Every spare moment, and many I could not spare, was taken up with playing, writing, listening to, and thinking about music. A year and a half later, as a high school junior, I was accepted to the University of Chicago as an early entrant. Sue was already there, a college senior and newly married to Boris, about to graduate from law school. In the Spring of 1954, they arranged a visit to campus for me. I went on the train by myself and tried to feel grown up in the big city. During my whirlwind visit there were interviews with professors, tours of the campus, and visits with Boris's Chicago family. On Easter Sunday, I had some time alone.

Dancing at Thirteen

On Easter the campus is desolate. By stepping through an archway on 59th Street, I found a spot that seemed most beautiful of all—a quadrangle, an acre or so, with tall gray buildings rising on every side. There are numerous slender black trees, and the long symmetries of rock-tile paths. I witnessed this under an overcast sky that added to the musty hue of the walls. Among these tons of stone and air, I was the only seeable soul. Each path led to its own door without looking back; the trees looked upon the rooftops and spires; dead ivy that had once been green and moving now clung to the gray, the brown roots lost upward into complexity. Seen from below by one who deemed himself invisible, the entire scene seemed to say, "I have looked this weighty way for many years and will for many years after you are gone." So when it was time to meet up with my new friends I left the gothic splendor to contemplate its own self.

Fresh from my seventeenth birthday, I was once more packed off on the train. That freshman year was delirious with romantic, academic, and musical episodes exploding around me in slow motion. To two romantic partners, I wrote pages of poems, none of which, singly or in aggregate, resulted in the loss of my virginity. Prose was limited

The Musical Knights

to essays and letters. The impulse to resume journal writing didn't show up until the spring of my sophomore year, when I was eighteen going on nineteen.

Journal from the End of Winter, 1956, University of Chicago
Volume I

The initial inspiration for this journal was Boswell's London Journal, written in 1762 and first published in 1950. I identified with the young man. He writes "a journal will improve me in expression, and knowing that I am to record my transactions will make me more careful to do well." But it is not only fascination with Boswell that has led me to contemplate this effort. Several months ago I became very high on many swallows of cognac. As I was lying deliriously in bed I reached over and traced on the wall with my finger the word YOUNG. Then, as inebriated, and other times as more sober, I have been almost happy to be over seventeen and under twenty. Last night I realized that, with the tax of years, I will lose such an enormous part of who I presently am that I can only hope to recapture a small part of it with this journal of my thoughts and actions.

Gigging at Sixteen

Thus begins a four-volume 711-page chronicle of the next six months of my seemingly momentous life. A discernible writing voice seems to emerge.

During spring break, on a trip back to our suburban Cincinnati home in Silverton, I went up the street to the village crossroads of Kennedy Heights to get a haircut at my boyhood barbershop, after which I decided to go home by the schoolboy's shortcut.

Thursday, March 22, 1956
After buying a Dairy Queen, and reading comic books in the barber's chair all through my haircut, I tramped home through the woods between Kennedy and Silverton. My mind began to work in terms of which tree to grab for balance, which stone to step on, which path to follow, but I felt too dignified in my camel's hair coat to be looking out for the really big guys.

A few days later I sat in on a jazz nightclub gig in the city. I played trumpet and felt I had arrived as a legitimate novice on the local jazz scene.

Sunday, March 25, 1956
The thrilling danger of the wet streets and the speed felt good to me as I drove home. We are most cautiously reckless when we are happy.

Back in Chicago, I had an insight about writing.

Saturday, March 31, 1956
This journal has become very time consuming, but it always comes first on my list of things to do. I'm still fond of it. Yet I mustn't let the knowledge that whatever important thing I do will be recorded (and thus must be remembered) spoil the beauty of the moment.

Monday, April 9, 1956
I just discovered a note I wrote this morning. I told myself to "just keep going, my life is too good for me."

Tuesday, April 10, 1956
As I was writing this afternoon, Seth came in, and with a congratulatory smirk informed me that the winner of the Matthews House Poetry Contest was my poem, "y o I u." I win $5.00. Even though the booty was small, the prize made me feel pretty fine; I think the poem is good and so does Connie, whom it was for, and to whom I am in debted for the opening line, *You and me duck foot*. Seth said the judges thought my title was obscene. I replied, "Damn right! The whole poem is as obscene as I could write it." I played piano for a bit, studied, listened to some music, and went to bed feeling like almost someone.

Just before I dropped off to sleep, I experienced a marvelous feeling of self-satisfaction. I was pretty nearly happy. As I became more and more excited, it occurred to me that if nothing else, I could contribute to the music world the terrific energy and purpose I was feeling just then.

Here is the poem that won $5.00 in the Matthews House Poetry Contest:

y o I u

You and me duck foot
walking down the lane,
night-rain smell the garden seeps,
child-wild the daylight leaps,
Who can taste the just-up sun,
Anyone?
You and me moony man,
WE CAN !

(and I transparent head encircling
your lips are the moonfruit
hovering succulence inside
I am the rind)

You and me pigtail
kissing on the lawn,
warm the moisty night-time is,
long the listening silence seems,
anxious-dangle the darkness dreams,
Who wants tingle-tangle fun,
Anyone?
You and me kangaroo,
WE DO !

(and the rain settles into the earth
which it dissolves finding welcome
after the delicious storm-breakfast
I am the melting snow)

You and me bass-string
playing in the park,
how we saw the world get old,
boasted grins and funny-faces,

danced with birds in sunny places,
Who made fun of the white-haired nun,
Anyone?
You and me beggar-kid,
WE DID !

So far, my journal writing shows the influence of my careful teachers in the College, of Boswell's eighteenth-century prose, and of a smattering of other writers including, evidently, e.e. cummings. But then something happened that had a deep, lasting effect: I read Truman Capote's *Other Voices, Other Rooms*. The moment I finished, I began writing with a new presence inside me. Was this Capote's voice, or my own voice that his raw intimacy had awakened?

Thursday, May 3, 1956
Reading, he forgot the other world and turned inside to the real one, to the young boy in the moisty hot swamp catching tree toads. He had never really seen a tree toad, but he cherished them as a love. The girl too, with the arrogant, just swelling breasts, was his and she slapped him softly when he bent to kiss her cheek. He lit a cigarette to enjoy more luxury. The words in front of him formed death fear young first almost love pink male skin hairless lemon smelling coolness or was it warmth. He lived the tale of Europe and Cuba in every sunbeam and particle of dust. The dreams of being real meant a lot to him and he knew that someday Dolores would outrun him; he could feel the formless touch of her fingertips on the nape of his neck. This Was The End. Am I me? The ending left its mark. He threw the book aside and turned off the light. *Boy was he ever queer.* No, on again. He put on some music, lit another cigarette, turned off the light, and lay outstretched. He saw the outstretched hand beckoning to him. Outstretched? No. Concentrate: strings, well voiced. Sleep? Eyes closed were tense, eyes open saw the non-existent images of his room. He was conscious of his mind, a fullness, Randolph's pink cheeks, snowflakes, and impact. He thought: a stupor that supersedes inspiration. *There is writing on the wall.* He could hear the clicks of the furnace pump below his room. How to write that? Click click click click click clcq clicq clicq clicqe clique clique clique clique, crowd, mob, no, don't start thinking about high school. Is the music in time with the clicks now?—that would be miraculous. No, it misses by a beat in twelve. His cigarette was down to a stump. He threw it on the floor. Now he remembered: Truman Capote. How was it pronounced? The music ended. He waited. There. Yes. That's all. Now, think. I have discovered this

before, it is *I*. I shall write *I* many times for *I* is me. *I I I I I I I I I I I I I I I I I I I I I I I I II....* Now the impact is...slipping—no there it is, I feel it. *Jesus, some people can write!* Try to sleep, no, think instead of *finding* oneself. Yes. It is a marvelous experience to read about someone else, especially if you find yourself to be someone warm and wonderful like a homosexual, or any kind of person with a beating heart.

I didn't keep the faux-Capote style in my journal prose for very long, but the heavy perfume of *Other Voices, Other Rooms* has stayed with me for life. It is like no other book, and came to me at a good time.

Friday, May 25, 1956
After dinner, Johnny, Arthur, Max, and I were sitting outside in the Gothic courtyard when four children, ages five to ten, descended upon us. We encouraged them with stories, jokes, and mock battles. Max amused them (and us) with his Lewis Carroll, not to mention his infant-wise personality, but soon we sank into the inevitability of horseback and war. For about a half-hour we had our fun on two levels. With the children hoisted on our shoulders clawing each other and us, we carried on sober-faced conversations.
"I got this suit at Brooks Brothers. Such expense!"
"Nice cloth. Tweed?"
"Yes, and I told the young man that's entirely too much to pay for a suit."
We spun and tossed the children about until we were exhausted, and when they cried for more we answered breathlessly that it was past their bedtime.

Saturday, July 7, 1956 [age 19]
I wish I could stop thinking about my journal as so many pages of printed matter: it should be a release and a problem-solver, not a potential publisher's prize. Joanne told me moths ago that *you owe it to yourself to keep writing*, and she has the right idea.

Tuesday, July 17, 1956
After dinner at home, I picked up Connie and we drove to the farm to take a night walk. All was as it should have been: clouds, stars, warmth, Nature. We embraced each other until we could come no closer. I looked at the moon then and asked her to marry me, and she said yes, and I held her so tightly I broke my watch band. Then we found a place in the pasture and made love, and it was the wonderful thing it always should be. I hope for a millennium of this.

Connie and Me

Friday, October 26, 1956

We had Margery [an old flame] over for dinner, but as soon as she left Connie began a tirade of insults, ending only with, "I hate her."

"Well, here we go again," I thought.

But after a spell we decided to ride our bicycles and it turned into a beautiful pre-honeymoon. Whooshing down the middle of channeled streets we revisited our old homes and saw our old ghosts lingering in doorways. The Chicago night was black, silent, and windless. We rode alongside each other talking in low voices. The day was saved. Riding back home, we were sitting still and the streets were sliding under us.

The journal, now up to Volume IV, abruptly ends on November 17, 1956, the day Connie and I went to the Cook County Courthouse to obtain a civil marriage license. The rest of my junior year and all of my senior year were consumed by disciplined academic study, composing audition scores for Stan Kenton, producing a tutorial thesis (*Changes in Jazz Styles, 1915-1955*), and composing a musical based on Molière's *The Imaginary Invalid*. The marriage, the music, and the academic work were all on an upward swing, but there would be only occasional and brief journal entries until I was safely out of college and traveling with the Stan Kenton band in early 1959.

PART TWO

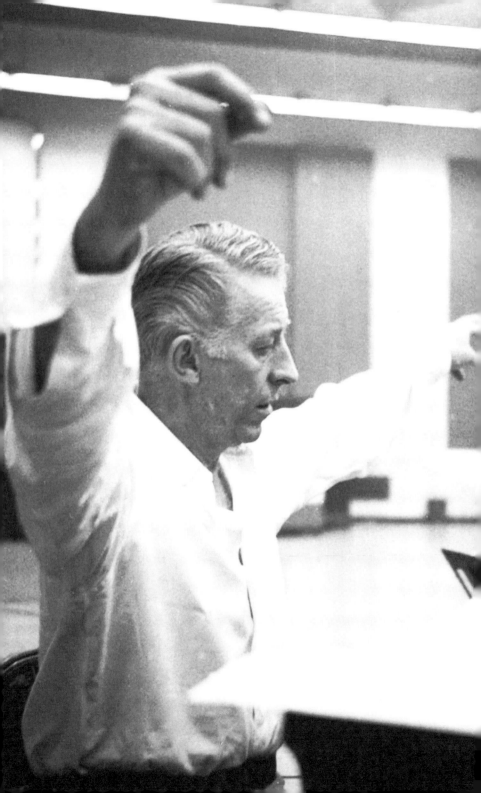

5

The Old Man

When I was fifty years old, I thought I had something book-length to say, but I did not have enough confidence in my writing skills to write a book. I read Natalie Goldberg's *Writing Down the Bones* and was startled to find myself in it as the teacher who told her that making music is ninety percent listening, an observation she applied to writing as well. She also said, famously, "Write what you know," advice that has guided the careers of many a writer. I, for one, took it to heart.

The story that was closest to my heart at the time was about the year I spent with the Stan Kenton band in 1959. I overcame the loss of the journal I had been keeping at that time and dug heavily into my memories, my memorabilia, and the memories of my musician friends. The experiences of the Kenton year went from the mania of applause and success to the despair of splintered love. The heart of the matter was that Kenton had become, by the time I was thirteen, a surrogate father to me. Following the usual course, I first idolized him, then recognized him, then deflated him, and finally accepted him fully for who he had been to me, and for who he was.

I wrote the story thirty years after it had happened, and it is now thirty-five years since I wrote it. Natalie was right! The emotional energy pulled sentences out of me I hadn't imagined were in me, and I read and reread my own writing with astonishment. Well, I got over that, and forthwith decided to get on with saying what I had to say about music. I thought I could do that in one book, but it took four— three of them for general readers and one tome weighing three-and-a-half pounds for serious musical nerds. The piece on Stan Kenton

I've saved all these years for just the right place in just the right book, and now here it appears in this very place in this very book.

Counting The Ways

> Now you are tangled up in others, and have forgotten what you once knew, and that's why everything you do has some weird failure in it.
>
> –Kabir, translated by Robert Bly

I am thirteen and it is a crisp autumn Sunday afternoon in a northern suburb of Cincinnati. My new brown jazz teacher has driven over from the other side of some tracks in his old wooden station wagon. He's big, and curly on top, and there is purpose in his eyes as he strides across the living room to the family Magnavox.

"Listen to this, Bill," he says, laying a ten-inch 78 onto the turntable. The new 1950-model automatic arm advances, dropping the stylus onto the disc with a familiar crackle. The opening phrase of music takes ten seconds, by the end of which I have risen over the roof of our nine-room house, out over the Ohio Valley, out of my family, beyond the conditions of my gentle birth and careful upbringing. Nothing will ever be the same.

This record is called *Maynard Ferguson* and is by the Stan Kenton Orchestra. What I hear is precisely this, note by note:

All by itself, a trumpet a perfect, brief high C into the air, then a loud, ringing F above it. This F is the highest note I've heard on the trumpet, an instrument I'd begun to play that summer. The F hangs briefly, then a powerful force lifts it up a whole tone to G; then it slips back through F to the original note, the high C. By this time (two seconds) all of my pubescent energies have charged to my crown and are waving in bright orange recognition. There is a brief silence, then the phrase is verified by repetition (two more seconds). A more dramatic pause.

The phrase is repeated once again, but the energy is more intense. My perception of myself, a boy in a living room with his teacher, vanishes. My inner ear has become a panoramic eye and it sees only this sound. Now the sound begins on the high F, rises resolutely to the G, stretches up to a clear pure A and leaps with immense white arms to a perfect double-high C. As it arrives there I am no longer hearing it, no longer seeing it. I have expanded into it. I am seated on a flying throne in a new wide sky.

Describing how he arrived at the theory of relativity, Einstein once said he imagined he was riding on a photon and from that position saw the universe in a new way. Riding Maynard Ferguson's double-high C did that for me.

The music unfolds. I stand frozen in my parents' house. The soaring cries of the Kenton trumpets are a lens through which the chaos of adolescence becomes focused and refined. At the end of the record my teacher is standing arms akimbo with a look of triumph on his face. He knows: I want more.

I am fifty-one now, living in the forest of my musical life, with foothills near and snow-lined ridges visible yonder. The other day a student asked me an innocent question about brass voicing and I answered by playing him Bill Russo's arrangement of "Fascinating Rhythm," recorded by Kenton in 1953. By midnight I was alone on the floor with my stereo and a dozen Stan Kenton albums lying face up. I listened to them in chronological order. I spent 1959 with the band as an arranger/composer and trumpet player. Men of my age are familiar with modes of nostalgia, adept at replaying life-tapes. On this night I ran my whole Kenton life-tape and, to my astonishment, found out something about love I hadn't known.

&

My father was cautious about his only son's fascination with jazz, but he searched out Buddy Hiles, the best jazz composer and arranger in Cincinnati, and offered him five dollars a week to teach me. Buddy, then in his early thirties, directed *the* black swing band in the area, and held odd jobs. After a few months, he had me writing for five saxophones and seven brass. He enjoyed watching me grow into his world, and we grew fond of one another.

I was one of the many kids across the county saving their allowances to buy the current 10-inch 78-rpm Kenton releases on Capitol Records. As I collected them, the sound of Kenton's world grew richer and more subtle, as did my identity with it. I discovered the trombones. Their five-tone chords were rooms in my dark mansion. Each room had a special resonance that made the walls vibrate and the black space between the walls glow. By identifying the notes of the chords, I became master of the resonances and the glowing spaces.

Our Baldwin spinet piano was in the dining room, five steps from the Magnavox in the living room. Many days after school, Mom would find me dropping the brown robot arm on the one exact groove of the record that contained the chord I needed to learn, running to the piano to duplicate the five tones, then back to find the next chord on the record, back and forth, racing and listening and opening to my true trombone nature. A fourteen-year-old's eyes can see the individual grooves on a 78-rpm record. That is where Stan Kenton lived, in those dark shellac canyons. As I plundered them, they turned gray with wear.

The junior high seven-piece dance band I started became the band of demand, and we played Kenton's *Intermission Riff* with flair. I was its pianist, learning harmony by memorizing dozens of pop tunes and standards, but I was in love with the trumpet, striving lustily for high notes that wouldn't come. All my teachers bade me stop trying to sound like Maynard Ferguson and practice fundamentals, but the lure was too great—I would try till I passed out and, when my head cleared, try some more. Mother was worried about my neck size. I wrecked my embouchure forever, probably, but the callus that formed under my lip I endured with pride. Someday I would *be* that sound and claim my right to the throne.

Behind my books in English class, I wrote music for ten brass and five reeds, hoping the cashmere girls who sat all around would respond to my true self. They thought I was weird. Terrifyingly painful migraines became an increasing part of my life. I discovered that loud passages of Kenton brass would numb the pain, transforming it into a shimmering fit of light.

Although my personality was being woven into the personality of Kenton's music, the idea of Kenton as an actual man with a personality this music mirrored had not occurred to me. Lying in bed late one afternoon, waiting for Pete Rugolo's *Mirage* to rescue me from migraine, I found myself staring at the cover of *A Presentation of Progressive Jazz*—a lurid publicity photo displaying Stan's wide smile and, on my copy, where the color printing was out of registration, green gums.

I propped myself up on one elbow, adjusted the light, and let my eyes sink into the green gums of an actual man. It was the flawed color, the obvious hype of Stan's pose, the misfired cunning of it all that enabled me to see the man beneath the image, and I said, "Hello, Stan." Still smiling hideously, the picture said, "Hello, Bill." Henceforth I looked deeply into all available publicity pictures, imagining what Kenton was *really* like and engaging him in nocturnal conversations too secret for words.

Around 11:00 one night, as I was listening illicitly to the radio under my blanket in my upstairs darkened room, a live remote of the band miraculously came in from Austin, Texas. *The Theme* played, Stan talked, and Maynard Ferguson played *Maynard Ferguson*. There, with the big tube radio under the stuffy sheet, my identification with Stan Kenton was complete. My own music in my private world. Suddenly—horrors—the reception was obliterated by the static of a nearby appliance. I rushed to the top of the stairs and, hearing my father's electric razor, leapt wildly down, flung myself into the bathroom, and yelled, "Stop, Dad, turn it off! Stan Kenton is on the radio from Texas."

Razor whining, Dad looked down more in astonishment than in anger.

"Why are you listening to the radio?"

"It's *live*. Maynard is playing. RIGHT NOW!"

Then he did get angry. He sent me sternly to bed. I guess he was just making his face smooth for Mom.

In electric rage, I lay awake hearing my own Kenton broadcast in my mind, with exploding brass climaxes and Stan's suave voice. A few days later, Dad casually invited me to go hear Stan Kenton at Orchestra Hall. "Well," I said coolly, "if you really want to go."

In that autumn of 1951, Stan was thirty-nine years old. I was fourteen. When Stan was fourteen, in 1926, he was "all music," he once said. "Nothing else ever entered my mind." He, too, had gained popularity in high school by leading a band. For fifteen years he jobbed around the West Coast, playing piano for a living, and was successful but unknown and restless. In 1940, he discovered that forming and leading a band was his best life choice, and he wrote a library of experimental music that turned his shy personality inside out. This was perhaps his greatest creative act. The new music was brash, fanfare-like, sometimes sweeping, often static. Though not dissimilar to other 1940s dance music, it was more elaborately punctuated, very loud, and, for that time, displayed a refined craft.

Biographer Carol Easton, in discussing the slim gate receipts of the Innovations in Modern Music tours of 1950 and 1951, says, "Attendance was spotty for the same reason that few art lovers would flock to an exhibit that combined the work of Andy Warhol and Norman Rockwell." The contradiction in this image might be cast over Stan's lifelong musical output. Stan was wedded to the outrageous and the prosaic. In the early days, the listeners and the dancers would even get into fights, Andy and Norman slugging it out. But Stan's Andy activated Stan's Norman. They needed each other.

Over ten years of enormous effort, Kenton's timely and masterful integration of these two impulses gained him worldwide fame and adulation. By 1947, the limitless energy he put into selling his band had become a legend in the music industry. No one could explain his stamina. Periodically he drove himself and his musicians past possibility into varieties of breakdown. But the rewards remained compelling, addicting.

Many other arrangers and composers came into his fold. The band stabilized at nineteen players—five trumpets, five trombones, and five saxophones, with bass, drums, guitar, and piano. Stan's leadership became flamboyant, majestic, larger than life. He developed a bountiful charisma. His demon work energy produced enormous crowds to cheer him on; he fed them with his embracing presence. His band was his body, and his band-body lumbered through America, inhaling applause and exhaling music.

When I was ten I caught a glimpse of President Truman and wondered about the light around his body. He was an ordinary-looking man; why should his body be limned with white light, especially at noonday? I surmised later that this is the light of large populations arcing back through their leaders.

When Stan walked out onto the stage of Cincinnati's Orchestra Hall that November night in 1951, white light was around his body. At first, I sat quietly in its glow, but as the music picked up momentum, I grew so excited that the woman behind me had to put her hand on my head, as if I were a child. The music was alive, the players magicians, their instruments magic fountains. Excerpts from Bob Graettinger's *City of Glass* were played. Maynard Ferguson played *Maynard Ferguson*. I noticed that the men were real. The beautifully sensual vocalist June Christy was real. The brass climaxes affirmed it. This was my life's work, my connection to the world.

After the concert, my father insisted that I say hello to Kenton and half-dragged me backstage. Kenton, at six-foot-four, appeared to be immensely tall. He wore his beltline high, exaggerating his long legs. In a moment, I was in his glance. He seemed to have been waiting for me. I introduced myself and blurted out, "I want to write for your band."

He motioned me to a protected little space near the light board where we could talk quietly. He put his left leg up on a chair, threw his right arm across the leg, and asked me questions about my schooling. I told him about Buddy Hiles, and composing music in English class.

"I think it's wonderful that you want to write for us," he said.

"Don't write whole pieces, just sounds, and label them 'Sound Number One,' 'Sound Number Two,' and 'Sound Number Three.'" These titles glistened with modernity. He told me to keep in touch, and when I was ready, the band would play my music. On the car ride home, when I told Dad that Stan would play whatever I wrote, he said, "Of course."

My courtship with Stan Kenton was a secret none of my friends could understand, and it gave me ammunition against the woes of my virginal adolescence. I wrote and wrote, whatever I could: an overture for the school orchestra, arrangements for Buddy's band and my own, fragments for any players who would rehearse with me. I played French horn in orchestra and routinely added dissonant notes—for modernity. When the conductor would point and say, "Wrong note in the horn," I'd shrug and say, "Difficult instrument."

The feeling of approaching greatness often stole over me. Every night, before turning off the light, I would listen to *Dance Before the Mirrors*, the most accessible movement from *City of Glass*. I could scarcely follow it, even after a hundred hearings, but it spoke a future language my marrow understood. When the Kenton band came to town, there would be me standing in front, looking up. And, within moments, Stan would look down and say, "Hello, Bill," and flash me his real-life smile with pink gums. He well knew that his recognition was the light of my life.

Stan lost a quarter million of his own dollars on the Innovations Orchestra tours of 1950 and 1951. In 1952, he was on the road playing dance music, but what dance music! The core of the book was by Bill Russo, Bill Holman, and Gerry Mulligan, and the new level of skill and subtlety drew me in. This was *happy* music I could grasp, not weird music over my head.

In the fall of '52, Stan and I made an appointment for June of '53, when the band would be in the large ballroom at Coney Island, the amusement park east of Cincinnati. I wrote music endlessly, on the bus, in class, or in bed at night with a flashlight. Sitting in History writing histrionic brass parts was power! Sexy sax voicings in Social Studies were power! Stan had lent me his power.

By June of '53, I was ready with *Sound Numbers One, Two, and Three*. My destiny was calling. Perhaps there was a little light around my body, who knows? Buddy Hiles and Dad accompanied me on the great day. Buddy couldn't get in the front door—blacks were barred. Kenton arranged to have Buddy arrive through the service entrance, then carefully rehearsed three of his scores.

It's late in the afternoon when Stan finally beckons to me.

"What do you have for us, Bill?"

The musicians are not amused to see a fifteen-year-old boy clutching his music. In the tired silence, I pass the parts out and show Stan the score for *Sound Number One*. It is a single whole-tone cluster for ten brass. Once and for all, I want to satisfy myself about the mystery of whole tones. Stan gives a downbeat, and the ten brass play the chord. It sounds very plain. No mystery.

"What's *Sound Number Two*?" Nonplussed, Stan looks down at the score. It is a trombone solo with a roving baritone counterpoint, plus some rooms from my dark mansion. The band plays it through. My ears get very large. I hear everything. It works! A few of the players sit up and look me over.

Bill Holman says, "Yeah, man, okay."

I ask to hear it again.

Stan says, "You count it off, Bill." It's even better this time.

Sound Number Three is an arrangement of a chorus of *Summertime*, with an improvised alto solo for Lee Konitz. Stan counts it off, and I clamber down the bandstand to the empty floor of the ballroom. As the band plays the opening bars, I back up twenty yards, the better to hear the blend. A new reality unfolds: real men playing music I have written for them. They are working, I am working. There is a pact. Konitz begins to play, and the scene is lit up. The special feeling of total rightness fills the great room. Big Stan is conducting; Little Stan is drinking it in. I know the rest of my life will go forward from this marked moment.

At the big climax, the trumpet player Buddy Childers plays the double-high Bb, and I go out the top of my head. I clamber back onto the stage, and Stan says, "You should be very proud of yourself, Bill." He calls in the parts, dismisses the band, and beckons to an alarmingly thin young man with cheek fuzz—it's Bob Graettinger.

"Take Bill over to the table and show him some things," says Stan.

Brushing by Lee Konitz, I say, "Thanks, man," and he smiles mysteriously as if he knows my secret and says nothing.

On a sheet of music paper, Graettinger jots down the first sixteen notes of the overtone series, pointing out that the fifteenth one "is an especially in-tune major seventh," the significance of which I understand two decades later when Graettinger is long dead.

I ride back to the band's hotel with Stan and a few of the guys. In the cool evening under a milky sky, the car winds along the green valley of the Ohio River, but the magic is gone. No matter how I strive to be among them, I am a boy among men. Small talk. Rushing wind. Stan asks me questions about the river and the town, but I don't know the answers. I haven't been knighted; there are no crowds, no auras, no big-minded conversations, just people in a car, resting. But it is okay. The innocent days of courtship are over.

Later that year, Stan lent me scores by Bill Russo and Gene Roland from the band's book, which I copied and returned. I started a rehearsal band. By now, I had some high-school clout. I was "writing for Stan." I put on a jazz concert featuring three Kenton scores with full orchestration, plus my own music. I was even going steady with a cashmere and making out in cars. On the crest of this success, my strongest impulse was to skip my senior year. I got accepted as an early entrant to the University of Chicago and called Stan.

"What should I do now?"

"Bill Russo is teaching in Chicago. Study with him and keep in touch."

With relief and smug arrogance, I kissed high school goodbye. Stan had got me through.

శా

In 1954, Bill Russo was twenty-seven; I was seventeen. He had been working for Kenton since 1950 as a writer and trombonist, and understood the nature of my bond. He was learning to be a teacher then, formalizing his skills and intuitions into a jazz pedagogy. He taught me music very well, but more than this, he helped me get past my blind love for Stan and the blind ambition behind it. The course of Bill's relationship with Stan did not run smooth, and though he was careful not to lick his wounds in front of me, he let me know he had them. I was amazed, appalled. I thought famous people were happy. Russo was my realist. Over many years, we tugged and turned until now, thirty years later, we are life-friends.

Russo opened me to a larger world of composition. In the 1950s, the University of Chicago had one of the great liberal arts colleges of all time. My Kentonitis abated. I spent a long, instructive episode as pianist for The Compass Players, which starred Mike Nichols, Elaine May, Severn Darden, Shelley Berman, and other brilliant talents from the Chicago theater scene. In an ecstasy of ripening, I got married.

Meanwhile, Stan was winning polls for Best Bandleader. The 1955 band recorded *Contemporary Concepts*, mostly Bill Holman's charts. In early 1956 there was a wildly successful tour of Great

Britain. Stan married his one-time vocalist, Ann Richards, who gave him a daughter, Dana Lyn. Mostly, though, he was on the road playing dance music.

By the spring of 1956, I had been studying with Russo for almost two years; it was time to display my hand again. I called Stan, and we set an audition date for June at the Blue Note, Chicago's jazz nightclub. Russo guided me, putting a governor on my excesses while coaching me in the larger game. If Stan must be the target, Russo taught me at least to discriminate in my selection of arrows. Often we disagreed. Once Russo questioned a title of mine, *Trilogy*.

"Stan's been known to choose a piece because of its title," he warned.

I thought a lot about that. How could it be? Book by its cover? Not Stan, surely.

I changed it to *Dialogue for Further Voices*. On the afternoon of the rehearsal, I felt like the man of the hour. During those days I kept a journal, and here is what I wrote that day, the first day of summer in my eighteenth year:

> *Thursday, June 21, 1956*
> Stan was late. He looked rushed and tired. For an hour and a half he slogged through five poorly written scores by other arrangers. The band sounded unbelievably bad, but as I looked straight into the footlights I saw success for myself. Finally Stan turned to me, introduced me to the band, asked me to distribute the parts and give him a tempo. The first score was played horribly; many parts had to be repeated; the reeds drowned out Carl Fontana's trombone solo. Halfway through, Kenton was called to the phone ("New York"). When he returned and finished the piece (starting from the middle), he said, "Well, that's an idea."
>
> The second score was played even worse. When it had been hobbled through and all the parts passed back I gave the pile of music a flick of ingratitude with my finger and felt everything swept in to the abyss. Russo left, saying, "It doesn't look too good." The rest happened quickly. When we spoke privately, Kenton made incoherent, irrational, illogical, mundane, and unfounded criticisms. First, the pieces were "the same." Second, they were "morbid." Third, they "lacked character." Fourth, they contained "too many minor sevenths." What he didn't say was that they weren't sufficiently obvious for the public taste.
>
> Fontana said he enjoyed his solo (*he* could hear it) and Bill Perkins complimented me extensively. I was surrounded by sympathy and did not understand why the tables had been so completely turned. All night in my dreams I kept rehearsing

passages that were vivid, and brilliantly played. "They are good," I thought, "why doesn't he like them?"

A few days of soul searching passed. More from my journal:

Sunday, June 24, 1956
I called Kenton, to thank him, and he answered me with mono-politeness, saying the band would be in town in August, we should get together then. He wasn't encouraging and I felt like calling him a bastard, with grit and malice in my heart. So far away from what we could have known.

Bill Russo tried to show me the larger picture, pointing out Stan's marital and financial difficulties and his circumscribed tastes. I just bit down harder and wrote a hard-punching minor-blues chart.

Friday, August 10, 1956
Bill Perkins wasn't there, and an impossible bassist had taken the place of Curtis Counce. Even though Stan was in fine spirits, I expected that nothing would come of nothing. Especially worrisome was an ensemble that rose to high G. Yet considering the lousy bassist, the band played my piece rather well. After Stan rehearsed some passages over, including the high ensemble, he folded the score, beamed, and squeezed my knee. "Much better," he said. "Bill Russo should be proud of you, and you should be proud of yourself."

But after the rehearsal, instead of mentioning figures, Stan said, "I want to put it straight to you, and be honest with you and honest with myself." As my eyes narrowed he went on that I should be very happy, etc., etc., but that he couldn't use the music, it wasn't record material, but he'd leave it in the book and blow it a few times. I thanked him and left immediately. Stan gave me what I used to crave—recognition, but not what I needed now—money. I called Bill Russo, who made things better. He told me by all means not to argue, as Stan is "very patriarchal."

Sunday, August 12, 1956
Almost at the end of the matinee, when I was resigned to not hearing my music in public, Stan made an announcement referring to "Bill Mathews, a young talent here in Chicago." About the piece, *Blues News*, he said, "If we do a good job we'll introduce him."

They did a fair job. The lead trumpet missed the G. Stan called me to the stand. As I rose to take a bow, the woman behind me went "O-ooh." Stan introduced me as a student of Russo's and paid me some compliment, to which I said, "Thank you very much." Stan then said that if I wanted to start my own band he would give me some phone numbers (to which I said, "Thank you very much") and put his arm around me, and all the people clapped. Then the band played *Young Blood* by Mulligan. I came home and listened to *Nobilissima Visione* by Hindemith.

Kenton was sensitive to the line between idolatry and devotion. His intuition was to put me down, way down, and then to build me back up enough to rekindle the process in a new way. With me as with many others, I saw him kill King Stan, stone by stone. Few around him thought he had this self-understanding, but he did recognize the practical limits to being worshiped. The surprising thing is that he was so unable to musically criticize or edit my scores. Today, reams of music later, "too many minor sevenths" still hurts, even when I laugh.

❧

In early 1957, Stan tried to resolve the road problem by claiming residence at the Rendezvous Ballroom in Balboa Beach, California, the scene of his successful 1941 launch. Paying customers were scant, and after a few months and great loss, the project was aborted. Stan simply did not know how to get beyond his band-body symbiosis, and evidently the band-body could stay alive only by endless one-nighters. By then, the big band business was a business of diminishing returns. Even as Stan was ecstatic over the birth of a son and was trying hard to grasp hold of a slipping marriage, he perceived the bottom line as the daily grind of dance music on the road.

I was not precisely empathetic to the life-problems of a complex, famous man twenty-five years my senior. I was in a creative and protected space. Dad paid the bills. I studied just enough to keep my B average and write "serious music," including a *Symphony for Brass* (which Russo tutored, then conducted), plus two musicals and a bachelor's thesis on the musical evolution of jazz. Conspiratorially, Russo and I planned another set of audition pieces, but this time it was all or nothing at all. Either I would work for Kenton or I would get an MA in English, my ace in the hole.

The showdown rehearsal was set for mid-December 1958, again at the Blue Note. My best energy went into these four scores. It had been, after all, eight long years since I had first rushed upward to greet Maynard's screaming trumpet. Two of these scores were pretty good (by my present standards; I knew it then, too), but I arrived at the audition in a grim frame of mind. Stan was older, more wasted. His band was tired, and its disconsolate playing barely gave shape to my music. Months, years of effort were garbled, like two radios playing at once. Yet I hung in, and so did Stan, bar by bar, until we had eaten through the four pieces.

Many years later—in fact, just the other night—Billy Catalano came over for dinner. I hadn't seen Billy in a quarter century, though he lives near me. He joined the Kenton band in 1957 as the fifth trumpet player and, by the time of my 1958 audition rehearsal, was locked in combat with Frank Huggins for the lead chair. In big bands—the Kenton band especially—the first trumpet job belongs to the strongest warrior. In cases of internecine warfare, Stan would often fuel the struggle with intimate encouragement to both parties, then step back and let the stronger man win. This did not seem cruel at the time.

I *loved* seeing Billy in my own house. He looked just like he looked at twenty-five, but he was fifty-five. I hoped he would remember that afternoon at the Blue Note, and he did, clearly.

"You were not humble," he recalled. "You were straight ahead, arrogant even, but he saw you as a genius. You had that air. I was taken with you just like he was. When you walked up onto the stand with your music, Stan looked into my eyes. He saw where you were gonna go—he predicted it. You were bigger than your music."

My memory is different. I felt like a captain going down with his ship. Each score got played once through, bing (gurgle) bang (gurgle). Then all the parts were called in and the band dismissed. Stan steered me to the kitchen, found a quiet place where women were fixing food, put his left leg on a folding chair, and threw his right arm over the leg. His silver hair was glistening. There was light around his tired body. His voice was calm and certain, with the deep resonance of a radio announcer describing an historic event: "Now King Gustav approaches the speaker's dais. He bows deeply to the King of Zanzibar. Now he receives from the Prime Minister a ceremonial pen for the signing of this momentous document. Ladies and Gentlemen, the National Anthem."

What he actually said was, "We will beat the Hotel Tropicana in Las Vegas beginning January third. Why don't you join us there and write for us? I'll pay you sixty dollars a week, plus your meals and hotel. Watch the guys, learn the sound of the band, and when we are playing one-nighters, you can come back to Chicago to write. We'll blow whatever you write and keep it in the book, at least for the time being. You should be very proud of yourself, and Bill Russo should be proud of you also."

He wasn't smiling, simply acknowledging that I'd passed a test and was free to advance.

"Thank you very much," I said.

He held out his huge meaty hand and shook my thin clammy one.

"We'll send you a ticket." And he was gone.

I sat down in the folding chair, eyes wide, absorbed in the calm of the women washing lettuce and slicing cucumbers.

Gradually, over the next few weeks, I let myself feel the excitement of joining the band. I had never been west of the Mississippi. When my plane touched down at the Las Vegas Airport, I went directly to my motel, set down my bags, and swept back the drapes to behold a rosy sunset arching over a desert landscape, something I had never seen. The scruffy ground lay flat from the back doorstep to blue and orange mountains a lifetime away. As a symbol of my journey into the unknown, I flung open the door and strode straight into the vast land. After two hundred yards, I turned around, suddenly wide awake and alone. The Del Mar Motel, slapped up like a billboard against the highway, looked like home, and I ran all the way back to my room.

The casino of the Tropicana was a world of a thousand lies, all believable. Leggy chorus girls with glossy lips filled me with loneliness. My new boss—the Old Man, as everyone called him—was careful to see that each of us was housed and fed, peeling off cash from a huge roll. The musicians had for their own use a large rehearsal room in the basement of the hotel, with flickering fluorescent light and an old Steinway L. Most of my time was spent there writing and, when no one was around, practicing Bach. Sometimes Stan would look over my shoulder, but he never offered musical criticism or advice. To aesthetic questions, the answer was, "You just need to keep writing."

Over this month-long period, eight of my new charts were rehearsed. Two were accepted into the book. The band performed nightly on a little stage in the Casino Lounge, and the first time the smoky hotel air filled with my music—an arrangement of *You Don't Know What Love Is*—I inhaled the moment, with its clicking roulette balls and clanking silver dollars. One was earning one's living.

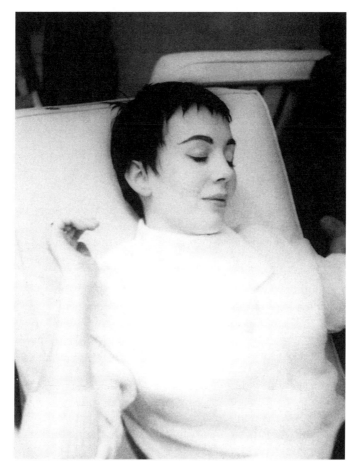

Ann Richards Kenton

The presence of Ann Kenton, Stan's wife, drove us musicians mad. She would appear at rehearsals made up like a mannequin, place herself with a pack of cigarettes and an ashtray on a chaise lounge directly in front of the band, half-close her eyes as if sunbathing in the on/off fluorescence, and with languid sexuality respond to the music. There was bad feeling between her and Stan, though they tried to conceal it. Stan asked me quietly one day if I would give Ann some theory lessons in their room—they had ordered a spinet to be brought up—and I said sure, I'd be honored. The next night, while Stan was conducting the first set, I knocked on their door.

I was nervous, and fighting fantasy. Ann seemed really sweet, very domestic. Humbly she asked me to teach her a few chords so she could accompany herself as she sang. She was a little slow to learn the names, and self-deprecatory, but anxious to show her seriousness. Her beauty, and her being Stan's wife, made me tremble. A few nights later, another lesson, more musically successful.

For the next lesson, I was early, and through the open ransom came her outraged voice, "You're old. I don't need you. Get out of here," and Stan's voice, muffled, trying not to be angry.

I ran away. When I came back later, Ann cracked the door and whispered, "No lesson tonight." The next day she went home, and I never saw her again.

The incident let me—or rather made me—take a new look at Stan. I considered his nature as a plain man, apart from My Man, apart from my elaborate investment in his fame. A kind of double vision occurred. One eye saw a gentle, tired worker, prematurely old. The other saw a statue, a silver-haired god, remote and other.

One night between sets, Stan was having a fine time at a front table with a heavily made-up blonde. He saw me approach and said, "Bill, this is Peggy Lee."

At the moment of introduction, a photographer's flashbulb went off, leaving a brilliant after-image in my mind forever: the heads of two legendary creatures smiling out from the page.

But the gentle plain man snuck up on you. Alone with Bach's Little Prelude in F Major one early A.M., I was interrupted by Stan, striding in to retrieve his coat.

"Listen to this," I said excitedly and played the piece, which had been saving my life that night.

Halfway out the door, Stan stood still as a freeze frame until the last sweet cadence, then nodded and smiled, amused.

"Good, Bill," and the door clicked after him.

That made me so happy! He actually *did* care.

I had written a letter to Bill Russo, and soon after, his came in the mail:

January 21, 1959

Dear Bill:

A letter from Polonius:
Don't consolidate your position too quickly. Don't decide who the good and the bad people are without thinking about it more. You must give Stan more of your psyche because, ultimately, he will

not be deceived by simulated or incomplete loyalty. Cool it and romanticize less. It is to your advantage not to stay away from the band at this time: it would be too easy to be forgotten. Otherwise the tone of your letter is encouraging and I am sure you will do quite well...

A recording session was scheduled for February 2, the last night at the casino, mostly Gene Roland charts. (It was later released as *Kenton at the Tropicana.*) One of my charts, *This Isn't Sometimes, This is Always*, a baritone sax feature for Billy Root, was recorded but not issued on the LP. (Years later, when the CD came out, it was included.)

The strife between lead trumpet players had come to a head: Billy's sense of big-band jazz style was better, but Frank had the chops. On the night of February 1, Billy punched out Frank on the stand, strode to his room, and packed his bag. Stan kissed Billy smack on the lips and said, "You'll be back." But Billy Catalano was gone for good. Another player, Joe Burnett, was sitting in the trumpet section by the next afternoon, and of course Frank Huggins was playing lead. But the February 2nd recording session seemed hollow. My piece especially sounded dull, beside the point. Stan knew I hadn't hit my stride, but he showed no impatience, just simple encouragement: "Keep writing." I was down. Then, somehow, on the way to L.A., I did the one thing a composer must never do: *I lost my composition book!*

"Oh, well," said Stan, "keep writing."

The band played The Crescendo in Hollywood opposite Lenny Bruce. I had no piano to write on and no dressing room. Behind the kitchen, under the back stairs, was a little corner where I tried to think chords. Sharing the space was a compressor engine that intermittently came alive with fortissimo clanks, about 144 per minute, so for two weeks I tried to write music at that tempo, with little success.

My sexual loneliness was absolute. Everyone else in the band was scoring easily, or so it seemed. One especially empty afternoon, I took a roll of pictures—from across the street—of the sweet beauties on the campus of Hollywood High School. An irate teacher pinched me by the sleeve and ushered me into the principal's office. The principal demanded the film, exposed it on the spot, and gave me a stentorian lecture about decency. At that very moment, I was certain, every last member of Stan Kenton's band was deep in coitus.

Up until this time, I had written sixteen scores, eight originals and eight arrangements, but nothing stayed in the book for very long. I didn't know how to make my music better, and rather than fix a score, Stan would junk it. When the band played a gig in San Francisco, I found my old music teacher Buddy Hiles selling cars on Van Ness Avenue. He was truly proud his boy was writing for Kenton. He showed me off to his boss and took me home for dinner in the Oakland hills. How could I tell him of the self-doubt I was experiencing?

The band went on without me, and I spent a week writing and walking in San Francisco, framing my adventures in the ground glass of my Argoflex. Billy Catalano, now an alumnus, gave me a tour of the beatnik haven of North Beach. Separated from the band, I was on my own in San Francisco, and innate joy broke the surface like a gulping fish. Music poured through. I wrote an arrangement of "The Thrill is Gone" that I *knew* was good.

I went back to Chicago to write. The band came through in March to play the Blue Note, and one afternoon we rehearsed *The Thrill is Gone*. Although the introduction didn't seem quite right, everything else was as I had anticipated. Stan's ears perked up. After the run-through, he turned back to the first page of the score and examined it for a long moment.

"The intro isn't in character. Why not start here?" he said, and pointed with his index finger to a certain black note on the paper. We tried it his way and he exclaimed, "That's a beautiful thing, Bill. What's next?"

For a bright, shaky moment, the ecstatic love of adolescence switched on like a sun. But on its heels, I told myself: You earned this. And Stan was immediately asking for more.

From then on, I was a living organ of Stan's band-body. The musicians needed me to nourish them. Stan's index finger pointing to a particular dot on my page full of dots meant: a gate had opened.

During that time in Chicago, the band recorded some desperately commercial music by Gene Roland. An especially grievous piece required the band to whistle in unison. Here was the bottom of a barrel past jokes, past complaints. The band was totally professional, like a Major League baseball team decisively defeated in the ninth and still hustling. I took a picture of Stan at the piano with the score spread out in front of him. The long arms are raised to cue the opening pucker. The parted silver hair is brushed impeccably back. The eyes are intently reading score but the eyebrows are arched, reinforcing the urgency of the approaching downbeat. He is in total control of a disastrous situation and is utterly relaxed.

The Thrill is Gone stayed in the book and became a showpiece. The next four scores I wrote were also successful, with one of them, *Willow Weep for Me*, reaching the same concert status. When the band was nearby, I joined them. One April morning in Grand Rapids, Michigan, I was sitting at a breakfast counter with Stan. We were on adjacent stools, leaning on our elbows, waiting for the guys at the booths to finish eating. Stan was telling me about other arrangers—Johnny Richards and Pete Rugolo—and defending Gene Roland. Suddenly I felt the big heart of the man in my own heart, and I took his big hand in mine and said, "I love you, Stan."

He flushed, looked painfully bashful for a moment, then said, "That's the kind of stuff we leave for the bars, Bill."

I protested—it would have been so easy for him to have said, "I love you, too," and at night, in the bar, he would have, reflexively.

A pencil and our receipt were lying on the counter. On the little paper rectangle, he wrote in minute, girlish hand, "Let's go," and smiled like a teenage steady.

Stan's seductive nature was legend. "Not gay," said Billy Catalano, "but sometimes you felt he wanted your body. He kissed us a lot." Now I was feeling that draw, absolutely not sexual, but indeed physical, a corporeal pact engulfing leader, player, driver, and bus. Had I stepped outside the pact with my naïve outburst? Stan delicately restored the boundaries of tidy courtship.

At a June rehearsal in New Jersey, another concert arrangement (*Lazy Afternoon*) was successful. On a rainy bus trip a few afternoons later, Stan was standing alone in the well, staring at the black ribbon ahead and exchanging simple sentences with Eric the driver. I joined them. There was never any lack of, or need of, conversation with Stan; it was easy to be with him. We all belonged together like fingers of a hand, idly touching. The hum of the bus and the water and the road were fusing when Stan quietly said, "Bill, why don't you start thinking in terms of an album of your music?" I woke up fast and showed nothing. The Old Man was gentle. He let me feel I completely deserved my own album, though no Kenton writer so far had gotten one at my young age—I was still twenty-one, with a birthday coming soon. He seemed to expect it, as though he knew all along how it would be. In fact, Stan's timing was perfect. He anticipated when I would find my sound with the band and gave the incentive for it to peak. Indeed, the next four arrangements I made went into the album.

For an exuberant month, I am a making-it young man in New York City. Success is: sitting at a cramped little table in Birdland with Bill Russo, listening as the Kenton band plays my music.

The band is on the Dick Clark Show at ABC-TV; my job is to re-score some old Kenton music for special choreography. Walk in from the street, tell the backstage doorman, "I'm with Kenton."

I photograph the city, and my heart expands.

There is a two-week stay at the Steel Pier in Atlantic City. The seaboard weather is gorgeous, the crowds are encouraging, the band is loose, Stan is smiling, and I am having the time of my life. For a couple of hours each day, I walk the town with my camera, dissolving into the summer flow. I am connected to people, I joke with strangers, and the alienation of my growing years thins into the Atlantic air. I still have those 2¼ x 2¼ pictures today: teenagers at the beach giving the high sign, old couples strolling on the boardwalk, lonely men, wizened women in bikinis, and in all of them I see my own face, the recognition of my own humanity. Aren't we all among one another? Like a light behind my crown is a calm, clear love for Stan.

And the Old Man is at his best, totally accessible to us, leading the gigs with easy control and constantly, constantly putting out waves of good feeling, wry humor, nurturing encouragement. The band rehearses *I Get Along Without You Very Well, Django, Lonely Woman,* and *Ill Wind*, all careful concert arrangements of mine. Stan is genuinely pleased. Everyone has a seaside glow. And the band is swinging.

Often, during matinees, I walk through the cavernous Steel Pier Ballroom or along the sunny walkways outside, loving the music of my pubescent dreams. Bare arms, airy dresses, and polka-dot shorts stream in all directions while charged layers of cymbals and brass sift through the ocean air. Success is easy!

By August, I had returned to Chicago for a long spell of writing. When the Kenton band arrived on the afternoon of August 9th, there was a surprise phone call from Stan. A new trumpet player had collapsed in front of the Cass Hotel. Could I find a replacement on short notice, just for a few nights? Sure, I'd try. I called everyone; no one was free. It was 5 p.m. The bus was to leave at 6 for a three-day loop around Chicago.

Stan said, "Could you come out with us just until we solve this problem?"

"I'm not a very good trumpet player, Stan."

"Well, just come and sit in the chair to help us out."

"Okay."

Fourth Trumpet

I'd wanted to play in the band since day one. At 6:10 the bus was on its way to Winnetka, and I, with my beat-up old King trumpet, was on it.

Actually, the dance book wasn't terribly difficult. I had the easiest part (fourth) and what was beyond me, I didn't play. My section-mates were sympathetic, even encouraging. Stan gave private counsel to avoid embarrassing me: "Hold your horn up, Bill. And stay out of the high unisons until you build some chops." I tried to keep out of trouble and enjoy the lark.

Lives pivot on tiny moments that appear without warning. On the bus back to Chicago, Stan unwrapped his big frame into the seat beside me.

"Would you like to stay on with us in the trumpet section, Bill?"

"For how long?"

"For as long as you like. We'll pay you $140 a week"—the base salary in those years—"plus your $60 writer's salary—$200 a week."

At home, my marriage had come apart. Two hundred a week was a big draw. I wanted to belong. I said yes. Who wouldn't? As it turned out, Stan's timing was not innocent. He saw I was ripe for a test, the kind he fueled his band with. The tiny moment was over. I was a trumpet player for the Stan Kenton band.

త

Stan would make you play for him better than you thought you ever could. His lanky conducting drew it out of you. Even in the Elks Club of an anonymous town in the middle of a remote prairie, we rode the magic energy of his long arms. Kazaam! The trombones. Abracadabra! The saxophones. Shazam! The rolling cymbals. Then a cry of sexual possession and the trumpets like lightning brighten the sphere. You are potent air, part of a stream that blows into the body of the big man facing you, larger than life, and out through him into the body of the crowd.

Night after night, it went on. I wrote whenever I could, on the bus, at rest stops, grabbing at the pianos before the gig, during intermission, after the gig. More than once, Stan had to shove me laughing off the piano bench so he could begin the next set.

In late August we rehearsed in Cincinnati, and more material was accepted for the record, this time my chart on *When Sonny Gets Blue*. But I was obsessed with the headline no one wrote: Local Boy Makes Good. The horde of cashmeres I'd fantasized didn't show. I promised Bill Chase, one of the great lead players of all time, a home-cooked meal if he'd give me a trumpet lesson. My folks said, "Invite Stan, too," and the three of us went to visit the old Magnavox in the living room, and the Baldwin spinet, and the space in between. I expected to feel an arc of triumph in this visit, but it turned awkward. How could I be part of Stan's body and my parents' body at the same time?

In the family den, Bill Chase was giving me a great trumpet lesson. The den used to be my nursery. I teethed there, and drew dots on duckies, and listened to Arthur Godfrey when I stayed home from school sick. Facing the golden energy streaming from the bell of Bill's horn was terrifying, humiliating. From the very beginning fly balls had fallen through my glove, and never had I scored a touchdown for my team. How could I expect to play the trumpet like this beautiful man? As he was popping high Gs and double Cs and Stan was talking the publishing business with my father, I was getting tangled up in the blue blanket of my childhood.

The visit home let me realize the specialness of the world Stan had created, the world of the bus and the gig, the world that sucked in adoration as it blew out streaming sound. I entered totally into this world, becoming Stan's hand, part of his brain. One day, when we were in the well of the bus, he said, "You know, Bill, when I first heard your arrangement of *The Thrill is Gone* I thought it was a bar of this and a bar of that, but now that we've played it a so many times I like it; it fits together." I'd shown him something?

I invented a bus game. I'd write one bar of melody, pass my composition book across the aisle, Stan would write one bar, and we'd continue to take turns until we either x'd out the whole thing like a "jack's game" in tic-tac-toe, or we approved it, a collective win. Then we'd find chords for our new melody. Nothing ever came of this exercise, it was just a way of passing time on the long journey. But of all times it was the best. It was like playing chess with your big brother in a storm. It was laughing in a private language.

I wasn't pulling my weight in the trumpet section, which meant, among other things, not sharing the high parts. The players tried to help me, tactfully at first. More than once I heard "Tune up again, Bill," instead of "You're playing out of tune," which I was. At a lunch stop in Altoona, I was sharing a booth with, among others, Charlie Mariano. A fine Count Basie chart came up on the jukebox, and I tapped time with my hand on the tabletop. Musicians exchanged glances across the table. Then in a quiet, protective way, Charlie put his hand over mine, imparting his own sense of the music's pulse. Charlie's time was laid back, resilient, yet strong like bone. Without missing any of the conversation, he kept the beautiful visceral gift alive until the record was over. No words. I never thanked him, but he changed my perception of time.

The long string of one-nighters ended in New York on September 21 and 22 with a recording session of nine of my concert ballad charts. The album was subsequently released under the title *Standards in Silhouette*. ("That's a good title, Bill," Stan had said in the well. "Did you think of it yourself?") In a cavernous studio, the band moved through my music with high professionalism, blowing cautious climaxes toward the metal ears hiding in the darkness.

Though Stan kept me in his sights and consulted me about blend and tempo, I felt strangely out of the process. From over my shoulder, an unseen disappointment brought me down. My music wasn't as good as Bill Russo's, or Gerry Mulligans's, or Bill Holman's. Was this the *it* of *making it*? Hadn't there been enough time? Or ability?

I wasn't conscious enough of my mood to hide it from Stan. He assured me the record would be a good one. In the end, flag inert, I accepted the victory with no parade. The truth is, I couldn't love my music the same way I'd loved Maynard Ferguson's opening summons one fall day in 1950. The throne of power had grown into some new shape, a shape I couldn't recognize. The wildfire was dying. Dying in the culture. Dying in Stan. My big moment had come too early for me and too late for him. Even without a parade, though, there was an outer accomplishment, and a sense that I could make better music for Kenton, closer to my Russo-Mulligan-Holman ideal, someday.

Coming up was a tour with the Four Freshmen and June Christy. June had been my adolescent heartthrob, and I respected the Four Freshmen's vocal mastery. Stan warned us that the five-week tour would be difficult. I thought it would be fun. But it was my undoing.

᷍

On September 28, we discovered in front of our hotel a sparkling clean new bus. Eric, the bus driver, was rested. His uniform was pressed. The bus even smelled new. Most of us had already boarded when Bill Trujillo took out a new stick of gum, flamboyantly threw the wrapper on the floor, and crowed, "First funk on the new bus." Everyone cheered, and the tour was underway.

All who were on that tour speak of it now with a special dread, its hardship and pain asterisked forever in our memories. Perhaps because I'd already gotten my own record, I began to see what I was seeing. And the first thing I saw was the nature of Stan's charisma. At that time I was reading Aldous Huxley's *The Devils of Loudon*, which deals specifically with witch burnings but, more generally, with mob psychology. It made me think about the way Stan radiated his energy outward and how it came back focused on him. I saw the engine his deep need drove, and I felt cheated.

But more than anything, I saw booze. Christy, Bob Flanagan, Jimmy Campbell, and Stan were the officers in a kind of drinking club in the front of the bus, and during the long miles a fearful amount of alcohol was consumed. At that time, I had never in my life been stoned (on anything) and had gotten drunk only once, alone, to prove to myself that alcohol was for idiots, weaklings. Each night, between the end of the gig and the predawn onset of his brief slumber, Stan drank a quart of Scotch. The night I realized this was dark. I couldn't discuss it with anyone, my prudery being as obnoxious to my peers as their vices were to me. Around 2 a.m., as the bus rolled through nowhere, Stan's eyes would become big blue pies. They glowed a bit in the dim light. And he seemed always to be smiling a little smile of happy astonishment. He never raised his voice or made a scene. He just gradually went away.

This began to hurt. I tried to solve the problem by pouring myself a shot of cognac, but then I couldn't read. But Huxley, Dylan Thomas, Voltaire, Henry Miller, and Eric Fromm could carry me only so far. I was lonely, disenchanted, tired, and the worst player in the band. As the strain of the tour mounted, fuses shortened. The trumpet section was hurting, and my weak chops didn't help. My sullen mood assured my position at the bottom of the pecking order. One sad night I was talking with the young good-old-boy Texan bass trombonist, who already had a genuine dislike of my egghead airs, about the sound of Miles Davis, whom, of course, we both admired. He maintained that Miles's *sound* was everything. I felt obligated to point out the intelligence of Miles' lines, his wit, and the content that gave his sound meaning. The *sound*, stripped of its content, would be meaningless (or so I argued). I meant to underline this by suggesting that even if someone with as poor a *sound* as myself executed Miles's ideas, the greatness would remain. But what I actually said was, "Hell, I *sound* better than Miles, but I can't make his ideas."

The trombonist leapt up in triumph exclaiming to the ambient stupor, "Hey, Mathieu says he sounds better than Miles."

"I did not," I cried.

He gave a mighty rebel yell: "YES YOU DID!" and the bus was in an uproar.

I had to put my arms up over my ears, like a schoolboy. Stan finally came back and told everyone to go to sleep. I was in tears.

"You, too, Bill."

The next night Ken Albers of the Four Freshmen spilled Scotch onto his clothes before nodding out with a lit cigarette. First smoke, then fire. We had to put out old Ken. I was getting desperate.

On October 10, the troupe recorded a live double album called *Roadshow*. June was in wretched health and marginal voice. The whole sloppy misery of the tour was inexplicably preserved on Capitol Records, the white noise of applause mixed with the tired desire of Stan's voice. You can hear us, organs of that desire-nature, blasting out sound-fodder. And when that concert was over, when every concert was over, it was back into the Ghost Bus for more tunneling through the night.

One dawn, restless and awake, I thought to go stand in the well and talk to Eric. Everyone else was asleep, Stan also, lying characteristically on his back across a double seat, long legs bent up at a sharp angle, shiny black shoes on the armrest. The seat opposite was empty; from there, I could look across the aisle and see in the early light the repose of his face. He was gone, all right. Red arterial lines were visible in his nostrils. His lips were thin blue, his cheeks puffy, his hair for once disheveled. Without the mask of wakefulness, he looked not like the Old Man but like an old man, asleep. My eyes sank into his face like rain into a garden. Love rose. Love like love for my very own blood, warm and suffused, not the love I had felt for the man who greeted me beneath green gums. This love had pain in it.

Over the weeks, my need for sleep became pressing. Try as I might I could not sleep sitting up. Strung across the back of the bus was a pole from which hung the band uniforms and the many Christy gowns. Beneath these was just room enough for a small man to stretch out *full length*. I rehearsed it one afternoon in the empty bus. All set. That night when the stupor gelled, I slid from my seat and snuggled into my private berth beneath the pink sequins. For a moment, I tasted the victory of a superior mind in an extended body. Then I heard the motor. Then I felt the heat. My bed was directly above the gearbox, the metal striping too hot to touch. When Eric changed gears, it was like being run over in your dreams. I stuck it out till morning, but that night was the nadir of my career with Stan Kenton. The next afternoon, I discovered that if I made myself even smaller, I could fit in the luggage rack above my seat. I perfected a sort of sleight-of-monkey technique. I don't think anyone saw me go up at night, and in the morning I waited until the bus emptied before leaping down.

Toward the end of the tour, the band began collectively to lose it. Mean little fights were common, there was a real depression in the music, and patches of weeping sprang up unnoticed, like weeds. One day a trombonist got a letter from his wife saying she was leaving him; that night, we wept openly. A saxophonist became violent— only Stan's touch restrained him. When things calmed down a little, I monkey-hopped to bed and slept well. At 8 a.m., I descended, grabbed my bag, and bumped sleepily forward. The bus was empty except for three figures in the front seat. The middle figure was Stan sitting ramrod straight. His right arm was draped around the violent man, now quiet like a baby suckling in his sleep, and his left firmly around the jilted man, whose motionless weeping produced no tears. In the pale morning, Stan's eyes were blue-gray beacons. He was a painting of compassion. I stood frozen in the aisle, my jaw down. His beacons met my own wide eyes.

"Take a good look at this, Bill," he said in a clear voice, totally conscious. "It's your scene someday."

I looked at the painting a moment longer, then shut my mouth and got down off the bus.

In early November of 1959, after the crazy labor of the tour was behind us, Stan found a talented trumpet player to fill my chair, then gently said to me, "I think you should leave us now." I fought for my position as a writer, but even that was slowly slipping away. Stan knew what he was doing. He knew how unhappy I had turned. He had given me what he could, and drawn out of me what he could. He'd been paid; I'd been paid. Now he peeled me off the body like dead skin. But we had seen each other, that was clear; young as I was, I knew we had seen each other.

At the Blue Note, two weeks later, we had The Chat, back in our old corner of the kitchen. Could I continue to write for him?

"Wait till you mature a little more, then come back with us." I was stunned by the clean sound of the gavel. I knew this work was finished.

"Will you do me a favor?"

"Certainly, Bill."

"Will you write Duke Ellington a letter of recommendation for me?"

Stan Kenton showed no surprise, made no groan, flinched not.

"I'd be thrilled. Duke is the greatest."

I thanked him, he left to conduct his band, and I sat down on a folding chair, biting the inside of my mouth.

He must have written a great letter because when I called Duke in December he said, unbelievably, "Sure, you can write for my band." Maybe Stan had said, "Duke, take this kid off my hands, will you?" Surely there was an exchange of professional courtesy. Duke opened his band to me, allowing me to use it as my instrument. He went so far as to record a couple of my arrangements, an act of such generosity that it allowed me finally to stop collecting bandleaders. So, as we parted, Kenton gave me a boost up to the next teacher, the next grade of apprenticeship. His demeanor at the end was kind but stern. I think he was disappointed that he couldn't take me past a certain point, and that I hadn't carried him past the high-water mark of my own teacher, Bill Russo.

But I was happy to be home, off the band, done with it. In a reactionary snit I referred to my Kenton scores as "juvenilia," and Capitol producer Lee Gillette got wind of it. He wanted to suppress the little ingrate's album, but Stan deterred him. Bitter to have been fired, I ascribed the weird failure of my music to Stan's own weird failure. Maybe I couldn't write *Fascinating Rhythm* or *Young Blood* or

Invention for Guitar and Trumpet, but Stan couldn't produce the composer who could. Sad, but true.

Three days after leaving the band, I rejoined my old University of Chicago friends in a theatrical venture called the Second City, which was to become a smash hit in no time. I became its musical director, carving out a different kind of success. I wrote Stan to thank him, and he replied in a princely manner:

March 4, 1960

Dear Bill:

I have had your nice letter with me for a week now and I am not only thrilled hearing from you but thrilled with the contents. The idea of your being with Duke is very thrilling. This too can be a part of your education. We both realize there is no doubt about Ellington being the biggest figure in the big band jazz world. I would watch everything about the man, absorb everything I could while you are together. In fact, I envy you, I wish I could be around him as much as you are. I think the working part of your relationship is also very fair. Let me say, I approve of everything.

I haven't really been home long enough to have a clear thought of what my problems are. I have been worrying mostly about the publishing business and trying to figure out ways to get enough income so that I don't have to be on the road for these long ugly periods. At the moment it looks as although we are going to Mexico, the middle of April, for a couple of weeks and then east for about three weeks before returning home. We will, no doubt, get a chance to have a chat someplace during the month of May.

Thank you again for writing and keeping me informed on your activities.

As ever,
Stan

I didn't think much about Stan Kenton for a while. In 1961, the Second City was playing on Broadway, I was writing for *Downbeat* under editor Gene Lees, and I'd begun *serious* classical study with composer Easley Blackwood. One early morning, after partying all night at Hugh Hefner's mansion with my theater buddies, I met Stan on Chicago's Michigan Avenue. He was window-shopping with a young woman whose black fringe hung down her red dress from belt to knees. Stan's white suit was clean, his hair was immaculate, and his blue eyes were pies. We recognized each other in the same instant.

An eighth note later, he said, "Hello, Bill, this is Rosie."

"Hello, Rosie," I said.

In 1963, I began doing *serious* acid, and my old mentor Stan Kenton kept appearing in trip-vision. After many drafts, I typed this letter:

Aug 1, 1964

Dear Stan,

This is to remind you that my gratitude to you remains unchanged over the years, and that you are one of the few men who (still) guides me on. Gradually, I begin to understand your position, and my feeling broadens.

My professional life is secure and I am using these years to study. Presently I am composing a Wind Quintet, practicing classical music and reading scores.

I hope that someday I will be able to perform for you a service of lasting and practical value. Nothing could give me more pleasure than writing music that would ease your financial burden, as well as further the artistic interests of the band. Someday (not soon) I may understand how to do this.

In the meantime here are my wishes for your continued vitality and success.

Sincerely,
Bill Mathieu

But I didn't mail it.

By 1967, I was a *serious* composer trying to integrate Pierre Boulez and Cecil Taylor. My new family and I moved to San Francisco, where I taught at the San Francisco Conservatory by day and at night played music for the Committee Theater. One evening in 1969, on the way to the gig in North Beach, my heart leapt to find STAN KENTON AND HIS ORCH on the marquee of the club across the street. At my intermission, I tore over there.

The club is quiet—no jukebox, even—with about forty small round tables, twenty of them occupied by singles or couples. Very young, uniformed musicians are standing around, as if waiting for the bar mitzvah to begin. The ticket seller shows me the open door to the tiny dressing room, green and brown. Inside is a couch the length of a bus seat, and lying on it, with his left arm thrown over his eyes, is Stan. His legs are bent sharply at the knees, and I see smooth skin above his black socks. Facing the couch is a folding chair in which I very quietly sit. This movie is in half-tones. The soundtrack is muffled. I hear the shallow breathing of the long man. We are alone. A minute passes. No phone rings. Stan's eyes are closed under his arm. His mouth says, "Hello, Bill."

"You recognize me!"

"I hear you wrote a symphony."

Could he mean the *Symphony for Brass* of a dozen years earlier? What has he heard? He takes his arm off his eyes and raises his head to peer at me.

"I'm working as the musical director of the Committee Theater across the street. I had to come see you."

His head lies back down, and he says, "I'm just resting here at intermission."

Helplessly I blurt out, "I'm sorry I fucked up your band."

Now the head turns to me with a hard smile of denial.

"You didn't fuck up my band."

"I didn't play very well, I mean."

Stan forces his body to sit up. His hands tie his shoestrings.

"You did very well with us. Come on, I'll introduce you to the band. Dick Shearer, our lead trombonist, knows your music very well."

I'm shaking hands with Dick Shearer, who says, "Oh, wow. I *love* your charts. *The Thrill is Gone, Willow Weep For Me*, some of my favorites."

The guys gather round. I'm a celebrity, everyone shakes my hand. Stan is rounding up the strays.

"Great album."

"Love your writing."

"Man, I've always wanted to meet you."

They look like my straight students at the Conservatory.

"Can you stay and listen?"

The musicians group on the stand. Some customers have left, a few new ones arrive. I stand in the back. The band plays a 1947 arrangement of *September Song*. My "places" call is in one minute. This doesn't feel right. It doesn't sound right. I zoom across the street and go back to work.

By August 1979, I had moved to a six-acre ranchette north of San Francisco, where I was composing and teaching. On the afternoon my Dad called to tell me Stan Kenton was dead, my family was out shopping. I hung up the kitchen phone and stood helpless, trying to find the missing part of my body. Eleven-year-old Lucy came bouncing in.

"Look at my new blouse, Dad. Dad? What's wrong, Dad."

"My old boss Stan Kenton just died."

"Who's Stan Kenton, *and* do you like my new blouse?"

৵

Over the next decade, the emptiness remained. I didn't examine the Old Man's death, or his death in me. It takes an innocent orchestration question by a composition student to start the process. I begin to hear brass in my head, and now I am sitting on my living room floor, surrounded by books and record albums with STAN KENTON on them, and tonight I've played the whole Kenton tape of my memory.

I'm fifty-one now, four years older than Stan was when I worked for him that long year. The Old Man younger than me, who would have thought? In his early forties, Stan included two monologues in the albums *Prologue* and *The Kenton Era*, and I listen carefully to these to get a fix on him. He's selling his band, do I wanna buy it? Do I believe his rap about the music, or is he covering a fat ego? Who is this guy?

Young Stanley bounds out of the speakers, impatient to be important, hungry for his music to be accepted as a cultural reality, not as a personal cover. The dam breaks and I am face to face with the shy fourteen-year-old suddenly vitalized by music, the eager-to-please pianist/arranger of twenty-six, the leader personality of twenty-nine, the national figure who has earned his precious success by the age of thirty-five. Like a big brother, I can sympathize with thirty-seven-year-old Stan, who had driven himself to breakdown with his visionary music—music that is, of course, both a cultural reality *and* a personal cover.

Stan discovers that the hands of the public stop clapping unless he drives himself beyond his own strength. If the hands stop, the money stops, and then, naturally, the music stops. And if the music stops, he has no self. What a dilemma. He enters psychoanalysis. Nice age to begin to figure it all out. He buys into the discipline and thinks, "I'll be a psychoanalyst." Naw. Too late. Then he figures a way to make "a real contribution to music" by upping the ante—the Innovations in Modern Music Orchestra. It tours across the country and loses *lots* of money.

Now, at forty-one, he fronts one of the greatest collections of musicians and libraries of music past, present, or future—the 1953 band. But the dilemma is still there: the road is a killer.

In 1953 the band bus crashes, people are hurt, the band goes home, and the bubble is burst. The dilemma won't go away. It never goes away. The band never regains its pre-crash peak, and Stan never stops driving past his limit. In this way he lives out his forties. Then his fifties, and he lasts through most of his sixties. Three marriages fail. Three children live hard lives overcoming his abandonment of them. In later life, two things assuage his loss of the Great Baton. At forty-seven he becomes an educator. Though he has to push even harder to give hundreds of clinics in colleges around the country, this "contribution" is incontestable, not a cover. Real value comes in. Instead of a constellation of stars, his band becomes a collection of virtuosi plucked from schools. The music, no longer a cultural mirror, is now a subculture of ensemble technique glistening with collective aggression.

Another thing helps him: he falls in love with his long-time friend Audree Coke, who nourishes and protects his later years. The arc of Stan's life comes into focus. The success: he really did mark American music in a beautiful way. The weird failure: his music was driven by desire for self, ever more godlike, bountiful sweet self. It never grew beyond that boundary into compassion and union. And self music is not soul music.

What driver whipped Stan from behind, I don't know. But the sweet siren that drew him showed up unexpectedly in my own life. During the 70s I directed a group called the Sufi Choir, which became well known in San Francisco. Those were the days of ecstatic dancing in Golden Gate Park. The Aquarian Age was giddy with self-recognition, and our reception at concerts was wildly high-spirited. I didn't expect that to affect me, but it did. I discovered how a leader, at the focus of the lens, channels energy. Countless high-frequency explosions of cheers and applause roar through his pineal gland and out through the back of his head to the members of the group. And a tidal wave of love rushes through the funnel of the leader's heart. After it subsides, you want more: the brilliance of it is addicting. The first time it happened to me I thought of Stan and said, "So that's it." As Carol Easton observed, "The curse of charisma is that it requires an audience." Stan was a rabbit, hounds at the rear, carrot in front. Well, it takes one to know one, and Stan knew a hunted, hungry kid when he saw one. He looked into Billy Catalano's eyes when I first walked on the stand as if to say, "Here comes another one." He saw himself in me.

And now I can see myself in him. It's 3 a.m. I decide to sit down and write Stan another letter. Tonight. I'll say Dear Stan, and chronicle the states of my love energy, and how they were transformed by his. I'll say how he killed my idolatry by telling me my music was too full of minor sevenths, and then propped me up so I could succeed in a new way. I'll say how he turned my love bitter by being human, and then opened me to a new musical life. I'll say how he tangled me up by dying on me too soon, before I was ready to be real for him. I'll say that his weird failure is mine, too, and everybody else's, from hobo to hero.

But just as my list of loves takes shape, Stan himself appears across the table from me. His large face is lighted from within and without. We are not in heaven, not on earth, but in vision, somewhere in between. I am looking directly into his gray-blue eyes, he is looking into my hazel ones, and our eyes are smiling. There are no words or names for anything, or stories, or time to tell them. Just this gentle smiling and these bright faces.

6

The Interloper

Counting the Ways was written in 1988, when I was fifty-one, thirty years after my work with Stan Kenton and thirty-five more before the time of this writing. Even though my journal from that year had been lost, I'd kept some old notes and itineraries and I'd often been interviewed about my Kenton years. So those memories played like a movie I'd seen many times, with editorial revisions each time. My Duke Ellington narrative, however, has never been written out until now, over sixty long years after the fact. I've often wondered: why such reluctance about putting Duke on the page? I think I know the answer now.

Psychologists have learned that each time we remember something anew, we change it, reliving it with our ever-new selves and then pressing "save" until the next time. To tell and retell a story is to gel it gradually; to write it down is to deep-freeze it. If I refuse to write it, the memory has a chance to be alive in my life, shaping and reshaping my psyche. And the most precious ones you want to keep quivering.

But there will come a time for the memorial service, and the words, some forgotten, some varied, stream out into their final order. I gave myself thirty years to shape those Stan Kenton days before I set them in print, then thirty more to read and reread them. As with a favorite book, upon each reading an older self is swaying differently to the same old tunes. For the Duke story, I've waited sixty years for the writing, and I'm glad because this story is now all wrapped up and ready for the deep freeze.

During our final talk in the kitchen of the Blue Note, the "chat" during which Kenton lowered the gavel for good, the idea of writing for Duke Ellington came to my mind immediately as a strategy for achieving an even more impressive success, thus warding off the inevitable despondency after my dismissal. But it did not occur to the young strategist to do a little risk assessment. When Duke said, "Sure, you can write for my band," I took it in stride, not realizing what an extravagantly generous offer it was. "Of course I can do this," I thought. At that time, Ellington was creatively bonded with Billy Strayhorn, so much so that it became impossible for future historians to ascertain who had composed what. Furthermore, their collaborations, with continual input from members of the band, accounted for most of the band's book. And, of course, Duke's band was segregated, primarily because it toured so frequently through segregated territory. His musical story was the story of Black culture, pure as the sun. The business end was usually white, often to his despair, but the music itself was a history of the African-American condition and had been since the beginning of his career. As far as I can trace, no white composer had ever been an integral, or even peripheral, part of the Ellington band.

Just to further burnish the chronicle of one young man's hubris, let me say that I hadn't done my homework, hadn't even enrolled in the course. Despite his enormous reputation, I'd rarely listened to Ellington by choice. I thought he was simply old-fashioned—a generational disconnect. But now the light had turned green, so I dug up some recordings and listened carefully. I soon became convinced that I would be able to write music more up to date, more thoroughly *composed*, for the Ellington band.

Something seminal had escaped me, however. Duke Ellington's music was a product of a musical genius utterly absorbed by and devoted to the anatomy of his culture. He knew its power, its depth. Of course, that culture and its music already had merged perforce with many aspects of Eurocentric culture present in American life. One of the most beautiful and persistent amalgamations of black and white culture, for instance, is the twelve-bar blues cycle, which arose in large part from the pentatonic calls and responses of the work fields and, in equal contribution, the harmonies at the core of the European canon. One form of the field songs comprised a solo call, its unison repetition by the others, and a completing phrase from the soloist. The characteristic tuning of the five-note scale—featuring what we now call "blue notes"—was new to Western ears.

Gradually these blue notes were braided into the familiar harmonies of Western hymns and popular songs, and that amalgam has become a common thread in the planet's musical tapestry, an enduring African gift. A commensurate gift to the planet is perhaps the most elegant of all European inventions, the grand piano, Ellington's chosen musical companion. In the music that poured from Ellington's band decade upon decade, all these cross-influences were so defined by the realities of American Black life with its very loud echoes of slavery that what one heard in the music was scarcely possible to be produced by a white kid from Cincinnati whose upbringing was that of an *open-minded* liberal—by which I mean deliberate *non*-prejudice, the self-congratulatory stance of tolerance. Sixty-five years later, I can clearly see that I aimed to burgle the power of Duke's band and, entitled as I felt, was entirely unaware of the theft.

It is now December of 1959. Duke must have received the letter of recommendation from Kenton, and it's time for me to make the call. Duke most graciously gives me the go-ahead and suggests I "write some things." There is a rehearsal scheduled in Pittsburg for a certain date in early February. He will pay for my plane fare and hotel. I should arrive with the score and parts around 4:00. He gives me the address of the theater. During the ensuing weeks, I compose quickly and hopefully, but there are many false starts and frustrating dead ends. What's wrong, why isn't this easy? My manuscript book is full of crossed-out staves, abandoned pages, but three pieces finally emerge complete and, courting optimism, I copy out the parts for each musician. In my mind's ear, I'm hearing the Ellington band playing my compositions exactly to my own tastes.

Early on the appointed day I take a Chicago-Pittsburgh prop-plane, then a taxi to the Stanley Theatre in the inner city's heart. I am carrying an overnight satchel and a fat bundle of music under my arm. I arrive just at 4:00, but the musicians are still straggling in; others are warming up, playing riffs, smoking. I approach Duke, who greets me with, "How was your flight?" He introduces me to the lead trumpet player, Willie Cook, who is cordial, and the primo tenor saxophone soloist, Paul Gonsalves, who mumbles and turns away. Mostly, though, the musicians are polite, if nonplussed—the boss must know what he's doing. Duke says I should take a seat, he'll get to my scores after a little while. I find the narrow stairway to the balcony and sit a few rows back from the rail. From this distance, I watch every move.

Around 5:00 the band begins its mysterious rehearsal process, a joint venture of questions, answers, instructions, brief side conversations, different groups playing over bits and phrases, putting things in sequence, maybe a full run-through of a piece, maybe not. Everyone seems aware of everyone else, and at the softest word or the simplest gesture from the leader, everyone knows what to do. It is a guided collaboration in which each, most active to most passive, plays his part, a living music organism. Ensconced in my perch, all my senses are inhaling. The theater smells like Cincinnati's old Cotton Club on Court Street between John and Mound, and now I'm a boy under Buddy Hiles's wing. I gradually feel more at home. This time I'm not a young boy, though, I'm a young man just beginning to recognize my presence as a generous if conditional free pass into a world well guarded not by choice but by centuries of societal cruelties I cannot imagine or fathom.

After about an hour, Duke passes out the parts to my pieces and the band begins to sight-read through them, one time through for each piece, no stopping. Although the actual sounds are blocked from my memory, I clearly recall the feeling of them sounding terrible to me: inchoate at worst, pretty at best, effete throughout. What painfully stays with me is the absolute passivity of the musicians. "I feel a draft," Lester Young used to say whenever he sensed the approach of a disrespecting white man, at which signal everyone in his band became poker-faced. As my music straggles ever on, Willie Cook, the congenial lead trumpet player, does try to lead when he can. But Johnny Hodges, the alto saxophone soloist, seems physically affronted by the piece I have written featuring him, and at its conclusion gingerly picks up his music and tosses it stoically onto the floor, the jazz musician's ultimate sign of disrespect for the writer. Duke himself is wearing a Duke mask, a well-honed nothing face.

The read-through of my three pieces takes less than fifteen minutes. The parts are passed to the band boy, who straightens them unsorted into a pile, folds the pile into the scores, and disappears.

Meanwhile, Duke is already passing out parts for a new arrangement by Billy Strayhorn, who appears on stage to take the band through his music. Everyone comes alive in a hurry, and the band plays on. Up in the balcony, I am coming alive, too.

ᔧ

The rehearsal ends just after 7:00, the places call is 7:45 for the 8:15 concert. Duke has immediate business to take care of with some men huddled in the fifth row. A few players straggle out for a drink or to scavenge the cold for a bite to eat. Many stay behind. I climb down from the balcony and join those on stage. Some just smoke and relax; a few gravitate up to the risers where Willie Cook is passing a joint around. I climb up there, supposing I'll feel more at home in the trumpet section than anywhere else. They are kind to me, offer me a hit. Like an embarrassed virgin at an orgy, I refuse. No one says anything about my music, and I dare not ask. Someone calls my attention to the stage, where Duke is standing at the piano, motioning for me to join him. A very thin, quiet man is seated at the keyboard. It is Billy Strayhorn. Duke introduces me as a young writer from Chicago.

"Why don't you show Bill some things at the piano?" he says to Billy.

I sit down on the piano bench to Strayhorn's right. He relaxes his hands over the keys, prepared to play. We are surrounded by quietly milling musicians and purposeful stagehands. Although I had barely studied the music of the Ellington Orchestra, I had learned quite a few Ellington-Strayhorn compositions that had already become revered jazz standards. At this moment, though, I sense that this small, self-effacing man, hands poised over the keys, is being compromised. I need to come up with a meaningful question.

"How do you find chords, Mr. Strayhorn?" I ask.

"Like this," he answers, playing through a beautiful sequence of chords.

"How do you know which chord is next?"

This is a real question for me, but it seems to genuinely perplex him.

"Like this," he says and plays some more, this time picking out a certain chord and demonstrating its resolution to various others. But I can't quite catch it.

"Would you show me that again, please?"

He plays something different. His shyness reminds me of when I was sitting at a small table with the similarly soft-spoken, alarmingly thin Bob Greattinger as he showed me, at the bidding of Stan Kenton after my debut rehearsal with *his* band, the fifteenth partial of the harmonic series.

Although Billy Strayhorn seems to have no words for his music, I can sense his big ears and capacious heart. The stage is being cleared for the performance.

I say, "Thank you very much, Mr. Strayhorn. I love your songs."

He nods that he has heard.

Again I climb the balcony stairs and sit in the back row with my overnight bag under my seat. The theater fills slowly with a mostly Black audience. The air is calm, yet anticipatory of a special evening. It is 8:40 when the faded red curtain goes up. To my surprise, the band is met not with unbounded enthusiasm but with the mutual love of old and trusted friends who are just now feeling complete. I sit like a lawn ornament through a long first set, an extended intermission, a longer second set, and five encores. As the evening progresses I become more and more deeply aware of the loving bond in the room, and I'm filled with wonder at the shared fullness of it.

Devi and I have a longtime friend, Benjamin Bagby, who is renowned for his stage presentations of the thousand-year-old epic poem, *Beowulf*, a linchpin of Anglo-Saxon literature. The poem, set in sixth-century Scandinavia, is about a great hero who lives and dies defending the land and its people against vicious attacks from monsters and dragons. Ben sits on a bench, center stage, holding a six-string medieval harp. Wearing the simple garb of a traveling bard, he recites, acts out, and sings; his voice becomes the entire dramatis personae. When I saw the two-hour performance I didn't know the story or a word of Anglo-Saxon, but I was riveted by the way every tone and syllable conveyed the visceral psyche of heroism. The energy, rising above plot and language, became a seamless transmission of pure mastery. This is how I feel sitting in the balcony of the Stanley Theatre, inhaling every nuance of Duke Ellington's concert. Simultaneously it is dawning on me that I haven't even come close to internalizing the core of Ellington's music. Whether or not a boy born in southern Ohio and raised inside the bubble of white privilege ever *could* is a debatable subject—*this* boy clearly had not. And in the midst of the ongoing rapture of the folks on all sides of me, that's what I'm realizing way up high in a Pittsburg balcony.

After the performance is over and the crowd has dwindled, I find Duke, who says we're about to share a cab to our hotel and have a late dinner there. The front seat of the cab seats three; Duke slides in next to the driver and motions me to sit next to him. From the pocket of his coat, he takes a small bottle, wets his eyes with its dropper, then gives me a sly look and says, "This is so I can see around corners." I almost believe him. Two band members climb in back with their instruments, close the door, and Duke gives the address to the driver. But just then, the back door opens and Paul Gonsalves wriggles past the stacked horns to get close to Duke's ear. There is the strong odor of alcohol. In a low voice, Paul is asking for cash. Duke needs to discourage his men from bingeing. Turning to face Paul, he speaks softly, sternly, and with finality, like the loving big brother he is. Paul slithers out of the cab, and we are on our way.

Duke turns toward me and asks, "How did you like our performance?"

How could I possibly tell him of the epiphany I just experienced, confess my fraud, the depth of my hubris? We are sitting so very close to one another.

"The band sounded wonderful," I say in my Stan Kenton voice.

&

When we get to the hotel, Duke asks the clerk to book a room for me. The clerk glances at me with surprise.

"I'm sorry, Mr. Ellington, but our hotel does not serve white people."

Duke suppresses his astonishment.

"But he's with me."

"We simply can't do it, sir."

Duke exhales, says, "All right then, he's my guest and he'll stay in my suite."

The clerk shrugs, hands Duke his key, and waves to the bellhop, who puts Duke's three bags on a dolly with my ragged overnight tote on top. We cram into a tiny elevator, turn right down a dim corridor on an ancient, still beautiful carpet to room 319. The suite consists of a large living room, a bedroom, and a bath between. The living room is spacious and pleasant in the way faded elegance becomes. There is a long couch, a coffee table, a round table with four chairs, and a fireplace with a gas log behind a screen. Three floors below, the streets of Pittsburg are still alive.

The bellboy leaves. Duke finds a menu, glances at it, hands it to me, and disappears into his bedroom. By the time I have decided what I want, Duke emerges wearing a luxurious light blue flannel bathrobe with a royal purple satin sash. On his head is a cap that looks like a nylon stocking done up with a neat knot, through which a few small black curls are visible down to the single strand. He reaches for the phone.

Dialing, he asks, "Know what you want?"

"Barley soup and a double cheeseburger."

I can hear the desk clerk's voice.

"The restaurant is closed, Mr. Ellington."

"There's got to be somebody there."

"No, sir, the restaurant closes at midnight."

We are both famished. "Closed" cannot possibly be a real word, and Duke shows his impatience.

"Go look," he demands of the clerk.

Long, empty pause.

"There's just the cleanup man, sir."

"Connect us!"

Pause.

"Yes, sir?"

"This is Duke Ellington in 319. What have you got in the kitchen?"

"Everything's locked up till morning, Mr. Ellington."

"Certainly you can find something to eat in a hotel restaurant kitchen."

"No, sir, no food. Only ice cream. There's no lock on the ice cream case."

"What flavors?"

"Vanilla, chocolate, and strawberry."

Duke doesn't miss a beat.

"Send them up."

"How much do you want of each, sir?"

"How much you got?"

"They're all in five-gallon containers, sir."

This time, a slight crescendo: "Bring them *up*."

Duke turns to me and says, "I hope you like ice cream."

"I love it."

"Me too."

Duke seems actually happy. He's made the best of it. I go to the bathroom. When I get back, the cleanup man himself has appeared with three five-gallon tubs on his cart and is placing them on the coffee table along with two spoons and two cloth napkins. Duke tips him the five dollars he did not give to Paul Gonsalves. He positions himself on the sofa centered exactly between the three tubs, beckons me to bring up a comfortable chair across from him, and hands me a napkin and a spoon. I see the vanilla tub is a quarter full, the chocolate not quite half, the strawberry mostly full.

"What's your favorite?" I ask.

"I like 'em all," he says, diving deep into the chocolate with a decisive downbeat. I pull up close and start with vanilla.

It is now 1:00 in the morning, I am sitting in a 19th-century hotel suite facing seven gallons of ice cream and a stocking-headed icon of American jazz. Ellington is in his young sixties, old enough to be Buddy Hiles's father, older than Stan Kenton by a half generation,

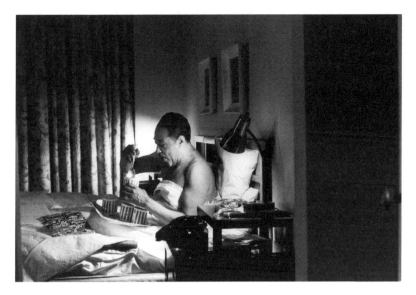

The Duke of Ice Cream

a few years older than my Dad. I am twenty-two and, in some ways, considerably younger than my age. As we suck up the creamy cold, our actual meeting begins.

Duke starts asking me questions about my upbringing, my parents, and my education through college. These are probing questions—he actually wants to know. I tell him about my father's publishing life, his bifurcated ambitions for his only son, my mother's reliable support, and about Buddy—a lot about Buddy—and Babe's nightclub (yes, Duke has been there "more than once"), and my times at the Cincinnati Cotton Club, where Duke started playing in the 1930s. I tell him about my vitriolic fourthgrade teacher, Miss Lucky, throwing books at Gertrude Turner, the only Black student in the school, about our segregated high school swimming pool, and about our *servants.* Face to face with Duke, I find myself suddenly able to articulate how invisible our ingrained entitlement has appeared to me and my milieu. He asks about the University of Chicago and its idiosyncrasies, about Bill Russo and, especially, about working with Stan. Duke is truly asking, looking at me kindly and earnestly. I think he wants to learn what he can from this talented, clueless cub.

Despite my passion for declaring myself, I'm not sure he knows what to make of me. As the conversation goes on, I'm wary that the gulf might be mutual. Most of the people Duke knows are gifted in some way, but they also share much common ground with him. I come to him on the bounce from across the big-band railroad tracks. I also know he's bound to a code of professional courtesy to his white doppelgänger, Stan Kenton. Perhaps these are merely self-doubts, my growing confrontation with my own racial and social values. Meanwhile, as we continue dipping into the ice cream, rotating flavors, the questions keep coming. Duke shows nothing but genuine curiosity. I don't know what to ask him in return that hasn't already been answered in thousands of interviews.

Across the vats, I study Duke Ellington's face. He is tired, yet wide awake. His focus on me is unwavering, his clarity unmistakable. And here, again, I see that light-around-the-body. Duke appears truly generous, and not just to me: that five-dollar tip may have been more than the cleanup man's salary for the day. But he is, like Stan, like Dad, like me, a very hungry man, a hunger we cannot discuss but freely share. That hunger is the sturdy bridge over the moat.

Given our singular dinner rations for this evening, we are as full up as we can manage. By now the coffee table is a mess, the tubs are half liquid, and both of us are sticky and tired. Duke gets up from the couch and says, "When you wake up in the morning, I'll be gone. In two weeks we'll be in Las Vegas. Call me then." He nods goodnight and disappears behind his door. I am suddenly so exhausted and overloaded that I don't even wash up. I roll up my trousers for a pillow, lie down on the couch with a thin coverlet over me, and immediately fade to black. By morning, the large room is full of light and Duke has cleared out. I put on my pants, wash my hands and face, catch an airport cab, and fly back to my Chicago life. By 9:00 p.m., I am sitting at my stage-left spinet, playing the Second City troupe into action.

I assumed Duke was done with me. We hadn't discussed the music I'd written for his band—there didn't seem to be a need to. But after two weeks I made the call anyway, and he seemed happy to hear from me. He suggested I provide new arrangements of the band's core repertoire since "we're tired of the old ones and need some new ones." We agreed on two titles, and I promised to send the arrangements soon. As I thought about it later, I realized that Duke had rejected my attempts at forging his band into my own compositional voice simply by silently not accepting them, then giving me some time to internalize the band's actual voice. Since new wine in old bottles would be actually useful to him, and I had a good track record as an arranger, his suggestion was worth a try. The two classics were "I'm Beginning to See the Light" and "It Don't Mean a Thing if It Ain't Got That Swing." In the midst of preparing songs for a new Second City review, and of my own composing projects, I wrote these two arrangements very quickly. The ideas flowed naturally from my new appreciation for what I was tasked to do. The variations on the old motifs, the new harmonies and instrumental voicings, the selection of soloists (yes, including Johnny Hodges on alto), and especially the climactic shout choruses—all came easily. These were good-feeling songs, and I wanted keenly to be part of the band's good feeling. In three weeks, the arrangements were finished, the scores proofed, the parts neatly copied out, and the package mailed via Special Delivery.

For three months I heard nothing, nor did I expect to, but in early June the phone rang. "This is Duke Ellington. We just finished recording two of your arrangements for Columbia Records. You'll get a test pressing in the mail from their office in a couple of weeks. I hope you like what we've done." Astonished, I thanked him. And when the test disc did arrive and I'd listened to it, I was even more astonished. What I'd written had been expanded considerably, and the tempi were much faster than I'd heard in my head. But the most significant change was wryly suggested by the album's title, *Piano in the Background*. The title was evidently meant as a euphemism: Ellington's exquisitely tasteful piano playing, which historically had indeed been mostly in the background, was featured prominently in this album. In my two arrangements especially, Duke plays abundantly like the brilliant soloist he is, with economy, wit, and commanding authority over the music's scope. I gradually came to realize that Duke had reshaped my music with the spirit of collaboration that had characterized the band from the very beginning. I'd given him a yard to play in, he'd done some creative landscaping, and he and his band proceeded to play marvelously therein. At the high point of one of the shout choruses someone emits a high shout of joy that remains, to this day, a jewel in my heart. I think it's the voice of Duke himself, but does it matter?

❧

What I carry with me most is the model of guidance that Duke planted in my own later teaching: an ideal of patience, discernment, and faith in the outcome. Only recently have I been able to identify with Duke's compassionate gaze upon the young boy I was, and with his ongoing, skillful guidance. He saw me as I was; he did not judge me. Then he let me do the real work, the inner work on my own, and was willing to wager the time and effort of his men that I would come through. In a subsequent phone call I asked Duke, "What's next?" He suggested I arrange some things for his new vocalist. We discussed her range and style, and the song choices. But I never wrote anything more for Duke Ellington's band and never tried to reconnect with him. Ellington had given me a fundamental life lesson, and I had given him a little something he could use. Fair trade. Curtain.

Duke first had taken the time to clearly read me, an arrogant young man from far away. When he listened to my music, he said nothing; when he listened to me talk as we measured out spoons of ice cream, he said nothing; when he'd given me exactly the work I could do for our mutual benefit, he said nothing. The music said everything. The entire vibe of transmission was so subtle, so subterranean, so psychologically and musically skillful that it has taken me decades to appreciate the whole of it. In fact, I hadn't, really, until now, writing out for the first time the story of those long-gone Duke days.

I see now why I left the Duke-thread dangling. From the vantage point of sixty years, it's clear that the movie was over, the credits were rolling. That may have felt inconclusive then, but not now, long after the house lights have gone up. What still remains of our fair trade is an ever-deepening gratitude that lives palpably in the space between my heart and solar plexus. And, of course, two tracks of exciting jazz.

In his 2013 biography of Duke Ellington, Terry Teachout says, in reference to the stormy if short-lived presence of bassist Charlie Mingus in the band, "Ellington almost never fired anyone, having discovered the secret of making unwanted players depart on their own accord before he was forced to cut them loose." I don't think I was an unwanted one, more like someone with whom the transaction was complete, but I definitively did cut my own self loose. Half a lifetime later, I have learned that such a strategy is often a key component in Sufi and Buddhist teaching.

Piano in the Background received little critical notice when it was first released, but over the years it has become a favorite of jazz fans and reviewers alike. The two arrangements I contributed are often singled out, usually for Duke's spectacular piano solos.

7

Just One More

In 1961, after having been recorded by Ellington and Kenton, I thought I'd be done collecting bands, but I wasn't. The electricity of Maynard Ferguson's high notes that I'd first heard eight years earlier had never quite left my body. By this time, Ferguson had long left Kenton to lead a band of his own. It was a smaller version of the Kenton band, thirteen players instead of nineteen, but it sounded full enough.

Maynard strove for a contemporary bebop sound, modern but not at all adventurous. No matter the ordinariness of his present musical life, however, I wanted to partner with the trumpeter who was my teenage god; that would be a most satisfying rite of passage. So in the fall of that year, when I was in New York, I approached Maynard at Birdland, where he was playing. He was cordial, suggested a visit, and gave directions to his new house just now nearing completion.

His address was at the end of the line—a three-bus, two-and-a-half-hour ride from Manhattan. When I stepped down from the empty bus, I couldn't see a city skyline anywhere. Where was I? Maynard's unfinished house, if that's what it was, appeared far across a seemingly deserted, scrubby plain. I didn't see a path, so, avoiding marshy areas and stepping around piles of building materials, I went straight for the structure. The scene appeared derelict and windswept: an unfinished house in the middle of empty real estate. I climbed the steps of the big porch, knocked on the fancy new door, and waited. Again I knocked and waited. Gingerly I let myself into a very large room open to new beams and a peaked roof. In front of me was a wide balcony with stairs leading up on either side, and hallways leading off to second-floor rooms. From somewhere came indistinct music. It was a stage set lit by afternoon light. I supposed it to be my cue.

"Hullo," I shout.

(Rumblings, thuds, off)

Again, "Helloooo."

(After a pause, the sound of two people approaching in slippers from stage right)

Now Maynard appears alongside a woman with long, uncombed blond hair. He is rumpled, walking uncertainly, peering out from an amused smile. She's just stepped out of a page of *Esquire*. They wear matching white bathrobes. Their eyes are large, and they are barely hanging on to the present.

Calling up to them I say, "It's Bill Mathieu. We have a date today at two o'clock."

Maynard squints, focuses with difficulty, then smiles sheepishly.

"Oh yeah, is this today? Here is...this is Janine.... Janine and I are just in the middle of..." Quizzically he looks at Janine, who demurely smiles and looks down. "An...*experience*. Could you..." He mumbles something to Janine, then turns back down to me: "Could you come back in a few hours?"

"I'll call you tomorrow."

"Okay, bye."

He shepherds her back whence they'd entered. I turn downstage and step out through the front door into the surreal afternoon.

In a phone call a few days later, Maynard unapologetically explained that he and his lady had been on an acid trip, and suggested that I set up a rehearsal for his band when they'd be in Chicago the following month. I knew I could use the Second City stage on a Monday night when the theater was dark. We agreed on the date. I said I wanted to write a concerto featuring his playing on valve trombone, French horn, and trumpet, each of his instruments for each of three movements. He said sure. I asked if it would be okay to leave out his trumpet's iconic high notes in favor of his superb musicianship. He said sure, and he'd pay for the copyist.

❧

All through my mid-twenties, I was wrestling with my identity as a composer. I loved jazz but also was internalizing classical and contemporary concert music, and that is what occupied my study and practice. I wanted to be the composer who wove the music of Stravinsky, Ives, Hindemith, Bartók, Boulez, Miles, Monk, Ornette, and Cecil—all my heroes—into a single fabric. As if I'd learned nothing from the recent past, I followed the same strategy I'd followed with the Kenton and Ellington bands for my debut with Maynard Ferguson's band: weighting my own aesthetic over theirs. This was perfectly reasonable from my point of view but hardly from the point of view of those bandleaders and their men. In an era when big bands were fading from the scene, Kenton desperately needed music he could sell; Ellington needed his voice to resonate with the emerging awareness of racial equality in the national psyche; and Ferguson needed to survive as the leading big band of swinging modern bebop. Over on my side of town, I was trying to integrate all my musical loves and obsessions into an authentic style of cultural synthesis. At the time, the odor of this conceit was clearly detectable by every jazz musician I met, but I wore it like someone who thought it a noble scent.

To be sure, I was far from alone in this endeavor. Certain works of Gunther Schuller, John Lewis, William Russo, and Leonard Bernstein, among many others, came to be known as Third Stream music (Schuller coined the term), and there was some narrow success. But in retrospect, I think the entire lot of us had difficulty discerning the difference between a lifelong internalization of influences on the one hand and superficial appropriation on the other. I, for one, may have been long on vision, but I was way short on homework. Over a half-century later, this intercultural stew still needs many more decades of simmering. Last night, however, my curiosity led me to burrow to the bottom of a pile of old scores and dig out *Concerto for Brass Soloist and Orchestra*, all forty-seven pages and fourteen minutes of it, in three movements. Maybe it's not quite as inept as I've come to remember, but, as you will soon see, we'll never know.

We have set the rehearsal to begin at 8:30 on the Second City stage. At 8:35, the band boy arrives in the band bus. By 10:00 he has everything set up: music stands, trap set, stool for the bassist, all in the band's familiar pattern. But only five players have shown up and most of those, including Maynard, have wandered off, leaving the pianist alone on stage playing quite beautifully for his own pleasure. By 10:30, seven of the thirteen are still missing. Most of the rest are warming up in a familiar pre-rehearsal cacophony. Now Maynard whistles loudly through his teeth, calling the men to the stage.

Having had to give up their night off, most of the guys are surly, stoned, or both. The stage lights are bright and the theater where I sit is dark.

Maynard introduces me. Some shade their eyes against the lights to peer into the emptiness. He passes out the parts to my concerto. The drummer appears and surveys his set-up; one more trumpet player shows up. Four out of ten wind and brass never do arrive. I have scored the first movement for alto sax, plus flute, clarinet, and bass clarinet, instruments the saxophonists routinely double on in their gigs. Maynard faces his band and is just about to give the downbeat when two of those players raise their hands. One says, "I forgot my flute," the other, "I didn't bring my bass clarinet. Sorry." "Well," shrugs Maynard, "just transpose."

The first movement of the concerto calls for delicate blends of winds and trombones, half of whom are missing, and two are trying with little success to transpose their flute and clarinet music to their saxophones. The thinned-out movement is played through. It is dull, incomprehensible. The second movement is supposed to feature Maynard's French horn, but with a glance at the score, he turns to me and says, "Oh, sorry man, I don't have my French horn with me." Pages rustle. The third movement, meant to feature Maynard's solo trumpet, requires good sight reading and careful rhythmic placement. With so many missing players, it becomes clear that this boat will not float, at least not tonight. Maynard turns to me sitting among the empty chairs and, with palms turned upward, shrugs. He turns back to the band and asks for the parts to be passed in. At this moment, the bass player makes an enthusiastic entrance. "I managed to borrow a bass," he crows.

The rhythm section of piano, bass, and drums is now complete, all ready to play.

This is a painful moment in my young life. Well rehearsed and performed, my concerto might have been a believable if not very compelling piece, a *noble* exercise in the merging of jazz sensibility and contemporary concert music. I've worked hard on it, placed my faith in it, and, in a secluded sector of my mind, idealized its acceptance.

Maynard has business with his men. Quietly he speaks to them about future gigs, itineraries, and travel arrangements. He allocates certain guys to pass on the information to the missing guys. There is a pause, some sudden restlessness arises, and someone calls out, "Let's play!" Someone else calls out the title of a tune, and within one minute there are five horns and a full rhythm section eagerly cutting loose the music they have had to restrain all week on the job. They sound happy, swinging, and astoundingly good. A few musicians leave. Not one has spoken to me. Maynard hands me the score and parts. Above the din, he says, "I'll call you." Sunken, I slink out of my own damn theater. By a week after the rehearsal, Maynard has not called. I call him. Briefly apologetic, he says, "It didn't work out." But then, in a replica of my post-debut conversation with Duke Ellington, he says, "Why don't you write a simple jazz chart for us, like maybe just a blues thing." Sensing this might be something of actual value to him and his band, and needing to salvage what I could from a messy failure, I agree. Within three days, I have composed, arranged, and scored a simple blues thing I've titled *Guess Again*. In two more days, I've copied out the parts, packaged it all, mailed it away. End of Maynard story?

❧

Three months later, I am more skeptical than amazed to receive a package from Roulette Records containing an LP album of The Maynard Ferguson Orchestra, and *Guess Again* is one of the tracks. I listen, it sounds all right, professionally played, a generic bebop chart many others in the field might have written at that time.

Simmering in my memory over the many years, *Guess Again* had acquired the aura of disappointment surrounding the night of the doomed rehearsal. But last night, I decided to check out the tune on YouTube. By Jove! There it sits, and to my present ears it sounds really good. At the time I wrote it, I'd been trying to compose a generic bebop chart for years, but my lack of total commitment to the style was the hurdle I'd always stumbled on. Evidently, though, the freshly drowned composer of twenty-four managed to pull off an intricate, swinging, yet absolutely generic big-band modern bebop chart. I'd contrived to write something not too simple, its complexity lying inside the perimeter of the band's style. And the musicians, especially Maynard, perform it with authentic brilliance, as if they actually love playing it. Check it out on YouTube, you simply can't miss it: *The Complete Roulette Recordings of The Maynard Ferguson Orchestra*, Disc 9. If you can fine-tune the cursor, *Guess Again* begins at 38:52 and lasts for exactly three minutes and thirty seconds.

❧

After I'd fully lived out my movie, *Stan, Duke, and Maynard*, I became capable of fully cognizing the obvious—I was using their fame to feed my own career hungers. In each case, these leaders guided me from self-serving composition to productive collaboration. I learned to see them as mere men, richly gifted and deeply flawed—even Duke (women, money). And I learned that I didn't need to use them, or anyone else, to satisfy my hungers. Sixty years after the action, I've learned to recognize the guidance that passed through my collection of bandleaders and on through me to my students. Internalized over my life, their impulse to guide me and the compassion of their teaching became indistinguishable from teaching itself. The characters and the parts they played disappear; what remains is the guidance, the kernel of wisdom to be passed forward. In that sense, my bandleader saga presaged the burglary of my Murshid's rock shrine, although I had to wait until—well, frankly—this very moment of writing to realize that.

There is a sweet coda to this romance. Since I first heard them in my early teens, I'd adored the sound of the Four Freshmen, a vocal group discovered in 1948 by Kenton himself, signed to Capitol Records, and thus catapulted to national success. The warmth of their blend resembled the harmonies of the beautifully in-tune Kenton trombone section, except that these harmonies come from men's voices singing from inside their own flesh. In October of 1959, when the Kenton band, along with June Christy and the Four Freshmen were on a cross-country tour, I asked the group if I could try my hand at arranging something for them. My arranging stock was high at the time, and they said "sure." We chose a popular song with pretty if frivolous lyrics and affective music, titled *Polka Dots and Moonbeams*. I already knew the song by heart and right away began writing the arrangement during the night-long bus rides to nowhere. I found that writing for human voices cultivated a kind of musical optimism in me. I took joy in my work and wrote without anxiety or doubt. About a thousand miles later, I handed the Four Freshmen my score. They said they'd take it from there. Sure enough, six months after I'd returned to Chicago, there arrived in the mail a new Capitol release of the Four Freshmen, complete with my arrangement. Accompanied by a tasteful orchestration in pop style, it was gorgeously sung, just like I'd heard it in my secret ear above the road noise of the bus.

The original members of the Four Freshmen have passed on, but a succession of excellent vocal quartets singing under the original brand name has endured for at least seventy years. My vocal score of *Polka Dots and Moonbeams*, sometimes enveloped in elaborate orchestrations, sometimes performed by the four men alone, always note-for-note as I wrote it, has become a classic in their repertoire. Quite a few versions are available online, performed by different incarnations of the Four Freshmen, and each one of them is rendered masterfully.

So my modest offering, conceived and written freely out of love for the music, flowed easily through me, through the singers, and outward to the wide world. Though it didn't seem like a big deal at the time, this happenstance became an important marker in my professional life. A decade later, I found myself writing music for choirs devoted to the music of their hearts and the hearts of their communities, and over the ensuing years dozens and dozens of songs have poured out. These songs just come through.

We can't always know when or how such transmissions actually begin. Sometimes it seems as though they simply happen through no traceable cause—they just come from somewhere and keep going on and on and on to somewhere else.

8

Chicago Gives Me a Dollar

My virgin LSD trip is the other life-memory I've been reluctant to write down. Even now, sixty years later, it's a toss-up, but I'm choosing now over never.

On an early November day of my twenty-seventh year, I was returning to our wood-frame house full of theater folk when a resident stopped me as he was coming down the outside stairs. Ed Yerxa, stocky, short-bearded, and congenial, worked the bar at Second City and occasionally supplied his friends with dope.

"Hey man, I've been saving something for you," he said, and pulled out of his jacket pocket a sugar cube wrapped tightly in cellophane. "It's an Owsely, man, the very best. Save it for a special time."

I'd been waiting for a chance to take my first acid trip, and this seemed to be it.

I entered my basement apartment, casually tossed the sugar cube into my sock drawer, and didn't think about LSD for a few weeks. Meanwhile, the frequent third-floor discussions, led by director Paul Sills, about ego and autonomy, the proper function of theater, Buber's I/Thou, and the individual's relation to God were ongoing. My housemates were all older than me, by just a few or as many as a dozen years. I was the youngster with big ears and little to say. They all called me Billy. I was very into my own work, practicing six hours a day, having frequent nights of stoned sex with available women, writing in my journal, writing for *Downbeat*—record reviews, interviews, and a monthly music-theory column—and listening to and composing tons of music. In short, I was deeply burrowed into a bachelor musician's life of work and introspection. I did bask in the third-floor intellectual camaraderie, but all those first principles and all that religious seeking engaged me only tenuously. I did think about Kant, God, Zen, and the rest, but my experiences with philosophy, with finding skeins of words for describing whatever it is that simply *is*, had been boring from childhood through college, and the disaffection was still fresh. My way of deeply knowing was through musical and sexual union. I wanted the ability to be fully awake to my experiences as I lived them, and was skeptical about hashing through first principles with others. I was hungry to go it alone. Like Huck Finn, I decided to light out for the Territory on my own. And now the Territory presents itself as a tab of primo acid.

On a Monday evening in early December, when the Second City is dark, I decide the time is ripe to test my self-knowing, to settle once and for all whether or not Man needs God. My friends are all aware of bad, and often dangerous, acid trips and repeatedly warn each other against solo flights without a friend close at hand. So, for insurance, I climb the porch steps to apprise my upstairs buddies, Dennis and Mona, of my plan. They roll their eyes. Mona says, "Okay, Billy, we're up here. Have a good time." Back down in my cozy basement rooms, I fetch the cube, unwrap it, examine it, then let it melt in my mouth. It tastes exactly like sugar. *Nothing to this*, I think, and proceed to take off my trousers, put on my warm bathrobe, and sit down at my table to wait.

Stanley Owsley was a mercurial, mysterious figure who was to become, a few years thence, the primo LSD maker for the Grateful Dead, among others. This particular tab may have been an early beta model for him; it was procured, according to my friend Ed, "from a friend who'd just returned from California." I'll never know the provenance of this melted cube of sugar entering my bloodstream, but I know that for fifteen minutes nothing is happening. So why not play my newly purchased Steinway grand? I get up from the chair. By the way, isn't it weird how everything from a standing position looks and feels so totally different? I gotta sit down. I try again and manage to center myself on the piano bench. I'll play Beethoven's "Appassionata" Sonata, a piece I've been working on for months. I begin, but the notes are not piano notes, they are notes on an instrument I've never heard before, notes that have distant choirs and bells in them. And the sequence of tones makes no sense. I lower my hands from the keys and wait a moment. I know—I'll play a record of my favorite Beethoven string quartet, Number 14 in C-sharp Minor. Turning on the stereo, locating the LP disc, removing it carefully from its slipcover, placing the disc on the turntable, and dropping the stylus at exactly that certain spot are sequentially heroic acts. I'll write an essay, I think, on the import of this with respect to...*evolution*. Yes. I settle opposite the speakers in my most comfortable chair. As the music begins, a miracle I never could have predicted unfolds, a miracle that transcends all philosophies, all talk of humans and gods, of secular and sacred.

It is now less than an hour into the trip. There's a welcome gauze over my mind. As the music begins, the string instruments, dancing through their frequencies, are secret, sublime messages sent directly into my brain. Now the sounds are no longer musical instruments or even recognizable as sound, but something transforming my body. I can plainly *see* the energy and feel it in my flesh, in my bones and joints. It is both my body and my perception of my body. Moment to moment, the miracle is presented. Wasn't it this very afternoon I'd read in Lao Tzu, *From wonder into wonder existence opens?*

The winter-dark of my basement studio is lit only by the glow of a 75-watt bulb above my head. In the front room, I've set the space heater on high, keeping everything warm, and now, it seems, getting warmer. Beethoven's string quartet is the very air quivering me more and more alive. Now the air itself is blossoming into a three-dimensional streaming mandala of never-before-seen beauty and complexity, with vividly iridescent rainbow-colored wavefronts intermingling with and through one another. The air is color-coded and shape-specific in ever-expanding, enveloping fountains of light. The waves are moving and motionless at the same time, *still moving*. There is no distinction between sound, sight, or sensibility. The air *is* the music, the music is the air, the non-air is the non-music.

Now there is a higher level. The streaming energy is more than itself: it is *code* for the whole of existence. It is coding for Being, for Source. It codes for our own *human* being, for us who have evolved to understand the code! I *am* the code, you see; the code and I are one and the same. Still as a stone, I succumb to wonder. The sensate mandalas are racing outward from a single source. Is the source the hi-fi speaker? My acid-soaked mind knows better. The source is this eternal moment. The Source is *Now*.

I'm so high that I nearly pass out. What I didn't realize then but know now is that the magic of this powerfully suspended moment will stay with me for as long as I'm alive. It will remain a primordial transmission from the beginning of time all the way through Beethoven's mind, then mine, and now the minds of everyone I've ever touched and been touched by. Dope or no dope, the experience stands.

Back to the basement. I'm so thoroughly and dangerously wiped out that I recognize this as the moment for seeking help. I get up unsteadily to my feet, secure my slippers, grab my winter coat and, leaving the record to play itself out, plunge into the winter night, up a flight of stairs, and knock on the door of my upstairs neighbors. It opens, and Mona, in mock surprise, exclaims, "Well, look who's here, it's Billy."

෨

We are sitting in a triangle, Dennis and Mona and I, on three chairs in their living room. I talk about what I am seeing now. It is my new opera, *The Dog's Brain*, which I'm at this very moment composing. I need to speak of it because it will heal humanity of its ills and follies. I describe the rapidly changing scenes appearing, in the pulse of a dog's attention span, before my eyes. Tasteful solos by Miles Davis are threaded throughout, along with scatterings of Ornette Coleman, Alban Berg, and the "Appassionata" sonata. My opera has everything in it without judgment, one vivid scene after another, an infinity of faces and places. It is my great masterwork, my contribution to the stream of life, my C-sharp Minor Quartet. My friends are partly kind, partly bored, mostly sleepy. Sometimes they talk quietly to me, and of course their sympathies become a featured part of *The Dog's Brain*. After about two hours of this, they figure they've talked me down, say it's time for bed, and tell me to go back downstairs and try to sleep. But they've underestimated Stanley Owsley.

I thank them and make my way down the steps, careful to avoid the dirty snow from last week's storm. I realize that now I'm finally on my own. I open the door of my basement flat and see a brightly burning flame in the corner of the front room. In an instant, the walls have caught fire, and I hear the unmistakable crackle of burning paint and wood. The heat pushes me back. In my slippers and winter coat, I turn around and run straight into the middle of street-lit Cleveland Avenue. For most of a city block, I run faster than a man can run. Looking back over my shoulder, I see an enormous conflagration reaching for the sky. "*Fire, fire, fire, fire,*" I bellow. Still running, I begin to lose consciousness. I feel myself falling.

This is one of those life-threatening moments when the movie goes into super slow motion, maybe even frame by frame. There's a reason for this: the mind is so lit up, there is so much to process, that the memory of it plays out like a mule pulling a weighted cart up a steep hill. Or, to be precise, like a very slow computer. In slow motion, then, this is what I remember: I am falling forward under a bright sodium vapor lamp. Instinctively I head to the left, away from the middle of the street, toward a strip of grass between the curb and the sidewalk where every few yards there are sturdy, newly planted saplings. I know, as I fall, that I must die curled around a tree, and I angle my body toward the nearest one. When my eyes are barely above the ground, I notice the tree is centered within an intricate mandala, its circular metalwork fixed above the drainage depression around the young trunk. It appears to me as an iridescent labyrinth inviting me to come to rest here, yes, here among the scattered patches of dirty snow. I hear sweet music of a deep silence, death's code. Then I'm gone.

I have no idea how long I lay there, but I am awakened by a big black boot prodding me gently. Rolling over, I find the sky lit with a celebratory display, reds and blues and rainbow patinas everywhere. Is someone expecting me? Backlit by a white sun, an enormously tall alien is looming over me while stimulating his genital area with his open palm. It is his language, I suppose, which I understand as a congenial Genital Test. His two companions are speaking Alien. They've found me! Their long search is over. I prop myself onto one elbow, and they tenderly hoist me to my feet. In muffled, coded barks, the three discourse amongst themselves. One consults a hand-held crackling box and, with music provided by cosmic rays, communicates with the mother ship. A woman's voice says, "Roger," a code I could crack if I cared to. The Genital Stimulator calmly ushers me up some steps into a metal machine I realize is skillfully crafted to resemble one of the Chicago Police paddy wagons often seen patrolling nightly up and down neighborhood streets.

Well, I won't be fooled. I sit on a metal bench with some other beings meant to look like me, except not so much. Some are merely skeletons, some wear badly fitting, poorly fabricated earth-like clothes.

I enjoy the ride, a movie of lights with a pleasant musical score of car horns, sirens, and rumbling sounds. I make a mental note: must use for *The Dog's Brain.* Some things look familiar, but this is not bothersome: some things in life do look familiar, that's all. Soon the pretend paddy wagon stops at a building marked Cook Country Jane, probably an old movie set, very clever. Then some muddled action, not very interesting, maybe I dozed for a moment. I'm tired. A number of us are led by Something into a very large room marked Holden Cell. There are high windows covered with vertical metal bars, and a single bare bulb hanging by a wire from the middle of the tall ceiling. Many beings are asleep on a cement floor that is sloped slightly toward the central drain. Others are laid out on waist-high metal slabs affixed around the perimeter. I claim a slab, lay my strung-out body down, and instantly go to sleep.

I wake up in a faint dawn. The Aliens are gone. All around me are clusters of unkempt men sleeping it off. We're all in the tank together, and I feel ecstatic, purified, and cleansed from the inside. I am overwhelmingly grateful for being here in the heart of Humanity, precisely here in *this* humanity that is rendering true for me the deepest suffering of this world. Yet I am simply another body among them, one more beating heart. I sit up on the slab. In front of my slippered feet is a massive mound of a man lying on his back. With each mightily achieved inhalation he snores with profound intensity, pauses, and whistles softly as he exhales. His curly stubble is gray on his pink face, his enormous length laid flat out. I scrutinize him from my perch. Where is his mother's singing, his father's kindness, his children's happy laughing, his wife's caress? My chest cavity hollows out, and its warmth envelops the good man at my feet, my best friend, my fellow journeyman. I am swept into a compassion I have never known.

I get up and kneel beside the giant for a moment, then lie down curling next to him with my arm across his chest. He smells of last night's gin and vomit. I feel the heaviness of his life, his failures and sorrow, and now, in his unguarded sleep, his open-hearted love. He is struggling to breathe, to survive, and I am aglow with loving him. An immeasurable compassion for life—for all of it—is palpable in each of my body's pulsing cells. I'm more connected to the world I live in than I ever knew possible. Radiating from my center, a golden light expands time and place, filling our metal and cement holding cell, the jail, the city I know, and all that is alive.

Equanimous within and without, I lie there conjoined with the spirit of my new brother. After what could have been an hour, I hear a nearby clatter, along with women's alto chatter. The breakfast cart is serving food to the adjoining cell. The men are stirring, coughing, spitting into corners, arranging their clothes—everyone seems familiar with the routine. The cart appears outside the bars of our cell. I get in line. When it is my turn, I am handed a slice of bologna between two slices of Wonder Bread. I'm hungry, I eat, and the meal is wonderful! I stand in line to drink real water from the real porcelain water fountain, *everyone's* water fountain, and the water is a river of delight, everyone's pure delight. I'm all set to be alive in a new way in a new day. I have no teeming emotion—everything seems perfectly in place, absolutely as it should be, and always has been, and always will be.

We are all waiting. The only sounds are coughing, nose blowing, some groans, a few whispers, a few subdued exchanges. Around 8:30 a warden enters the cell, calls my name, and escorts me down the hall to a small room with a plain wooden bench, a chair with a leather seat, and a guard standing at casual attention. The guard tells me to sit on the bench and wait. I feel perfectly calm, self-contained. I want nothing, need nothing. With perfect concentration, I examine the pattern of cracks in the stone floor. Presently, the door opens quietly and a pair of soft leather shoes, pointedly styled in the Italian fashion of the day, appears in my field of vision. Looking up, I see a short, nattily dressed man with olive skin and shiny hair brushed sharply back. He glances at me briefly with professional acuity, sits opposite me in the leather-seated chair.

"Where'dja get the stuff?" he begins in a sharp voice.

At the time, LSD was not illegal. Few people besides the beatnik community and a handful of research chemists had even heard of the drug, much less an Owsley tab of it. The detective must have thought I'd taken meth, then rampant on the street. At this point I am cogent with acid morality: to wit, I know I have to lie in order to protect my friend—that is beyond question—but at the same time, in a true world, a human being pure of heart would never lie. I look up into the eyes of the detective and seek his soul.

Very slowly, as if receiving a message from beyond this earthly pale, I intone, "Y. R. X. A." *Okay,* I assure myself, *you left out a letter from Ed's name, that's not a lie.*

He asks again, "Who'dja get it from?"

I narrow my eyes and, from a galaxy far, far away, I say the same thing. Disgusted, he picks up his papers and leaves the room. The guard stays, unsmiling.

Now I begin to feel a rapidly rising anxiety: *Have I burned up my friends?* Softly I address the guard. Is there any way he can find out if a fire last night at 452 Webster Street has been reported? He opens the door, motions to a guy with a clipboard, speaks quickly. After three minutes, there is a soft knock, the guard pokes his head out the door, then turns back toward me. "No fire there," he says.

At 9:15, I am ushered into a courtroom with some other folks who, like me, had been scooped off the street so they wouldn't freeze to death in the Chicago winter. I am playing my part in what is clearly a morning ritual. When my turn comes to stand before the judge, he looks up from his notes. I've been charged with disorderly conduct. I make sure my winter coat is closed. He studies me seriously for a long moment.

Then the judge leans forward.

"Do you have a home to go to?"

"Yes, sir."

"Then, young man,"—more forward—"Go. To. It." Now barking: "Bailiff! Give this man a dollar."

Matter-of-factly the judge brings down his gavel.

"Next case."

In those days, the local law required the court to supply released defendants with bus fare to the extent of the city limits. The bailiff hands me a dollar, and I'm ushered out through heavy doors into the cold morning. A few cabs are waiting. I get in one and explain my plight to the driver, promising to pay him upon arrival. He shrugs, "Where to?" Once home to the perfectly intact wood frame house at 452 Webster Street, I find my basement door wide open. I bolt inside, retrieve some cash, and pay the driver the $2.75 charge, plus that very dollar as a tip, plus another of my own. Back inside, I turn down the space heater, turn off the hi-fi, throw myself onto the bed, and sleep soundly. Mid-afternoon, I awaken fresh into a newly purposeful life.

The same afternoon I clump up the steps to my friends. Only Mona is home. I thank her for her kindness and ask her to relay my thanks to Dennis.

"We were just, like, staying up with a sick friend, Billy."

I begin to tell her what happened but stop myself before saying a word. This story has to cook for a while. A really long while.

Over the next few days, I tried to put together what happened. I knew I'd had a psychotic break, but I also felt both viscerally and spiritually affected by some new reality I needed to learn. First, just like Alice when she woke up from Wonderland, I tried to trace the everyday physical events that triggered the hallucinations. I realized that when I'd come down from my friends upstairs, the flame visible from the grate at the bottom of the space heater and the unusually high heat of the room triggered the illusion of an enveloping fire. The stylus of the hi-fi had been going 'round the same groove in Limbo Central, and the static of the needle-in-groove became the crackle of burning wood. Furthermore, I noticed that the two very strong night lamps of the neighborhood fire station half a block away could easily diffract in the misty dark of a Chicago sky, hence the conflagration. I also reasoned that someone must have called the police, since paddy wagons showed up rarely in our tidy, middle-class neighborhood. It was below 20 degrees that night and I could have died, no kidding. And when I inspected the grillwork over the drain of the very tree I had chosen to expire around, I was happily surprised. All up and down Cleveland Avenue, exquisite little iron mandalas graced every tree. And indeed, the brown iron of the grillwork does irridesce under sodium vapor lamps in a way that suggests the patterns one sees when rubbing one's eyes, or when passing out from an overdose of a psychedelic drug. And what lovely deaths those can be.

The most meaningful hallucination to me, however, was how I experienced the Beethoven string quartet. Mandala patterns of every sort are common under the influence of hallucinogens, as are varieties of synesthesia. Their beauty has influenced visual art from ancient Aztec paintings to hippie comics, light shows, posters, media advertising and, especially animation from Disney on. We recognize it when we see it. But this episode was special to me because, with eyes wide open, I saw those music-driven hallucinations as patterns of actual air in real time. The experience triggered an unfolding realization: music is mutually external and internal, and it reveals the nature of nature, including us, in a way nothing else can. The ongoing epiphany is that music does not come from somewhere else, but that we *are* music, and in the process of learning music we are learning ourselves. From this point of view I have developed a particular way of making and teaching music, described in my book, *Harmonic Experience*, in which the primary concern is the subjective experience of the reader. When people ask how I teach music, I say, "I don't teach music, I teach people." From my earliest years, the open window of my self-knowing has been music, and the transcendent range of that psychotic night six decades ago has given me a crucial ongoing insight. From that crazy moment on, the whole world and everything in it has become music.

There are many ways to break open a human heart. The mere presence of a beloved teacher is often the best way. A love affair gone right or wrong is another. Spiritual practice may serve. Drugs can be pivotal also, but it is quite problematic to appraise chemical wisdom. What about those musical mandalas, that somatization of all vibration audible and inaudible? Useful as that wisdom has been for me, it nevertheless was instigated by a hallucination. The little death of passing out on a freezing Chicago night became a useful narrative of ego death, but it was triggered by psychosis. What about the infinite compassion I felt for the mound of flesh lying on the floor of a jail, sleeping off the alcoholic annihilation of his sufferings? That was not a hallucination. However, the victory of the body surviving the toxins of a psychedelic drug commonly results in a feeling of elation and human connection. So is this drug-wisdom or survival? Well then, is a forty-day retreat in an isolated monastery cell that nearly drives you crazy or damn near kills you, or both, an imposed formulaic structure, or is it a true rebirth? I'd say it could be neither or both. I know that practice is good and sometimes even crucial. After all, I'm a practicing musician. Yet when one has developed illuminated consciousness, every moment of every living day is practice: that is, practice qua practice disappears. What remains is an illumined life.

As far as my LSD narrative goes, I'm truly grateful for the psychedelic vision of the nature of vibrational wisdom via Beethoven. It has become a crucial ray of insight, an über-musical mode of knowing. But the love for a snoring old guy laid out on a cell floor has been a primary template for living a beneficent life. It is not about that guy, bless him. It is about the sudden blossoming of compassion, the primordial harmony we are given to feel by virtue of being fully awake.

So, from serendipitous circumstances, wisdom appeared. I'm glad I recognized it as an inseparable part of my own capacity, and I can be open to it at any time in any guise. The feeling for that big man on that long-ago morning has been an enduring touchstone, a chemical collaboration I'm very fortunate to have experienced. Doubtless, I should have stopped there.

But my dance with psychedelics wasn't quite over. There were several subsequent episodes featuring cannabis, LSD, peyote, and psilocybin, with markedly mixed results. There transpired some deep transmission, all right, tough as nails. But in the end, the message was *enough, did it, done, over and out.* What I've received has taken the form of music improvised and composed, words spoken and written, and unfettered presence with those I'm with. But no more psychedelically induced wisdom for me. I got mine in my oh-so-earnest youth, when the getting was good. From now on, I'll take it just as it comes.

9

The Journalist

My journal, now up to Volume V, resumed in 1958. At twenty-one, I've just received my BA from the University of Chicago. Since my career as a composer/arranger for the Stan Kenton band appeared to be dead, or on hold at best, I decided to place my postgraduate fate into the hands of the university's English department. That was the plan, but that's not what happened.

When, in late December, Kenton invited me to join the band in Las Vegas, I hastily withdrew from the university, packed my bags, tried to pacify my anxious wife, and flew off to the desert, score paper and journal in hand. During that year, I filled my journal with pages of vignettes from the momentous year I spent with Stan's famous band. When I returned jobless to Chicago in late 1959, I was immediately hired as musical director of the fledgling Second City Theater. Connie and I were soon divorced, and I subsequently lived the young bachelor's life. Volume V thus became engorged with pages of blood-red poetry and the purple prose of rapture and loss.

On a trip to New York in late 1963 I stayed in the sublet apartment of a friend, and when I packed to leave I evidently left Volume V of my journal behind. By the time I seriously missed it back in Chicago, my friend had cleaned out the sublet and moved to a new place. When I asked him frantically about my journal, he had no memory of it. Much of the story of those years has been retrieved from memory, but the pulsing prose of Volume V has vanished forever beyond the great beyond.

Volume VI picks up in mid-December 1963, a year before the LSD experience of Chapter 8 in this book. By then, my writing has had an eventful young adulthood to mature. Its voice seems to have both more subjectivity and more objectivity. It takes place in a bigger room. There is more dancing with words, more fascination with ideas. I'm reading Martin Buber and Alan Watts, smoking lots of dope, and making love with like-minded women. I sense that I'm writing for a wiser future self, probably my own, but maybe I'm beginning to sense somewhere a still wiser Self, a more universal ear to hear these words.

Whatever I did learn in those days, and however I found the language to articulate it, I am so very glad to have written and preserved these journals. There is a kind of youth-to-age wisdom in reading them today, sixty years later, when I'm beginning to make some sense out of my life, out of life in general, and, by projection, everyone else's life. I still recognize the young man writing these passages, though. He is centered in his head and his gonads, but he is honestly seeking his heart, and I do understand his desperation. I feel close to him. I lean in and say with a smile in my eye, "Keep writing."

❧

Volume VI
December 1963 – October 1966
Age Twenty-Six through Twenty-Nine

December 9, 1963
Volume V has been snatched by the journal snatcher. In it among other things were entries from the summer of 1959, including a long chronicle of the Kenton-Christy-Four Freshmen tour, a running commentary on my awakening social and musical consciousness, and recent heart-breaking paragraphs about infatuation and separation. I found a draft of one poem:

> In the night before spring
> the cold roots of trees and grasses
> are the silent throat of the land.
> They are listening to the lonesome cries,
> waiting for their cue.
>
> When it thaws they will answer.
> When breath becomes sound
> there is no doubt in the voices
> of the willow buds. Their song says
> love is a covenant with the frozen earth,
> and the sun does shine there,
> underground.

Scraps from my desk:

~The idea of death stealing closer until it is infinitely close, at which time life and death need and support one another.

~All the streets are the same until you get there.

~The Kennedy assassination has made me realize that "I" is not safe (as fantasies had heretofore led me to believe) from the holocaust.

~The Way becomes all. Success—*any* culmination whatever—shrivels.

~Why has God SINGLED ME OUT to be just like everybody else?

~God made Bach,
            then sighed.

   The cellists are piercing
   the timpanist with their bows.
   The triangle player goes
ting.

   At the Serkin recital
   this Sunday afternoon
   students looked at their hands
   in despair

On Giving Janet a Metronome for Christmas

   Saints dangling on like a carrot
   whose clip-clop donkey we are,
   rivers running, birds blooming,
   God's glory and the fly in my skull
   go tick.

February 5, 1964
The little bit of wrong in each thing is manifest while the rightness hides. My own normalcy, my own unmarked place in the community of lives, my own brief life, my subtly aging body (rheumy jaws, a brilliant gray hair in the barber's this afternoon, a constant bodily unease, a rectal message of doom), the enormous

lack of love in my life, the vacancy of no Thou. I am not unhappy or peevish, but my tolerance for the unpleasant is low.

March 31, 1964
Today, after four months of procrastinating, I called James Burney at whose apartment I stayed in New York. He had moved, and my journal, with no name or address identifying it, has gone down his garbage chute and been incinerated by now. The journal *snatcher* and the journal *writer* are seen to be the same. Somehow I have deliberately lost my past. The subconscious influence so much against my conscious design maddens me.

Friday, April 10, 1964
Now Granny Clara is dead. During the eulogy at the funeral Dad and I leaned against each other and played tic-tac-toe on my sleeve. In our way we played taps for her. Aunt Bessie, jealous of Clara since childhood, waited uncounted years to be able to stand tall and speak at her little sister's funeral. She did. Gesturing toward the rabbis he said, "I heard him *every time* he said Clara. *Her name rang like a bell.*"

April 27, 1964
High as I was last night, I think I saw many things, one of which is that I ought to be living in this wet and dark-sided spring morning and not writing in it.

The tension between living out one's life and making art about it never goes away. Even if one lives life as a committed artist, no one's life actually *is* their art. I know that now but couldn't quite say it then. I got only so far as the discontent, the nag between the two.

May 13, 1964
The point of music is the understanding that we are not perfect, and that it is possible to seek perfect union by artificial means in order to come in touch with the divine. If we were perfectly divine: no music. Or everything would *be* music.

October 19, 1964
The good composers are really good. The standards are higher than anyone except the best practitioners know. What an awful way we have to do things sometimes: years, perhaps, of not

loving full. I want fullness but I am a child yet, ungrown, on an allowance, pausing for words.

October 20, 1964
In Cincinnati I went in the late afternoon to haunt Walnut Hills High School where I saw the *stuff* from which my former life was made; the banisters, the lockers and doorknobs: to *touch* the same touch, to run my fingers against the same green curved wall, and feel again the enormity, the *totality* of the auditorium in which *every single one* could fit—and there is the stage—MY stage. All this as a way of adjusting memories, nightmares or just dreams for a mode of merely present being.

Weed and hash played a significant part in my life at this time. Often as not, I wrote in my journal high as a kite, so cosmic lightning would strike, and I could briefly enter mystical states of union. I intuited some of the central concepts of holistic philosophy, including Buddhism, and felt the need to articulate them, which meant discovering a new language. These were cannabis-induced insights, however, concepts only, and not the realized experiences of a lived-in life; such experience came to me only decades later. The following entry is a surprising précis of Buddhist thought, namely the unity of unbounded potential and cognitive knowing from which compassion arises. Although a language does appear for the *ideas*, there is scant voice for those ideas being lived out through the sieve of experience. I wonder how often wisdom, especially writing wisdom, appears initially as concept, but then takes many seasons to ripen into active fruition.

October 27, 1964, stoned
God *is* the unknown. Existence is unknowable, *ergo* "divine."
I have a conception of a passionless existence within which we passionate humans move. Whence this passion? Self-generating and self-apprehending, like consciousness, an evolutionary process.

December 28, 1964
[I'm referring in this entry to the events described in the previous chapter, "Chicago Gives Me a Dollar."] Two weeks ago, around December 15th, was the LSD experience about which I am motivated to *not* write—it can't be written. Exorcism, that's all. One sees: self is not the means of living. Like a rat in a maze, that

direction causes pain, and one learns to say no to it. Life is with people, life is life, humans are human. Our first commitment is to our humanity, our common field of human being. *From* that is drawn art, secondarily and subsequently. Being *for* itself is apart from human life, which must be being *in* itself.

The LSD fire has died now, and though I do see it occasionally I'm free to make everyday choices. The fire tells me nothing more than of its own impartiality—it cannot choose for me.

It's best not to write about this part because the LSD has to be absorbed into each moment, with no revelations retained in writing. I don't want to crystallize the episode—I want it to stay wordless inside, to ripen as pure feeling.

New Year's Day, 1965
There is only: *the generations*. Life passes through us, that is all.

April 27, 1965, New York
Last night at Carnegie Hall I heard the world premiere of the complete Ives Fourth Symphony, with Leopold Stokowski conducting the American Symphony Orchestra and the Schola Cantorum. It taught me some, and gave me more reason to continue as a composer: Ives saw images as unfeasible as mine. Also, after uncountable hearings, I heard as if for the *first time* Beethoven's Fifth. Sitting a few feet from the concert-master, having a sense of the human-ness of the event taking place, the dead man baring himself and preaching to us skins and bones who had come to hear him—who had *gathered* to hear him—I received a profound knowing of Beethoven, who at one time was flesh, not an historical figure. And near me a lady of forty-two, so proud, so alone, and so utterly filled with her love, which Beethoven had heard...

June 21, 1965, Chicago
Sitting alone at the bar after work tonight, I said to my impassive waitress friend Madonna, "Madonna, I'm so unhappy," and she replied, "So what?"
Wise, that.

July 12, 1965, Cincinnati to San Francisco
My flight out to San Francisco was a partaking of this epoch's madness, and madness it is. Champagne, good spirits, painted women, good food elaborately prepared, and all of us captives in an enormous and dangerous machine. Meanwhile, I'm tracking the earth below on a big map of the U.S. I can see the ground as a circle one inch in diameter gliding under me, and thusly I navigate our flight. My preoccupation with the irony between our

smooth progress through the air and the rugged determination of the covered wagon settlers to reach the coast 140 years ago is doggedly present.

July 15, 1965, San Francisco
Last night Barbara and Roland Pitschell treated me to a good dinner (hers) and then to Mount Tamalpais to see the red sun set over a sea of fog we had just ascended through. The sun made a red arc over 100 miles. I climbed and stood on a boulder and found my breath gasping in—the same impulse that wrote YOUNG on the wall a decade ago. Still young, still approaching the pole in the middle of the field, still *awaiting*, still sucking in my breath in order to grow, to survive.

After the boulder we roughed it over many trails in bright, bright moonlight arriving finally at the Greek Theater, a small semi circle of seats hewn from rock, square rocks built up quite high, with soft sod for a stage and a flat rock for a forum and, for a backdrop, sylvan mountain woods, fog, moon.

[Enter] Horsemen at a gallop.

I sat on the bare rock; we smoked more. I lay back in the rock bed and looked at the clear stars. I saw my childhood again. Then I knew my body, the rhythm of my muscles, again. I journeyed through an unexpected affirmation. I sighed and panted and convulsed with joy—the pure joy of being a human creature, here, in my skin—HERE—the *miracle* of being here. Farther up the mountain there was a lookout, and from there I saw the coast of California like a map, and the coast was very real and clear to me—the meeting of land and sea made such a necessary and beautiful shape. Then I saw a bright yellow orange shooting star burn up in the atmosphere. I did not care that it was not a sign—it was I who saw it, perhaps no one else—charmed, charmed life...

And then off we went down the mountain roads, miraculously arriving despite the great hazards to which I surrendered and—still miraculously, I sit here writing.

August 7, 1965
Listening to North Indian ragas again—the sitar leads you *on* in the music and *in* to single stroke affirmation of life.

August 24, 1965
    The fly in my skull
    dreamt it was dreaming
    woke up
    & keeled over.

September 19, 1965
To my father: SUCCESS IS A WASTE OF VALUABLE TIME

I think: if a man fully accepts the most basic thing he knows, that he exists *as he is,* then he would not pursue a theology. There is nothing more difficult to understand than the gift of one's existence, yet there is no need for certainty for nothing else is more certain. How odd to think that God could be thought of as separate, or spoken of apart, or given names.

I have a growing sense of myself as a member of the historical (albeit fine-print) human canon; but even more so as one among many human bodies. Also a knowing that at twenty-eight boyhood is being physically passed by. In its place a growing social, humanistic commitment, and a belief in work and daily living.

At the piano, a big technique boost. I see how awful some virtuosi must feel. Once you get it, it's a big cheat, not the real deal.

November 14, 1965
My public exposure threatens like an incubus. MY public exposure. MY orange juice. Although the premiere of MY Woodwind Quintet Oct. 26 was an uneven success from first to last, I know I have written a good piece, made a useful statement in a tough field. Yet this musical language I am using right now, this fractious mode of self-definition, is what threatens the spirit from within and without. I know The Good. The only question becomes: can I face it? Or must I forever catch myself turning?

November 16, 1965
One must learn, I see, not to smother feelings of self and thusly suffer the consequent pain, but to learn our distinctly human form of being: adjusting, cajoling, persuading, one's self *into*—and one's fleeing from one's self *into*—the communality, the human harmony. This is moment-to-moment business. Giving and taking constantly become a single action, then diverge, only to then become indistinguishable: to divide, disperse and coalesce.

January 15, 1966
This period is characterized by a surcease of mysteries. There is no pondering of mystery because everything is given by the same grace—one takes each thing at a time. I have no questions. Existence reveals *itself,* but we find a language for things via philosophical treatises and summaries.

This is a splendid example of a hashish-induced insight that proves unsustainable in lived-out life, although I did seem to recognize that at the time. A few days later I wrote: *Hashish puts me in contact with The Good, but doesn't let me be inside it, or be active from it.* For someone living in a surcease of mysteries, though, I sure did have a lot of questions:

January 24, 1965
I have been given so much in relation to everyone else—how can I give back?

Can I act individually upon the necessity of all of us to give? If so, how? How can a social morality pass through me?

How is it possible to be unattached and still whole? To wholly love without passion?

The ego is a fiction, an *idea*, like *words*. True, egos and words have a kind of reality, but my truest existence is without an acting self. I can live this *some* of the time to *some* degree. Some wee degree. At least my musical activities now seem less problematical.

And then, a fortnight later when I was making up my mind to ask Kay, the woman I'd been courting and breaking up with for three years, for her hand in marriage, I wrote the following poem:

Lord, How We Turn

Planet by grace turning
turns Earth,
who, turning, turns ribbons
of chains of spirals
of fire atoms forming
next fire atoms
of kin
into seeping, wiggling
fractions of sponges
then sponges,
still turning, turn
fishes, snakes, apes,
then humans who see
the Earth turning
and turn to reflecting thus on their nature.
Thusly we turn.

February 13, 1966
Just soon some future day I will better remember:

To be alone, to seek the self, now appears WRONG, it is itself the very FIRE, it is the dark place that says no, it is headache, spasm, amour-propre.

March 23, 1966
The wedding service, flanked by Minister Shifflets's professionally blue eyes and Kay's still blue eyes of survival fixed on me, was staggering, and called on all our faith. Nearly fainting, full of import, we made our vows.

August 6, 1966
I'm twenty-nine, and going up against certain manhood. My music work is formed by its calling to me and my response. My improvised music is the re-marking on the flow of Being through my being. My written music condenses and solidifies that mark of Being. We are vessels here to purify our selves, to *not obstruct* what comes through us.

My day-to-day journal tracking ends shortly thereafter, and except for The Canada Journal in 1971 (see Chapter 12), a brief resurgence in 1975, The Bali Journal in 1989 (see Chapter 17), and a few brief travel journals, and for sporadic therapeutic purposes, the daily discipline has not resumed. Many other autobiographical forms have taken its place, however: a camcorder bought in 1991 with which I've made artsy films about travel and home life, a passion for black-and-white still photography, and a spate of five books, counting this one. Up to and including this very day, the task of every living hour has been to find enough time to do justice to the music streaming through my ears and fingers.

10

Theater Music

My first involvement in theater dates from the mid-1950s as a newbie in the extracurricular University Theater, a small stage with room for an audience of sixty, where both classic and original plays were performed. At first, I was the youngest one in the room, so I broke into my theater shoes by watching and interacting with people more mature and more advanced in their craft. As my theatrical experience widened, gradually and inevitably I became a peer, then a guide, then an elder teacher and, currently, an available memory trove. There have been many theatrical generations since the courageous beginnings of theatrical and musical experiments in free improvisation, and a varied array of forms and styles has arisen. A slew of books has been written about those early days in the 1950s and 60s and the subsequent evolution of the quintessentially American art of theatrical improvisation. The chapter you are reading now draws sporadically from five books in which I am quoted: *The Compass* by Janet Coleman, *The Second City 40th Anniversary Book* by Sheldon Patinkin, *Improv Nation* by Sam Wasson, *Ensemble* by Mark Larson, and an oral biography of Mike Nichols, *Life Isn't Everything*, by Ash Carter and Sam Kashner.

I've been interviewed, not only for these books but for various other worthy projects, on the condition that the interviews be transcribed—for accuracy's sake, of course, but also because I wanted to speak this history before writing it. What follows is derived from such interviews, but also from raw, newly unearthed memories that tend to emerge whenever I reminisce about those ancient days.

The Compass

In the late fall of 1955 I found my way to Jimmy's, a bar just south of the UC campus, on 55th Street, in order to audition as the intermission pianist for a new type of cabaret that was opening soon. At eighteen, I was under age, and this was not my turf, so I was half wary, half excited. I was ushered into a long room with an elevated stage along one side of which actors were rehearsing. A woman and a man (author and actor Roger Bowen) were on stage improvising a scene. They were apparently on the deck of an ocean liner. The man, trying to pick up the woman, was casting about for an interesting activity that would engage their mutual interest. He placed two chairs side by side, and they stood on them so as to be able to look down into the ship's funnels.

With a shudder, the woman asked, "What are those black *things* down there?"

"Those are filters," answered the man gently, turning full-face to gaze wistfully at her, "like the hairs in your nose."

I was impressed: the situation was so absurdly comical, the simile was so clever, and the improvisational wit so seemingly effortless. Best of all, the scene didn't end on that line—it kept going as the characters continued to discover new things about each other, and we about them. Once the rehearsal was over, I did audition on an ancient upright piano (that *smelled* decrepit) for David Shepherd, the director. He heard a few bars and asked if I wanted to be the intermission pianist for The Compass Players, opening in a few weeks, five dollars a night, drinks at cost. I said yes. I was socially young for my age and perhaps overly awestruck by the actors' prodigious talents and mysterious processes. But I wasn't the only one awestruck. When we opened, and word got around, there were many who came to see us who recognized the Compass as not only a new level of freedom in making theater but also, more tellingly, a new level of creative social thought. We became the darlings of the university cognoscenti, especially the social scientists. One day, a scene between Mike Nichols and Elaine May came up for serious discussion in my Social Science class. Something new was clearly in the air.

An Historic Mistake

At the Compass, I was very quiet, absorbed it all, and played the piano only when I was told to. It never occurred to anyone, least of all me, that the intermission pianist should become a part of the

Mike Nichols and Elaine May: First Date

show, even if only for cues. I was marginalized but affectionately so—a kind of company mascot. I watched the actors on stage and off. I began to understand that periods of tedium and stretches of mediocrity went along with periods of full, manic brilliance. Mike Nichols, alone among the actors, had friendly sympathy for me as the awkward musical kid I was. At six years my senior, he became a kind of protective older brother, and I adulated him. Reciprocally, my wife Connie and I frequently fed him in our 57th Street apartment when he couldn't afford to buy dinner, which was often. Watching him work, whether in monologues or with Elaine May during inspired improvisations or in ensemble with the company, I felt a halo of greatness around him. There was always a knowing glow, a smile that you could see only peripherally. From time to time, he would impersonate the German director Erich von Stroheim on stage, ending some absurd directorial satire by crying, "Print!" and I would think, "That's prophecy." There was no doubt in my mind that he could change the world.

One night, during intermission, when the actors were planning the improvised set, Mike said to me, "We're going to do a scene in a Paris café. Will you play background music, like *La Vie en rose*?"—a song which I scarcely knew then and still don't know, except that the tune sounds a lot like the opening bassoon solo of Stravinsky's *Rite of Spring*. (I wonder if they both got it from some old Russian folk tune.) When it came time for that scene, as the lights went up, I began to play—pecking out the melody and hunting for the chords. Seated at my white grand piano situated at floor level facing the audience, I had no idea what was happening above and in back of me on stage, and why should I? I was trying to figure out the damn song. Mike and Elaine, improvising a boy-meets-girl scene, were making conversation at their little table and needing to speak louder and louder over the music.

Mike began to say things like, "Isn't it interesting how loudly we have to speak in this café?" but I was absorbed in *La Vie en rose*. Finally he fairly shouted, "Garçon, piano player, you there, could you play softer?" I realized, *Holy Jesus, there's a scene going on back there,* and I did quiet down. It was an embarrassing turn for me, but never mind, because as far as I can ascertain, it marks the Very First Moment in the long history of pianistic accompaniment to professional theatrical improvisation. So I flunked the first test, but that was okay—things could only get better.

After the scene was over, Mike was gracious in his way, saying that it wasn't *really* my fault that the scene didn't work. It was my first glimmer that if I were to be part of the company, I had to learn to play in the service of the actors and the scene, a lesson as valuable on stage as in real life. It was the beginning of a fortunate education for an eighteen-year-old striver like me, and I needed to be taught it over countless subsequent scenes. I'm still learning the life part.

Mike had alopecia universalis, which means total baldness everywhere on his body. He had to go through a daily ritual of gluing on his wig and eyebrows. I knew Mike's true feelings about his hairlessness: the disease was a source of childhood shame he carried with him into adulthood. But Mike had learned to laugh so he wouldn't cry. One night, Mike and I were in the theater men's room; he was combing his wig in the mirror, and I was peeing.

Mike, peering critically at himself, asked me, "Do you think they'd all laugh if I tore off my wig?"

Mike Nichols: Author at the Local Garden Club

It was a serious question.

"At first," I said, and he laughed a cynical and authentic laugh.

That laugh characterized Mike's stance: the comedic covering the traumatic, both magnified into as grand a public spectacle as his fame could afford.

Rumi says the wound is where the light enters you. Much light came through Mike Nichols' wounds. As his fame as a director grew it was instructive, especially for those who knew him, to observe how his jujutsu of pain into mastery resulted in so many brilliantly directed plays and movies.

Over the next year, the Compass went through spasms of discovery, each member of the company facing his or her personal void, as all explorers must do. Audiences left the theater sometimes exhilarated, sometimes bored, sometimes both. The theater was losing money, and the director, David Shepherd, embroiled his company in theatrical and political structures that did not serve the actors well. In my junior year of college, my studies were desperately calling me. I left the company, and soon after that the company folded. It didn't take long for the stars—Mike, Elaine, Barbara Harris, and the stand-up comic Shelley Berman—to open a much slicker show on the North Side's Rush Street. I got a postcard in the mail advertising their opening night, which I tossed without hesitation.

I graduated with a BA from the University of Chicago in 1958, spent 1959 with the Kenton band, and met Roger Bowen at a campus concert in the late fall of 1959. He suggested that the next day I make my way Near-North to 1842 Wells Street and try out as musical director for a brand-new cabaret theater.

The Second City

As I arrived at the theater the next afternoon, Barbara Harris and Eugene Troobnick were on stage rehearsing a scene. Roger introduced me to the director, Paul Sills, who was very gruff in those days, abrupt and almost pugnacious in guiding actors toward insights about themselves. His mother and mentor was Viola Spolin, the maven of trust-based improvisational theater. Immediately Paul handed me a sheet of lyrics by David Shepherd.

"Put this to music," Paul said, "write it for Barbara."

I didn't even know her range—I had to guess. The lyrics began, *Everybody's in the know but me / knows who Eisenhower has to tea....* Then the refrain, *If you don't like your drink, the next one will be better / the lights will be brighter, the songs will be louder....* There was a small spinet stage left, and the rehearsal was still going on. I softly touched some notes to make sure and wrote the song in ten minutes.

When the rehearsal broke, Paul called out from the back of the house, "Are you ready, Mathieu?"

"Ready," I called back.

He walked on stage.

"Teach it to Barbara. Bill, this is Barbara. Barbara, this is Bill."

I recognized instantly that Barbara Harris was a highly musical being, and in ten minutes she could sing and act the song perfectly. When Paul heard it, he said, "That's the opening song." The next thing I knew, there were more things for me to do, and then more. I don't remember ever being hired; I was simply a part of the company. It was an immediate understanding. It was obvious. It was fabulous.

The way the little stage was set up at that time, a truncated Wurlitzer spinet was partially snugged into a little alcove at stage left. Inches to my right, the scenes would play out on stage. The audience would be able to see my face and the back of the piano, which had a shawl hanging down the back to cover the bare wood. The alcove had a niche where I could stash books to read during rehearsals when I wasn't involved. It was my own semi-public nook, me and my little piano. Only partly seen, I could even smoke during performances if and only if I exhaled the smoke slowly to the left. Since there was no exit stage left, once on stage the pianist stayed on stage. But that was fine by me. I was getting an education that I never thought I would get and certainly couldn't purchase. It was informative, and I took to it, understood it. I understood that there is such a thing as *theater music*, and I was becoming one of its practitioners.

In a recent interview, the mime Paul Sand remembered: "Bill got it. He would play completely intuitively with everybody. He was a wonderful inspiration with his music. He was just one of the players, part of the group. He improvised along with us. He wasn't waiting for anybody, but would just play intuitively when he felt like it. Just like when we actors would speak up when we felt like it. And he would make subtle musical comments during the scenes, kind of like Harpo Marx in his own way."

Alan Arkin added, "We did a twenty-minute faux Mozart opera absolutely seriously. The only reference to it being a comedy was the fact that it was sung in gibberish, but the gibberish was all written out. It was a fake Italian that we had to learn. I could sing it now. I could sing the whole thing now." For my part, I just loved and admired everyone involved—the actors, the staff. I was enamored of them.

It's curious: when you're making history, you don't necessarily know you're making history. We didn't know. We were just doing our work on a day-by-day, scene-by-scene basis, whatever was in front of us to do. And when you're working that hard, sometimes people take notice. Then you're on local TV, and then you're part of a *Playboy* deal, and then you're part of this, and then you're part of that, and then you're in *Time* magazine. We were all gifted people doing something we loved together, and we were more surprised than anyone by our sudden ascent in popularity. I don't think a single one of us imagined how influential our experiment in collective improvisation would eventually become.

Those first few months of the Second City were special in the lives of those who lived them and, by extension, special to the history of theater. A new societal mirror was being cast that enabled us all to see ourselves openly and critically in real time. The new theater was based not only on the immediacy of daily social and political life, and the humor to be found in those, but also on solid trust. The actors had to develop the capacity to tell themselves and each other the truth, to accept what was given, and to trust the audience to understand and accept it also. Much is made over the social and political prescience of the original Second City Company, but enough cannot be said about how crucial was this new consciousness of trust in the moment. It created an overall feeling of value and high purpose, although we didn't talk of it that way. The immediate, practical point may have been whether or not a scene worked, but, more broadly, the feeling that came over the room when an improvisation was in progress was palpably one of mutual trust and understanding. It was a new and valuable kind of collective high. The audience was in on the act. Audiences and actors alike, through this new reflective process, had a share in reframing our lives.

As our audiences grew and our fame spread from local to national, the immensely satisfying feeling of good work well done also grew. This doesn't mean there weren't harsh words, or even fistfights, because there were, but animosities evaporated quickly. What was at stake was too valuable to lose. For me, one of the most important indicators of value was the temperament of the staff—waiters, cooks, ticket-seller, and hat check girl. We were all glad to get to the theater in the evening, glad to be in each other's presence, glad to be party to the audience's delight and, especially, glad to party when the audience went home. Our after-hours parties were celebrations of being young on the flying edge of the world. On the best nights, the staff would present send-ups of the actors' scenes. One gag running from night to night was provided by one of our waiters, Todd Cazaux, who would walk unpredictably in and out of scenes as a hyper-dignified waiter in the style of a Bergman film. There were uproarious and obscene man-on-the-street interviews, spontaneous operatic arias and choruses, and appearances by all manner of world leaders and thinkers, from Hoover to Wittgenstein. I especially remember one never-to-be-heard-again song improvised by Barbara and me about a beach resort named Snickering Sands. Sometimes we would all become entangled in a manic collective improvisation. These events could be genuinely hilarious or merely boisterous, but they were a measure of our esteem for one another and our engagement in the work.

The Second City Sinfonia

There's no doubt that Paul Sills' energy drove the show. He could look like a bulldog of a man, and sometimes his manner was snarling or worse, as though he had continually to defend his genius. Sometimes it was genuinely good-natured and fraternal. But mercurial as it was, it was always probing and discerning. Occasionally his direction was so brilliant I was open-mouthed. How could he have known what he knew? (It turns out that it was in large part thanks to his mother, Viola Spolin.) At other times he was a bully, unnecessarily perhaps. But as the months went by, the outcome was a series of brilliantly cohesive shows whose unified voice was wrangled from a company of actors with widely diverse talents and sensibilities. Paul Sills became an authentic teacher for me, partly because he was an intellectual in the best sense: not a scholar, surely, but a man passionate about ideas while at the same time enormously capable in the real world of making collective art. Later in life, his heart opened in a wonderful way. In the 1960s, Paul introduced me to theologian Martin Buber; in the 1990s, I introduced him to Persian poet Jalaluddin Rumi, who became a source of guidance to Paul for the rest of his life.

Viola Spolin

Viola Spolin is, according to my lights, the hero of the entire saga, the Great Mother of trust-based improvisational theater. A broad woman with a commanding presence, she created a milieu that could produce improvisational companies; she produced Paul, and she continued to refine and proselytize for her aesthetic until the end of her life. It rankles me that many who should know better have not recognized the generative power of her work or the place all of us had, whether we knew it or not, in carrying it forward. My most creative contact with her came in the early days of our newly built, larger theater next door on Wells Street, when she was teaching teenagers on Saturday afternoons. She asked me to come and do some musical work with the kids, and for half a dozen sessions I did. I began to look more carefully at the theater games as Viola played and taught them, and an exciting repertoire of musical games began to appear. I didn't realize at first how the new musical games could be used beyond their instructive value, but eventually they had the cumulative effect of musicalizing the theatrical process and helped shape (as we shall soon see) the "long-form" improvisation called Harold.

Trust-based games changed mid-20th-century theater such that by 1980 or 1990, nearly all contemporary theatrical training had been influenced by Viola's work. If you were familiar with the training, you could identify its results on most any stage or screen. Nowadays, you can scarcely attend a drama school, or even a high school drama class, without doing exercises or playing games that originated from those we learned and developed under Viola's discerning eye. For me, they have become an essential tool in making and teaching music.

Pygmalion

In a 1961 letter, my father asked me what I was *actually doing* with my time. I replied by describing how I'd spent that very afternoon and evening.

> When I arrived at the Second City about 3:00 in the afternoon, a tall, beautiful young man with an expressive craggy face named Paul Sand (a protégé of Marcel Marceau), and Barbara Harris, a lovely young woman with white skin and lyrical body (ex-wife of our director Paul Sills), were running through the beats of a pantomime called *Pygmalion*.

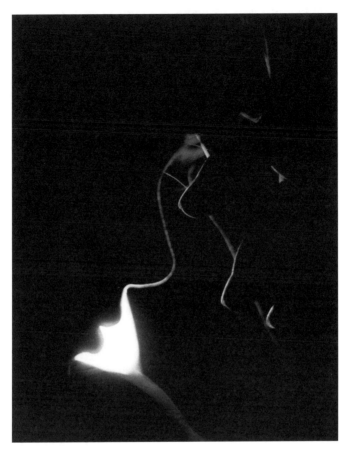

Barbara Harris in Silhouette

"Ah, here's Bill," said director Paul, "we need music."

"Okay, run through it, and let me watch," I said.

Here is what I saw, all performed in silence.

As the lights come up, Barbara is discovered standing on a chair in the pose of the Greek statue. Paul Sand has just finished sculpting her. He chips a little here, a little there, is pleased with his work, circles it, smiles. Then he goes to the window, pulls down the shade, and with a long and lovely gesture kisses the statue on the neck. Then he slaps himself back to reality, turns his back on the statue, and begins to make himself some coffee. Barbara's eyes move. Paul senses a movement in back of him, turns around, isn't sure, turns his back, looks suddenly over his shoulder. Now Barbara blossoms into life. Paul is ecstatic, gives her his hand. She steps down lightly from the chair, and they do a little pas de deux around the stage, ending with Paul sitting on a different chair and Barbara at his feet, looking up into his eyes. Paul gets up suddenly, raises the window, lets in some fresh air, pours himself a drink. He offers some to Barbara. She pours out half, takes a sip, belches delicately. There follows another pas de deux, more willowy, a beat longer, more lyrical than the first, but in the course of their dance, Barbara's hand brushes against the stove. She stops suddenly and looks at her fingers. They are covered with dirt. She goes to the window and looks out. It is New York, dirty, busy, everyday. She looks around the sculptor's studio. It's filthy. Paul desperately starts to clean it, kicking things into closets, sweeping away the dust and dirt. Barbara shrugs a little shrug, as if to say that the ugliness of his life cannot compete with the world she has just come from. She waves a small, tender goodbye. Paul offers her a red rose—shockingly, a real one, not mimed—but she refuses. It is not enough. She climbs up on the chair again and begins to go back into her statuesque pose. Paul is frantic with despair, disbelief; he dances around her, entreating. And then, very simply, she makes an inviting gesture for him to join her in her own world. *Me?* Paul points to himself. Barbara reaches out, *come.* Paul goes slowly to her, stands at her feet, his head on her bosom. Her arms begin to enfold him in her embrace, but at the last minute, something catches his eye. As Barbara's arm comes into his line of vision, he notices something wrong with the thumb—a slight imperfection, to be sure, but an imperfection just the same. He swings free of her, takes off his coat, picks up his tools. Barbara's eyes follow him. But soon she has returned whence she came. As the lights go down, Paul is chipping away as he was at the beginning of the scene. It's as if nothing had happened.

To this action I had to improvise a score. In two run-throughs, we are satisfied.

We play the scene that night, and at the end can hear the audience let out its breath.

By this time the entire company has straggled in, and director Paul Sills begins a little lecture about making rehearsals on time. As it turns out, Barbara has an appointment with her psychiatrist and has to leave in fifteen minutes. Since she is the worst offender for being late to, or absent from, rehearsals, she begins to defend her appointment.

"I'm not talking to you alone, Barbara, I'm talking to everyone," says Paul.

As usual, those two begin to go at each other. (Their divorce became final last week.) Barbara becomes more and more

Barbara Askance

defensive, Paul more aggressive.

"Why are you always blaming me?" wails Barbara. "Everyone is always blaming me in this theater."

"For Chrissake," cries Paul, "no one's blaming you, just shut up for a minute."

Barbara won't shut up.

"Come on, Hon," I say, "the guy's just talking," and someone else says, "Jesus, Barbara, just listen to what he's saying."

And now everybody has a word for Barbara. She stands in the middle of the room, and her world collapses around her. She flings her arms and shouts wildly, "Me, me, me, me, everyone's always picking on *me*. I won't stand for it. I hate it. I hate this whole fucking theater."

And with that, the charming nymph of minutes before gathers up her belongings and stomps from the theater, having to stoop to pick up her fallen key ring as she exits. Dead silence. Somebody sighs loudly.

"Well," says Paul Sand the mime, "she'll certainly have a good session with her doctor today."

Two hours later, Barbara calls her ex-husband and offers apologies. He then tells the assembled company in a confidential tone, "Look, I was married to her for three years. Barbara is going through a stage that's very dangerous for her and everyone else. So just handle her and yourself carefully, and she'll be okay. Okay? I know what I'm talking about."

Nobody says a word. And later that night, during performance, it was as if nothing had happened. Nothing *had* happened.

ॐ

The Second City was so successful that its management was tempted to expand its horizons. The new theater next door had a larger capacity, a full kitchen, a full downstairs bar, and a brand-new, honey-sweet Mason & Hamlin grand piano perched offstage left. The first production there was a new musical, *Big Deal*, based on *The Beggar's Opera* and centered on Chicago politics. The book was by David Shepard, my songs were played by Fred Kaz, and Alan Arkin starred as MacHeath. The cast was good, Alan sang marvelously, Fred's piano playing made everything shine, but the piece was burdened by a dreary, overlong scenario about Chicago corruption.

Soon after *Big Deal* faltered and folded, our producers saw a chance to take our stellar improvising company to The Royale Theatre on Broadway. There was much trepidation about this from the company, which turned out to be fully justified. A new company was brought into Chicago to replace the original one, my dear friends went off to New York, me along with them to find a replacement for myself, and when it became clear that our Broadway partners did not want improvisation to disturb their remunerative Broadway norms, the actors became increasingly rigid in their set scenes. Barbara Harris, the ingénue of the show, had been the most nervous about the move. A few months into the run to half-filled houses and half-enthusiastic audiences, Barbara wrote me a letter.

Thursday, November 30, 1961

Dear Bill,

Thank you for writing. I'm so conscious of your name, broadly spread across the Royale billboard, and whenever I sing *Hoboken Story*, or hear Mina belt out *I Got Blues* (she's taken it over) it's almost as though you're breathing all over us, silently stalking the wings, wincing at Larry's often unkempt chords, fretting or applauding at our wailing group. How could we forget you?

Impossible. You instill our scenes with tension and drama long after we've dried up emotionally.

You know how people take on the look of their mates after years of union with them? I envision you looking somewhat like a piano. I don't know exactly why except when I think of Chicago and you I think of Chicago and you and a piano too. There you are, looking more like a piano every day. I'm imagining, from your piano, the words, the improvising, the minds, the scenes you've encountered these past years. I'm overwhelmed just thinking about it. Jealous too, because I'm not in on it anymore. What can I say? Here we sit at the end of a dead voyage. Our material squeaks from age like a dried up tree. The question is how long can the branches hold up under the weight of eight deadweight people. Sounds bleak. Just depressing a little not to be thinking and creating something, even the smallest thing. Well, we make money, so we get analyzed instead. It's okay. There's some talk of a club opening up here. I'm not even sure if it's a good idea for me anymore. I almost think I should turn to other things, if possible. Like acting for example.

Maybe. I go on readings, and some of the things I read for are really interesting. The problem is landing a job. No small matter here, knowing something about my hungry competition. It's nice to know I might have a job always waiting with Second City.

In general though, everyone in the company is well. You ought to get Second City to finance a trip for you. As though you'd heard a rumor that we'd gone down the drain musicwise. Which might be true for all I know. And you? I hope the winter has permeated your cheeks and nose and stayed away from your soul. Take care.

Much love,
Barbara

Seedlings

All through the '60s back in Chicago, the big old wood-frame house at 452 Webster had served as a kind of Second City commune. On the third floor lived Paul and Carol Sills, on the second lived Severn Darden's ex-wife, Anne, in one apartment and in another, Ed Yerxa; directly above me on the first floor were Dennis Cunningham and his wife, Mona. I had four rooms of basement with my Steinway grand in the middle one, and across from me Fred Kaz had a small studio with a Knabe grand taking up most of the space. In common, we all (under Paul Sills' guidance) had Martin Buber, humanist philosopher who preached connection, the word "yes," waves of yeses from one person to another, and the I/Thou relationship between God and Man.

At the back of our house was a big yard where we built a sound sculpture, a tall jungle gym of junk with resonant objects we would discover and haul in from everywhere. Someone scored a casing from a nuclear warhead that made a loud, pure soprano bell sound. We residents and our friends would bang away for long improvisations. Musical sounds mix; words do not. Ensemble playing is the soul of music; in contrast, several people cannot sensibly talk at once. I wanted the actors to learn—and teach me—how the collective musical mind could operate in the actors' milieu.

Meanwhile, Alan Myerson, who had briefly directed the Second City in the early '60s, founded his own company in San Francisco, the Committee, in collaboration with his then-wife Irene Riordan (later known as Latifa Taormina). Soft-spoken and highly articulate, Myerson was also teaching improvisation at San Francisco State and, with his students, was experimenting with brave new collaborative improvisational processes. The hope was to escape the prison of individual sketches. Sometimes these experiments would coalesce into cohesive improvised plays. The question arose: What did this reveal about the nature of spontaneous, collaborative mind?

At the same time, Del Close, the on-again-off-again director at the Committee, was working out new games and ideas for formal structures that would harness the most honest, unguarded extemporaneous play possible. But he was so bipolar, so up-and-down, that glimpses of genius appeared among arid stretches of nothing. He was an unpredictable mystery man who was into drugs like Charlie Parker and Miles Davis were into drugs—you couldn't separate the psychotic breaks from the work itself. His utterances were mystical, sometimes garbled, sometimes profound. His genius was half boon, half problem.

In the five years from 1962 through 1966, I worked in Chicago with a succession of new actors now playing on the less intimate, larger stage. The new faces in the new, expansive theater were still drawing Chicago audiences, but the genius of the original company had dissipated its energies into Los Angeles and New York. Alan and Mike became enormously successful. Barbara was now well known, Severn, Andrew and the others less so, but working. Back in Chicago, the light had dimmed for me.

After the assassination of President Kennedy, and during our disastrously escalating involvement in Vietnam, the American zeitgeist had changed. Satire had become increasingly difficult; parody and low physical comedy had become the default form of humor. Our references used to be Ibsen and Proust; now they were the Partridge Family and Elvis Presley. True, I had a lovely new Mason & Hamlin grand, and an aisle through the audience to escape the stage when necessary. I enjoyed composing the many songs we performed. I was paid well. But what actually kept me in Chicago was that the theatrical work was sufficiently easy to afford me the six-plus hours a day I craved to practice piano, learn the language of the European canon from Easley Blackwood, my newly acquired composition teacher, and compose *serious* music.

Kay and I were finally married in 1966, and I adopted her two young children. Back in San Francisco, the Committee Theater was thriving. I knew its musical director, Ellsworth Milburn, because he'd married my high school sweetheart. In fact, I'd recommended him for the job at the Committee, and had given him some coaching, and he flourished there. In 1965 he invited me to come sub for him so he could take a vacation. I fell in love with the city I had not seen since my Kenton episode six years before and was impressed by the daring, the political will, and the brilliance of the Committee's actors.

They were raw, creative, trenchant in their satire, very funny, and their uniquely collaborative spirit was a perfect reflection of the beatnik zeitgeist of the city. The lure of San Francisco became greater as my life in Chicago seemed to wind down. Kay and I made the momentous decision to pick ourselves up from our Midwestern roots and head west. All the way west.

The Best

My successor at the Second City was Fred Kaz, who, by virtue of his kindness and the probity of his musicianship, became a primary teacher for me. His musical truth has been a clear chime sounding in every part of my life. He could drop as deep into a zone of pure music and fly as high above the mind as any musician I've ever heard. The Second City actors cherished him. But in 1992, after twenty-five years devoted to enhancing their work, he was, to his despair, let go. It was claimed that he was too old-guard, too untutored in contemporary ways, including electronic keyboards. But the Second City bought him a seaworthy boat that he lived on near San Pedro (north of San Diego), happily content with his new wife Helen, from 1992 until he died in 2016. He continued to perform from time to time in LA, but it's quite possible that sailing made him happier even than playing music. In any case, he was a great maestro of jazz composition and improvisation, the very model of musical mastery. I just saw a video of a solo concert he played in 1997 and it was pure joy. He was simply the best.

❦

Our family of four arrived in San Francisco in January 1967, found a second-floor flat near Haight-Ashbury, and Kay and I produced two children of our own. I split the Committee Theater gig with Ellsworth and soon landed a job at the San Francisco Conservatory. We arrived just in time for the Summer of Love, thus managing *not* to have to live through the Chicago Riots of 1968. And at The Committee Theater, a longtime, adventurous collaboration was underway.

The Committee Theater and Beyond

By 1968, I was teaching musical improvisation at the San Francisco Conservatory to a select troupe of actors, instrumentalists, and singers, merging Spolin's games with my own. Our mantra was ACHAAT, an acronym for Anything Can Happen At Any Time, but "anything" was cradled by trust-based games and techniques. We formed a performing group called The Ghost Opera Company. The "ghost" was meant to be the narrative that arose autonomously in each member of the audience, each narrative unspoken and untranslatable. Sometimes amazing, cohesive pieces would arise out of processes that were musically analogous to theater games. What on earth was happening?

Alan Myerson, Del Close, and I came together via the Committee's stage in the summer of 1967 to look for common ground in the search for trust-based, long-form, game-structured, free-play stagecraft. Comparing our notes over several months, we recognized some commonality in our devotion to our ideals, and similar expectations for the emergence of a newly shaped theatrical mind. We knew we had something viable but didn't know how to stage it or sustain it again and again. To truly develop and evolve this magical form— whatever we called it—we would have to have some built-in options, the flexibility to revise on a moment's notice, and a pliable structure guiding the improvisation itself. Through the fall of 1967, we rotated the company through workshops, with the three of us pitching our theatrical ideals.

I was—and am—a musical idealist in the sense that I believe music at its purest and best is its own narrative, and that listening to it in its absolute state is its own absolute reward. But when I tried to train the company to be guided by this musical ideal, the actors proved none too thrilled. They needed to embody an identifiable character. They needed a place to act in, a "where-am-I," not an

"I-am-on-stage." They needed a story, and a motivation for behavior. In short, they needed theater. The more I tried to get the actors to wean themselves from these earthly phenomena, the more they rebelled. At the end of one contentious workshop, the actors rose up and fell upon me like the cards at the end of *Alice in Wonderland*. They didn't hurt me, of course, but after licking my imaginary wounds I began to recognize that they needed to be *actors*: grounded human beings moving through human spaces who can discover themselves as real humans in real time. At another memorable workshop, Del was sitting at his little table, strung out in yesterday's clothes, watching the improvisers struggle and fail to implement my musical abstractions. Periodically he took sips from an industrial-size can of Del Monte apricot juice he'd lifted from the kitchen. When the exercise was over, he carefully poured every drop of the half-full can over his head. Sticky bright orange rivulets ran down his eyelids and cheeks, seeped into his shirt, dropped onto his crotch, and pooled onto the rug. The actors, vastly amused, took his point and merrily departed, released from musical jail. I was deeply offended, but I did finally learn that I wasn't allowed to turn actors into abstract motion and sound, at least not this time around. Dancers, maybe. Actors, no. Well, perhaps yes for brief moments—but as passing textures only, one of many textures welcome on stage. I had to be taught that abstraction cannot be the dominant aesthetic of theater. But actors *can* learn to hear stage life *as if* it were music, and thus bring to themselves and to their audience a fragrance of the union that only musical ensemble can reveal.

Del Close held to the ideal of psychological transparency, of ego loss, of a sufficiently clean mental state to be able to receive whatever comes—with a heavy emphasis on one's most terrifying fears. I knew Del well enough to know that underlying his schematically brilliant methods was a core belief in the primacy of human connection. I never heard him say, "We are each other," but it's reported that on his deathbed, during a staged pre-death wake, he came close.

Alan Myerson most definitely could say we are each other, and did, and maybe even said we are loving kindness. What we three shared in common was revealed in our immersion in the collaborative process itself. We all knew that Viola's games, plus our ever-new ones, were not enough. There needed to be a more architectonic method, a method by which top-down and bottom-up structures could merge in a singular whole structure. The open secret was that discovering the method was itself the method. The very seeking is what was sought. At its best, this method brought forward our latent human imperative for cooperation. How to evolve the specific processes that revealed this was the challenge. The three of us needed each other to make real the answers as ongoing, illuminating theater.

We attempted many performances in front of alternatively bored, confused, or exhilarated late-night audiences. Most of these attempts bombed, yet even when two or three out of ten were successful, those two or three could be brilliant enough to make us happy to be alive. They were truly improvised plays with kaleidoscopic social narrative, ironic comedic situations, spontaneous poetry, sudden changes in venue, character, and style (Shakespeare, Ibsen, Pirandello), all threaded through with improvised songs and an underlying musical score. And when a true jewel emerged, everyone was whipped up into the next phase of discovery.

We Have to Name This Thing

Many months of this ensued. One afternoon, after a particularly productive company workshop, a few actors hung around analyzing the day's efforts. We all knew we were on to something. Alan was not present on this day, but Del and I were.

Del, sitting apart at his little bistro table, announced, "We gotta name this thing."

Immediately I had the image of some guy named Harold sitting in his undershirt with a dead cigar in his mouth, watching a test pattern on a black-and-white TV, and I said, "How about Harold?"

I thought it was kind of cheeky, like when a reporter asked George Harrison what he called his haircut and he answered, "Arthur."

"Bad idea," said Del, but the actors loved it. They wouldn't let it go. It stuck. As long-form improvisation became widely known as The Harold, Del claimed to be the originator of the name as well as the form, but he was the originator of neither. We all were.

Is It Real Music?

My favorite scene in which I appeared on stage was one that Ellsworth began and the company and I refined over many years: The Emotional Symphony, known familiarly as Emo Symph. We asked the audience to give us suggestions of an emotion suiting each actor in turn; I then lined the actors up from negative to positive emotions and, using each emotion's full palette of vocal sounds, conducted a faux piece of music. The emotional range went from tantrums of rage (in eighth-note bursts or prolonged shrieks) all the way to sexual ecstasies (quarter-note gasps to lengthy orgasmic cadenzas), plus everything in between: discontent, boredom, reluctant agreement, all with the full dynamic range from pianississimo to fortississimo. We had a few preset hand signals for swift entrances, certain ensemble textures, and so forth, but there were two crucial, generative techniques. First, the actors played it straight. With utter concentration, global listening, split-second timing, and musical sensibilities, they *became* trained musicians. Second, I was composing on the spot a *serious* composition, my Magnum Opus. The result was easy to hear as real music, or rather as an amusing and knowing send-up of the same. We on stage knew how to do this, and the audience knew how to play its part. In a theatrical sense, The Emotional Symphony *was* real music, an astonishing high for the audience and the players alike. We ended our improvisational set with it every night for years, and it was never not fun, not once.

Sitting There

During the two decades I spent with the University of Chicago Theater, the Compass, the Second City, and the Committee, I watched the unfolding of events from the piano bench, a singular vantage point. Siting there, I often felt marginalized, bored, and desperate to be spending my time in creative work that was more essentially musical. But I also came to recognize the newness of the great experiment, its importance in the development of creative collaboration, and hence its value to the community at large. It turns out I was learning more from the actors than I realized at the time. Now, fifty years after the Committee folded its wings and my chapter in theater came to a close, I realize how much of the actors' wisdom I carry with me.

When Freud was queried as to the purpose of psychoanalysis, he answered, "To discover the universal elements of our everyday lives—those elements of our seemingly private and unique experience that are, in fact, archetypal."

We are far more the same than we are different. Improvisation can be seen as away of finding and sharing solutions to the problems we share communally, and savoring the joy of such collective discoveries. Even more than most actors, *those* actors had a heightened way of seeing people, an empathy that required enhanced receptive powers. From within the human communality they had the ability to become transparent. What might come *out* on stage as aggressive, spontaneous satire went *in* off stage through a patient, porous observer. One of the seminal rules of improvisation is that a "character" is just a magnified piece of you, so be you. I never had the knack for this, but because of all those thousands of hours watching dozens upon dozens of actors inventing character after character in scene after scene, I've come to see people differently. I've become more transparent to and sympathetic with the universality of persona and personality, to *those elements of our seemingly private and unique experience that are, in fact, archetypal.* I feel more connected to people and enjoy them more. They're both funnier and more profound.

And the memories of those extraordinary moments of discovery in rehearsals and performances—those brilliant lights never dim.

Evolution and Devolution

Just before the Committee Theater went under, I was offered a job on the full-time faculty of Mills College teaching music theory. My exit from the Committee was in the summer of 1973, and though one toe will always be in the theater and its music, everything I see that is happening in the theater world I see now from a distance, more from the perspective of an American consumer than an engaged participant. What I see is that the high ideal we all cherished at the beginning of this journey has bifurcated into a low road and a high road.

The low road is ubiquitous, all too easy to see. Driven by a mercilessly commercialized industry, comedians go for cheap laughs, accursed laugh tracks deafen our wills, and it's the rare movie that digs deep. Laughs and violence sell; depth not so much. Improvisatory workshops are seen as tools for getting ahead in the business, and the profit motive of the business world reigns supreme.

The high road is there for all who look for it: high-school and college drama departments worldwide, playing theater games; savvy directors who know what game to play next and how to play it; myriad actors serious about spontaneity in their craft; many beats in many (if not most) movies that have been worked out through improvisational techniques; the prevailing understanding in the business that improvising through the situation implicit in a scene is the way to find the soul of the scene; as well as the many folks who come together simply to play theater games—not to get laughs, not to get jobs, not to be brilliant, but for the pure release of being in an atmosphere of trust, of adventure, of not knowing and then knowing, of the sheer joy of play. Trust-based theater games have influenced the way theater is taught today as much as, if not more than, any

Viola Spolin

other way of learning how to be on stage.

Best of all, after a decade or so The Harold long-form improvisation found its basic, though highly variable, form. Decades after its first performance in 1967, it's grown a shaggy white beard and can serve as a kind of comforting but still spry uncle. One can find long-form improvisations being performed all over the country, either as an evening of audience delight and participation or as a class or course given under the rubric of a theater or school. There are also several books and descriptive internet sources devoted to the past and present of long-form improvisation. If you find yourself visiting a large city, the chances are you can check the local listings and find a Harold Night playing soon in a theater near you.

If you want to know more about theater games or Viola Spolin, just Google them and her and you'll see an abundance of books and references, most notably her own classic *Improvisation for the Theater*. The many available sources notwithstanding, Viola's groundwork and the little stones we all added have fallen under the strata of generations. But perhaps that's as it should be. The work in our lives is ultimately not ours to claim but part of a great circle of work.

If improvisation has taught me anything, it is to honor the way newness unfolds between the strict discipline of trust-based acceptance (Yes And) on the one hand and ACHAAT (Anything Can Happen At Any Time) on the other, and to have the courage to allow what comes. That openness is what I appreciate when I see it on stage, that's my own ideal as a musician, and that's how I try to live my life. All of us first-generation improvisation folks have done the pathfinding work we've done, and we've found our varied ways of navigating the rest of our lives. Fewer and fewer of us are still alive. What is happening these days in the convoluted web of the theater world is what is happening these days.

And now, Amenable Audient, having said all that, we ask that you, yes you with a torn ticket in your pocket, we ask that you please wait expectantly for this timely beat to pass—and now this one additional beat you sensed coming—and NOW (*pause*)...the last line—and *now*:

BLACKOUT
Laughter
Music up
Applause
Lights up
Music segues into next chapter
Music fades under

PART THREE

11

Murshid

In the spring of 1967, my San Francisco theater company, the Committee, was scheduled to be on *The Tonight Show*, so we all had to trundle to Los Angeles. Most of the cast would take the shuttle flight, but Nancy Fish, one of the actors, needed to make some stops along the way and asked if I wanted to drive down with her in her VW bug.

"Sure," I said.

I liked Nancy. In her late thirties, she was the company elder and spoke with a no-nonsense level gaze. I always believed her on and off stage.

The first stop was just south of the city.

"It's my godfather. He's a wonderful man. I really want you to meet him," she enthused.

We were greeted in the foyer by a clean-shaven, short, barrel-chested man of about seventy named Samuel Lewis. Nancy and the man embraced briefly, and as they drew back to look at each other, their eyes shone like new stars.

"This is our pianist and musical director," said Nancy.

The man nodded to me, then gestured to a triangle of chairs in the living room. The moment we were seated, Nancy and Mr. Lewis began a love-fest of current events, family, and mutual friends.

They were utterly wrapped in each other. I took the opportunity to look around the room—mostly bookshelves containing a neatly housed, extensive hardcover library. Solid old furniture. Family photographs and Buddhist art. Couldn't help but notice that Nancy's short skirt was even shorter as she happened to casually cross her legs. From my chair, I could see oh so far up Nancy's shapely thighs, but I made this discovery as an oh-so-innocent moment in the arc of scanning the room.

This continued until a lull in the conversation.

Looking at Nancy with a quizzical little smile, Mr. Lewis asked, "Who's your friend, the wolf?"

"Oh, Bill Mathieu, he's our wonderful musician," she replied, and she went on to laud me. Her godfather glanced in my direction, the conversation changed, and we left soon after.

Driving south, Nancy asked me, "What do you think of my godfather?"

"He's a nice Jewish man," I replied, a remark of deliberate neutrality that one Jew makes to another about a third.

On Wednesday evenings in the fall of that year, I stayed home with the kids while my wife attended meetings in Marin County, just across the Golden Gate Bridge from San Francisco. After a few weeks, I asked her about the nature of the meetings.

Her reply was, "You'd better meet this man."

The next week, I asked her, "Who is 'this man'?"

"You'd better meet him."

So the next week, we hired a babysitter and I went along. We crossed the bridge, found the road in Larkspur, and walked up the many wooden steps of an old wooden home stilted on a steep hillside. On the deck were neat rows of shoes and sandals. I had never seen this nicety before, this regard for others. To one side was a box full of diverse wooden flutes, dozens of them, please take one, and from inside the large room adjacent came the alluring sound of mysteriously tuned flute music.

We picked out our flutes and entered, joined the cloud of shoeless flute sounds, and for a few minutes I gave myself up completely to the holy tootle. When I did look around, everyone seemed brightly awake, but casual. Everyone was welcoming and warm. Each one, strangers all, looked familiar. I had never had a family of such mutually loving peers before, and I became brightly awake myself.

People arranged themselves to be seated. As we quieted down, I noticed a little old guy with a circle of folks around him. He walked to the front of the room, sat facing us in the chair that had been placed for him, and *it's the same guy.* Except now he's grown a white beard and he's wearing a green cotton robe. What I saw this time was a voluble teacher whose teaching had a recurring self-reference and self-importance that I found suspicious. People were rapt, listening and still, but I was put off. Another crazy Jewish uncle I did not need. And he'd had the chutzpa to call me a wolf! In such a frame

MURSHID

of mind I endured the evening, even though it seemed like some fascinating things were said. Things that. Caught. My Attention. Things I thought *a lot* about later.

Gradually I came to realize that Samuel Lewis had a deep knowledge of the traditions and practices of Buddhism, Islam, Judaism, Hinduism, and Christianity. A profound scholar and world traveler, he was a teacher of increasing influence. He was also a direct disciple of Inayat Khan, the first teacher to bring a coherent Sufi lineage to the West. Lewis called his followers "seekers of the heart." Although I recognized the value of such things, I still didn't like *him*, his brusque ways, his abrupt vacillations between loving guidance and self-protective boasting. It didn't feel right to get too close.

At the following meeting, a special event was announced: the ceremonial opening of a Sufi Khanka, a house of cooperative living. This much-anticipated celebration was held on a Sunday at noon in the large back yard of a suburban house in Novato, thirty-five pre-freeway miles north of San Francisco. The men were dressed in casual but freshly laundered clothes, white or solid-colored. Mostly long, clean hair, sometimes tied back, like mine. The women were ravishing in their beautifully sewn, colorful, flowing dresses. There was a certain joy along with that casualness again, devotees in their twenties being themselves. No need to be nice—their being was nice.

The teacher led some circle dancing, some chanting, more dancing. Then a huge buffet was set up on one side of the yard. We lined up at a long table of potluck dishes. At the end of the line was the teacher, Sam himself—whom everybody called Murshid, a Persian word for teacher—blessing the food with his outstretched hands and exchanging eyeball-to-eyeball glances with each person. Evidently, if you wanted lunch, Samuel Lewis was gonna bless your food. I watched the others. Someone told me that the eyeballing was called *darshan*, "the glance," the moment of mutual recognition of one another's essence. Something was going on during that glance, something I wanted, but I was uneasy about getting *too close*. When it was my turn, the green-robed man blessed my food with his strong hands, but when the moment came to exchange glances, he swiveled his head sharply to his right, showing me his scraggly bearded cheek, and waved me on.

I don't know if I've come to imagine what happened next or if it actually happened, but my clear auditory memory is of a huge gong sounding with full force throughout my skull. Murshid had truly seen me! He had seen my resistance to him play out again and again, and all, I thought ruefully, because he had begun by calling me by my true name. I'd thought I was invisible to him, but he gave back in full measure what I had given him. In unison, then, we'd recognized one another. What a perfect darshan!

After lunch, I listened up, and thus my path toward discipleship began.

The Murshid and The Man

What follows is not a biographical summary of Samuel Lewis's life, but rather a highly selective view of certain aspects that pertain to my own life. Cited passages from the writings of Samuel Lewis have been lightly edited for contextual clarity. Definitions of non-English words are parenthesized. Passages quoting Neil Douglas-Klotz are from *Gardens of Vision and Initiation*.

Lewis had an extremely tough early life. He was roundly rejected by his businessman father and had a complex relationship with his mother and brother. His parents demonstrated little affection for one another. He was small, unattractive, internally focused, and generally quite unlike the other members of his family. Because it was possibly true, and because it could explain so much, there has long been the supposition that Samuel was not the son of his nominal father, Jacob. Jacob Lewis evidently thought so. Of course the mother denied it, but in her late sixties she confessed to a friend, "My son is named Samuel. Do you know why? He was born a prophet, and he came into the spiritual body first." One interpretation of her meaning is that one's spiritual body is married to God, and she felt married to God when Samuel was conceived and born. The historicity of this story aside, Samuel was considered the black sheep, ostracized by his wealthy father, despised by his brother, and only intermittently protected by his mother.

Whatever his lingering suspicion about his paternity, Samuel wanted desperately to be accepted as a true son by his putative Dad. In 1925, when he was almost thirty, he wrote a poem called "A Prayer for My Father," containing the following lines (the italics are mine):

> O God, give me strength to aid my father.
> May my next years bring happiness to his heart.
> Make me a source of pride and joy for him,

Murshid Sam Lewis

And may the future show the way
That he may see in me a son of his,
And I see and treat him as my father.

Murshid's hunger to be a true son extended through the decades of his life. In 1956, at age sixty, he was living for a time at Anandashram in South India and had accepted its guru, Swami "Papa" Ramdas, as his own. In his journal, he remarked how Papa "uses all-embracing love first," that is, primarily. In a later memoir, he marvels that "from one point of view, I am a Muslim being a Sufi; from another point of view, one could call me a Buddhist, for the whole life has been co-mingled with the intellectual and spiritual pursuit of the Buddhadharma. And yet, with Papa, I was his child." Swami Ramdas was, at long last, a father figure who gave from an endless fountain the paternal love that Samuel most needed.

In 1958, at age sixty-two, Samuel Lewis began to work with Dr. Blanche Baker, one of America's first "client-centered" psychoanalysts, in order to heal the trauma of his nuclear family. Here is an account given by Samuels' close friend, Gavin Arthur:

He had this fearful inferiority complex, which she cured. I believe she really did, because after Sam got through with her course of psychoanalysis he emerged a very, very different person. He no longer had a chip on his shoulder all the time. And because he had devoted all of his time to seclusion, when he felt the world hated him, he was drawn into his shell. He made good use of the loneliness by becoming a tremendous scholar.

Dr. Baker had a most remarkable gift as a psychoanalyst. I think she helped Sam orient himself and find out why he had been born into this unattractive body and unattractive nature, where he mostly antagonized people.

Every man, if he wants to be a philosopher, needs a priestess like Socrates had in Diotima. You have to have a woman like that. And Sam didn't have any woman like that until he met Blanche. I think this was the turning point—meeting a woman that he could talk to absolutely in depth, as he would to a man.

Douglas-Klotz concurs. Speaking of the evolution of the Dances of Universal Peace, he writes how Lewis, by 1960, had come "to fulfill various needs for personal relationship through the dance, and then finally became disenchanted with anything except a deeper aspect of it. As he speaks of folk dance fulfilling for him a 'father instinct' and a 'husband instinct,' the influence of his therapy with Dr. Baker becomes clear."

Most of the influential teachers in my life have been musicians, but Murshid Lewis, not a developed musician, has been the most influential of all. Many accounts of Lewis's life are hagiographical to a substantial degree, and delineate the efforts and accomplishments of a man—a prophet, even—with worldwide influence. My interest at this writing lies in how Samuel Lewis modeled the qualities I've needed to pursue an active inner life. But there is also something else: the father hang-up in my life has not been dissimilar to Murshid's. Young Samuel hungered to be seen as a true son; I longed to *not* be infantilized as the child my father had so deeply loved, but rather to be seen as the actual adult I became. As Samuel Lewis repeatedly encountered surrogate fathers, he garnered initiations into numerous spiritual lineages; in my quest for father-musicians, I assimilated a wide range of musical initiations from diverse cultures. Murshid Lewis's search continued until he realized he had become like a sympathetic and forgiving father to his own father; I eventually realized the same thing about myself and my father. Finally, I believe, Murshid came to understand that he had become the very teacher he'd been seeking all along; that is happening to me also.

The salient difference here is that my life has been (so far) relatively easy. Samuel Lewis's journey was far rougher, its hills steeper, its roads often closed. I am most curious to know how a man who survived such early unpleasantness—who thrust that unpleasantness back into himself and out onto others for so long— how this man learned to recognize and heed the guidance of his teachers, and his own inner guidance. How did he become a man whose dark spirit brightened into radiance and whose transmission came so alive for a thriving community of seekers? Considering I have *as yet* to scatter my father's ashes into the waiting wind, I remain resonant with this part of the story.

Pain Into Love

By the end of 1961, Lewis, age sixty-five, was able to report to his journal, "I am closing the most edifying year. Everything has turned around and I think every upset of every earlier part of my life has been reversed."

By 1966, young people flocking to San Francisco were beginning to listen to him, to take in what he had to give. In aggregate, they gave Lewis the psychological feedback he needed to know himself more deeply. The exchange between a man nearing seventy and young adults in their twenties was intergenerational, and the more creative for that.

During this period, Lewis articulated his insights by writing extensive letters to his Pakistani goddaughter, Khalifa Saadi Khwar Khan, with copies sent to his Pakistani Sufi Pir, Barkat Ali. The following excerpt, in which he refers to himself in the third person, is from such a letter.

> *May 13, 1966*
> Then there is the matter of touch and sex relations, which are so different in all parts of the world. Your Murshid did not take kindly to touch from either man or woman for a long, long time. Eventually he learned how to evaluate people through the touch, but far prefers evaluation through the breath. Indeed it is this subject that is more interesting to him than anything else. So if he uses the breath and not the touch, it is because he finds something both scientifically and spiritually far more interesting.

It becomes as if all touch relations were for the children of Allah and the breath relations for the wise of Allah.

Douglas-Klotz picks up this thread. By his early seventies "it becomes more and more clear to Lewis, who is now functioning as a Sufi Murshid, that through divine guidance he is addressing and healing his own lifelong issues with intimacy, touch, love, and joy through his work with his young California disciples."

In a talk Murshid gave to his disciples, he divides love into five different planes: animal, human, genius, angelic, and divine. He begins by pointing out how the divine is seen in the animal kingdom by foxes or birds, "who take care of the young and each other":

> I don't think that human beings who indulge in animal love always have the intelligence of fox love at all. Or dove love. I am not speaking out against animal love, I am speaking out against human beings who indulge in animal love without having the wisdom of the animal.
>
> Now we come to human love. You know, I've had romances, but I never got married in this life. I think God didn't want me to, but it doesn't make any difference. I'm satisfied now that I'm just a papa or a grandpapa to everyone. Every now and then I used to fall in love. Now I've stopped that because I'm in love with everybody.
>
> When we come to the love of geniuses, it is based on more than just love and companionship. It is based on common ideals, common purposes in life. Here it's not a discipline, but a natural evolution.
>
> Now we come to the angelic love. And there, people love because they love, and you either love or you don't love, but that's all there is. Nothing else but that. That's the higher heaven called *deva-loka*. It's made up of love.
>
> Beyond that is the divine love. In divine love, there is no other self. There isn't you and me and God—and there is you and me and God. Only which is which? That's the divine love. This is my field, not the human love.... The lesson to be learned here is to extract love from time and link it to eternity. And when we link it to eternity, we begin to have the real knowledge. Defined love is incomplete love; it is love's shadow. In timeless love we *become* the other.

To extract love from time and link it to eternity: I am asking myself, and I am asking you, what would be the quality of our lives then? Timeless, Loving Reader, what then?

Vision and the Unseen World

Where did Samuel Lewis's guidance come from? It is difficult to separate out the various sources of Murshid's spiritual guidance, especially his *self-to-self* guidance vs. his *unseen world-to-self* guidance. Douglas-Klotz remarks, "By natural predilection, family history and/or training, Samuel Lewis undoubtedly possessed prodigious psychic powers, however defined." In early life, Lewis himself wrote, "One learned to transcend the time and space and even to 'see' into the future. I often rehearsed conversations with the Messiah and later, when I was eighteen, with the Master. But when I awoke to the realization, it was almost impossible to reconcile the dreams and musings with the objective reality. This has been the wonder of my life."

When Lewis was twenty-nine, Khwajah Khidr, an Islamic guardian-angel figure who is said to offer wisdom to those in need, appeared to him in vision. "He offered poetry or music," Lewis later recalled. "I chose poetry, wherein I felt there was a promise and an inspiration. There was a long argument: why was the poetry chosen and not the music? Years later the music did come, and it is coming, and with the dance, but these are different stories."

Lewis was ever cautious about such visions, however. Inayat Khan himself had already written in a 1911 letter to his American disciple Murshida Rabia Martin, "I never want you to have the feelings of having magical powers like those who have the spiritual craze and see wonderful sights. I want you to find out the God in the usual things that you are experiencing by your five senses." In a letter of his own to Rabia Martin, Lewis wrote, "I have not had many visions or phenomena, but the greatest of phenomena has been the opening of the door of my heart." Many decades later, recalling his young adult experiences of Japanese Buddhism, Lewis added a caution: "One learned to transcend the time and space, and even to see into the future. My friends, do not seek such faculties. It will bring you enemies. You will be misunderstood. Find your true nature first and then, if you will, look a little."

Murshid often clarified this by saying that reality is to be found not in visions but in real-world activity, "in the fruits of your labor." When, at age sixty-eight, Murshid found himself in the hospital with ptomaine poisoning, he had a vision that demonstrated the wisdom of this insight. "Allah came to me in vision and said, 'You are the Teacher of the Hippies.'" Allah had thus *spoken his name*, and Samuel Lewis heard his name thus spoken, and his subsequent labors bore fruits for multitudes in the real world.

Fudo

As a young man, Lewis understood intellectually the notion of righteous anger. At age twenty-nine, in his description of the Japanese god Fudo, his erudition is on display: "Fudo is Jesus driving the moneylenders from the temple. Fudo is Jesus castigating the scribes and Pharisees. Fudo is Jeremiah standing before the king. Fudo is Bodhidharma refusing to praise the Emperor. Fudo is the wise guide who does not confuse sentimentality with love." But as Gavin Arthur reminds us, at that age Lewis walked through the world with a ready chip on his shoulder. As his love refined, not only was his conceptual understanding commensurately refined, it was put into action as well. The story is often told that in his last years, when Murshid would sometimes seem harsh to a disciple, he would afterward turn and say to the nearest person, "Feel my pulse," which he knew would be normal. I never saw Murshid actually angry with anyone from ego alone, and his righteous Fudo energy typically produced salutary results in his disciples.

Murshid sometimes did resemble a *madzub*, a person intoxicated with God. At age sixty-five he writes a friend about this seemingly nonlinear behavior: "There is a rumor going around that I am mad and I answer, of course I am mad, but my madness is the same yesterday, today and tomorrow. Other people have Sanity No.1 on Monday, Sanity No.2 on Tuesday, Sanity No.3 on Wednesday, and another Sanity next week." But just months before he died, he told a class, "If you've got any awe about me, I'd go mad. I've made mistakes. I've dropped dishes in the kitchen. I've burned the rice. And so I've asked God not to be perfect, to function with all my faults." Murshid Lewis wanted to be seen as just a man, and indeed he was just a man, an imperfect man with an ideal of divine love.

Harvest

In 1958, at age sixty-two, in a letter to his dancer friend Leonora Ponti, Lewis described his vision of a future that would become a reality ten years later: "To bring nations of the world together by eating, praying, and dancing is one facet. Another facet is to help feed the multitudes. I am working all the time at it. It has placed me under both strain and joy." Three years later, he writes, "I have learned to treat the world as a whole single body, and to appreciate the hearts and minds of other people. So I do not travel as a stranger." In 1970, he writes, referring to himself by name, "Sam was influenced to maintain a diary after reading the words of Thomas Jefferson, Ralph Waldo Emerson, and Papa Ramdas. But in retrospect, it must be said that the more one considers it, there is no diary. There is only the fulfillment of the Divine life through what would appear to be an ego personality, but which is nothing but a mode of God expressing itself outwardly. And daily Sam seems to find that there is really nothing else but this divine life."

This is surely a great realization, namely that there *is* no story. One is here and then one isn't. A light turns on, then off again—not much of a story. Ah, but the light! Where does the light go? *Where the Light Goes* is a story that belongs to everyone.

I came into Murshid's life at the season of its blossoming, the end of a very long movie, and it has taken me, and many who knew him, the better part of our lives to fill in the rest of the picture. We know a large part of ourselves through him, so the quest, like any mother-figure or father-figure quest, has actually been the search for one's own authority, for possession of one's own autonomy, the lifelong road to self-realization. Such is a measure of a teacher's wisdom—that his students become whole by learning to parent themselves. And such is my transmission from Murshid Lewis, a long and patient teaching completed fifty years after his death by disappearing himself from my lovely shrine. What a fox!

An Invitation

In the early spring of 1968, we still lived in San Francisco. I was thirty, surrounded by three children, a pregnant wife, and two frisky whippets named Maggie and Braxmoose, all of us equally needy. Nonetheless, on Wednesday nights, we hired a sitter, and off we went. Murshid's meetings were joyous and illuminating celebrations of circle dancing, singing, discursive and provocative teaching—yes, teaching by that same guy with the beard in a chair. But that guy seemed to be mellowing as his bond with his followers—and the bond *amongst* his followers—grew warmer and wider. At one meeting in 1969, Murshid tried out a musical idea he had: a four-part polyphonic chant. The music was almost childishly simple but nonetheless affective, thrilling even. My intellectual composer-mind wanted to know how that could possibly be true. I found the *idea* of polyphonic chanting new and intriguing, and I wanted my chance at it.

After the meeting, I asked Murshid if I could try my hand. Before I could finish my question, he boomed, "Sure!" as if he had been waiting for me to ask. The next day, I strung together several chants the group already knew into a round that was easy to sing and learn but elaborate in its polyphony. The following Wednesday, I found it easy, natural, even *casual* to be teaching a long piece to my new family. First, we learned it well in unison; when we finally sang it as a round, the large domed room filled with a kind of communal ecstasy I'd never heard or felt before. Nor, perhaps, had anyone else. The air was glowing. When it had subsided, Murshid simply proclaimed, "All right," and without further comment went on to the next event. The rightness was in a quality of feeling that spoke for itself. A few days later, Murshid did speak of it in a letter to Anandashram: "It was introduced by the choral master. It was all-powerful and was marked by the descent of the Holy Spirit upon this person. It took one up into spiritual consciousness."

When I arrived at the next week's meeting, about twenty people had already gathered in the room. Murshid directed everybody in chanting, *Welcome to the Maestro, welcome to the Maestro.* I wasn't sure what was meant by this, but after the same thing happened at the next two gatherings, I thought to myself, *I must be the Maestro.* Once again, Murshid had named me. He recognized not only how ripe I had become to occupy that niche but also how the musical aspect of his longed-for desire to fulfill Inayat Khan's mandate—to bring Sufism, with its highly developed esoteric traditions, out of India to meet its Western bride—was playing out. That is how I became, for that time, the Maestro of the Sufi community.

Gradually I came to realize that many of my new friends playing their guitars, enjoying their folk music and their own songs, had beautifully in-tune and open-hearted voices. Could we form an actual choir? With everyone's contributions and my arranging and composing experience, we could build a repertoire of music for circle dancing and even for concerts. The energy of this thought flowed like a mountain stream. "Sure!" boomed Murshid when I broached the subject, so I consulted the more gifted of the singers, and about twenty people said yes. We scheduled a Tuesday evening rehearsal at 7:30 in our basement studio in Marin and to my amazement, Murshid himself showed up to sing bass, and quite passably at that. Likewise the second Tuesday. At 7:25 on the evening of the third rehearsal, he called to give his excuses and blessings. Likewise the following week. By the fifth Tuesday, the Sufi Choir had found its voice, and when his call came at 7:25 I said, "You don't have to call anymore, Murshid. The seed has sprouted."

The rest of this story is told in a later passage (in Chapter 18) devoted to the Sufi Choir, but I will add here that at age thirty-two, after twenty-five years of life-molding musical training, this was exactly the dosage of devotional music I needed. The clarity of Inayat Khan's prescience was not wasted on Murshid, me, or his musical disciples. This was a direct transmission from an ancient tradition born of Asian soil now sprouted in America. We were doing what we were called upon to do, our music filled the needy air and the hungry ears—more and more so over the years as we grew one with the sacred sound, the sound beyond sound.

A Forward Pass at Lama

In June 1970, Murshid spent some weeks teaching at Lama Foundation in the mountains of Northern New Mexico. One of the first and most enduring of the spiritual communes, it is still in full flower today, more than fifty years after its founding. We guests and the residents alike spent much of our time making adobe bricks for the now-famous meeting hall with its spacious geometric dome and grand octagonal window looking out over the San Cristobal plain. Murshid beat a drum under the hot sun to encourage us laborers sweating in the mud fields. These were high times, suffused with lofty ideals and hard work, a combination that has sustained many of us over our lifetimes. In the daily meetings, I was called on to teach new songs, some of them written that day on texts by "Lama beans," as we were called. One day I received a message to appear at the "teacher's hut," a small, round, modestly domed wooden room tucked into the mountain. The outside temperature was very hot that day, and it was hotter inside the hut. Murshid, in his underpants, was sitting at a table; his secretary, Mansur, was taking dictation on an ancient typewriter.

Murshid nodded as I came in, bade me sit, and continued a letter he was writing to a colleague in Pakistan: "During the dancing classes, we intersperse the rest periods with chanting. These are apart from the new type of Qawals [a style of ecstatic singing]. Now the next thing is the evolution in Western music of the day from popular music. The inspirations from Allah seem to blend in these modes with the chanting of sacred phrases. Now we come to the next phase. A disciple, William Mathieu, joined us. I am at this time giving him the spiritual name of Allaudin."

After the letter was finished, Murshid slipped his green cotton teaching robe over his head, smoothed himself out, signaled for me to stand before him, and began a formal ceremony of initiation.

Hierarchical initiation means different things to different people, but to many, including this lineage of Sufis, it can be one stepping-stone on a long path. It is partly symbolic, a sign that there is an outward recognition of an inner purpose. For some, initiation is a promise to bond with a teacher forever, but one of the reasons I was attached to this particular lineage is that its disciples typically are passed on from teacher to teacher. It is the teaching itself that holds the continuity; the teacher is the agent, the bus driver, the mail person, the friend who brings over a home-cooked meal when you're laid up.

Murshid began by saying a blessing and then we recited in unison a prayer by Inayat Khan. Then he asked the required question: "Do you accept me as your spiritual teacher?" but went on to add in a loud, no-nonsense voice, "FOR THE TIME BEING." Eyes wide, I heard myself say yes. With his finger, he drew onto my forehead a winged heart, a Sufi symbol. We exchanged *darshan*, and then Murshid said, "I hereby initiate you, William Allaudin Mathieu, as my disciple." There was another prayer. Murshid took off his robe.

Not being a fan of ceremony, I didn't think I'd feel any differently, but I walked down the mountain a different man. After Murshid died, and as various teachers passed through my life, the phrase "for the time being" took on a greater significance, as we shall see.

Travels With Murshid

In the middle of our two-week stay at Lama, Murshid invited me to accompany him on a tour of some spiritual communes in the vicinity. One of these was for Gurdjieff disciples, one for itinerant hippies, and one apparently was simply for lost souls. The young communes themselves were in states of desperation and confusion. As Murshid talked to the residents, he displayed an uncanny sense of what needed to be heard. He tried to get the listeners to do some circle dancing, and had me try to get them all to chant or sing together—all this with varying success. But Murshid's energy remained optimistic and bright, and everyone did seem buoyed up. Even the Gurdjieff followers, hugely suspicious of traveling spiritual teachers, didn't kick us off their farm. In fact, Murshid brought light into some very dark faces.

Murshid had also been invited to give a presentation at the University of New Mexico in Albuquerque, where quite a crowd joined in the dancing and singing. And they listened attentively to the idiosyncratic traveling teacher. This was new to me—there was joy in the eyes of the dancers, hope in the foreheads of the listeners, devotion in the throats of the singers, and we were somewhere other than Marin County, California. Ours was not, of course, an entirely singular vision, but here in this vibrant room was clear and present experience of its passage from heart to heart. Murshid's energy and positivity were transformative, and seeing him in action was, for me, transmission of the clearest kind. When he answered questions he went straight-arrow to the question behind the question. This caused astonishment in the questioner because the hidden question had been so immediately exposed and answered. I learned that we are not ordinarily conscious of what we are truly asking. But Murshid was.

A clear and discriminating teacher has the ability to read the psychological state and life quality of another. Murshid could not have evolved into this clarity had he not come to a resolution of his earlier traumas. His early life was torture, but his seeking was pure. He didn't quit or become disheartened. He was possessed by the call to rise above his personal suffering and become resonant with the woes of others so he could address the suffering of multitudes. The call evolved into a functional wisdom teaching, a wisdom I have sought in my own teaching, in my music, and in my life. He modeled it directly into me, recognized my own recognition of it, and waved me on down the line.

Over the months that followed, we grew to trust one another. When I brought a question to him, or a proposal, he most often said, "I'm not saying *any*thing." And because I always brought the best to my teacher, he never once reprimanded me. Well, maybe once. At the end of a class of instruction on the chakras—how one begins with the lower chakras and becomes aware of the qualities of the higher ones successively—I asked him whether, if you have experience of the crown chakra, you could meditate on it. "Yes," Murshid replied, with a stern look and in a loud voice, "if you have realized the others first." I sheepishly thanked him and reminded myself (again) to stop asking pride-of-knowledge questions.

My connection with Murshid Lewis was deep but not particularly personal. I didn't seek private time with him. Most of his disciples asked for one-on-one interviews for guidance in their personal affairs, but I got what I was looking for in the words Murshid spoke and wrote, in the example of his teaching, and in the way he was cultivating a cohesive spiritual community. My part of the bargain was my service via the choir under the guiding eye of his heart.

Nonetheless, I thought I should ask for a private interview even though I had no personal laundry for him to wash. When I showed up in his office one sun-filled autumn morning in 1970, he bade me be comfortable in the chair opposite his desk and inquired about my family. I gave him a brief update—my family was doing well at that time. Then he said, "Did you hear the one about the double-bass player in the opera orchestra?" Brightening, I said, "Well, no, I don't believe I have."

He dove right in. "For twenty years, a double-bass player worked in the pit orchestra of his city's large opera house without ever taking a night off. One night he asked his three section mates if they'd mind if he took the next night off. They encouraged him enthusiastically, so he did. He spent the next morning at the beach. In the afternoon he went to the zoo. He ate a luxurious dinner at an expensive restaurant, and since he didn't have any plans for the evening, he decided to go see his buddies at the opera. On the program that evening was *Carmen*. He sat in the center of the first balcony and enjoyed himself immensely.

"The next night, when he showed up for work, his section mates asked him how was his night off. He said, 'I came to see you guys.' They asked what he thought of the performance. 'Absolutely fabulous!' he said. 'You wouldn't *believe* what goes on up there on the stage. Do you know that place where we go...'" and Murshid sang with gusto and accuracy four bars of a routine-sounding bass part—all quarter notes, with a half note at the end. He continued, "And they said, 'Yeah, yeah, yeah,' and he said, 'Well, there's a *fabulous* melody that goes over that...'" and Murshid sang with operatic bravado the first few bars of "The Toreador's Song."

This is a funny joke, but well told by a musician for musicians, it is more than funny. You have to get that the bass notes he sang are the actual bass notes for this melody, that the song is one of the best known in the operatic canon and, crucially, that pit musicians hear poorly and, in some cases, see not at all what is happening on on stage. This is especially true for the double-basses, who are often standing in the back row of the orchestra, facing the audience, and with the front edge of the stage above their heads.

The story also understands the trials of musicians-for-hire, particularly those laboring in pit orchestras who balance economic security against the musical myopia of their gigs. It has empathy for the choices they have to make, the choices few professional musicians are lucky enough to entirely escape. Few people who are *not* professional musicians could fully know the dark psychological brunt of this. For Murshid, telling that joke so well to the maestro of his choir meant that he had intuited one of the most ironic conditions of our professional lives, and smoothly pulled off his interpretation for my benefit. After the mirth subsided Murshid said, "Well, someone's waiting to see me," and the interview was over. I walked away grinning and grateful. Once again, my Murshid had seen and met me in my own world, as I had faithfully done unto him. He showed me once again the powerful blessing of mutual recognition between teacher and student.

Affirmation

In the first days of 1971, Murshid took a fatal fall down a straight flight of stairs. He suffered a concussion and a brain contusion. He was hospitalized in a deep coma for eighteen days before he died, occasionally emerging, especially in the first week, to speak. We took turns caring for him. When my turn came, it was dinnertime, but Murshid could eat only Jell-O, which this evening was cut into little cherry-red cubes. A tiny white plastic spoon came with the dish. I took over the shift from one of our choir altos, who instructed me to feed him only when he opened his mouth. Murshid, lying fitfully on his back, had rashes on his skin he would reflexively scratch. He would be restless, then motionless, then his mouth would open and I would drop a cube of Jell-O into it. After several cubes and a spell of motionless quiet, Murshid suddenly boomed forth, "I SAY YES!" It was the voice not of a dying man but of a confident leader, a voice thrilling in its conviction. Then the scratching, then the opening of the wizened mouth, then the sliding in of the Jell-O cube with the plastic spoon, and then the quiet again. I waited for the next outburst and it came a few minutes later, like the first: "I SAY YES!" Then twice more at longer intervals until my hour watch was relieved.

Gentle Reader, what we have here is, on the one hand, red sugar cubes dropping into the dying blackness and, on the other, the eternal power of Murshid's final acceptance. Consider for a moment the balance between these. Consider how Samuel Lewis, tiptoeing on the brink of his own mundane extinction, manifests the words that are the essence of creation. This is a good life lesson to remember, a good lesson to realize on each breath.

ॐ

In a final letter, dictated upon briefly coming out of his coma, Murshid reported to his Pakistani Pir, Barkat Ali, that his transmission of divine wisdom, the commission given him by Inayat Khan forty-five years previously, had been accomplished: "For I believe to have representatives in all purity and goodness of which Allah is capable and which will now be presumed done forever." He passed away thirteen days later.

Passed away, they say.

Away indeed.

Where does the light go when it turns off?

Murshid Samuel Lewis left a flourishing organization of Sufi followers with many moving parts, schools within a school, including a branch for righteous living with Gaia and another for direct aid to suffering communities. The organization as a whole is called the Sufi Ruhaniat International: *Ruh* is a proto-Semitic word for breath or spirit. Most of its members do think of it as a kind of university, albeit a "spiritual" one, if you will, rather than a theological one. It teaches the ideas and immerses you in the practices of the major religions of the world, attempting to expand and refine the sensibilities of its initiates. Its curriculum is based on experience, not concepts. There are some healthy splinter groups, not all of which are initiatory. The Ruhaniat and its associated groups facilitate camps, centers, dance and prayer circles, and varied forms of instruction in twenty-one countries (as of 2021). The ideas, practices, and pedagogical modes of Samuel Lewis are now a worldwide reality.

I consider the Ruhaniat my beloved Alma Mater. For about thirty years I taught under its rubric, most of these as an active Sheikh, but no longer. In my present teaching, and in my life in general, I've found it more helpful to eschew most names and forms generally ascribed to both exoteric and esoteric knowledge. For me, it proves best to meet each moment, each breath, and each *cadence* (to use the musical term for breath) as unique and indefinable. Music—music in all its seductive mystery, most blessedly *wordless* music—is my agency. As a psychological digging tool, music works well. More broadly, music is a medium of somatic connectivity to other humans and to worlds beyond ourselves we could not otherwise imagine. I appear as a Senior Teacher when asked, and I keep au courant. But mostly, as Murshid foresaw, I follow my own eclectic road. One thing that has remained steadfast, however, is my sense of family, of all of us being

Conducting the Choir at Murshid's Funeral

ourselves together at the same time. Many years after Murshid has died, and many others have died, and more and more others have arrived, the familial bond shines like a sun that never sets.

And I am so very thankful also for the music we of the Sufi Choir made and recorded during the dozen years after Murshid's death. It has legs, as they say—keeps being fresh and meaningful to listeners, keeps filling hearts around the world, keeps filling me with praise. And sometimes with tears. For all of us, it was a high and lucky time to be together. This is just one of myriad stories being told right now, of course, but somehow the music of the Sufi Choir seems so often to go beyond the story into plotless, wordless connectivity. *And this praising sound fills the air*, says Rumi. Then as now.

12

The Canada Journal

The Canada Journal, from 1971, features a kind of run-on writing I was experimenting with at the time. The style was an attempt at panoramic vision, a psychedelic inclusion, with an affinity for fragments and flippant grammar. The journal is also an autobiographical acknowledgment of the twenty-year relationship I had with Kay, my second wife and the mother of our four children.

After our on again/off again courtship, I made the *decision* to ask Kay to marry me. Kay kept her own counsel for two weeks, then invited me to go for walk. "About this *idea* of yours," she began, and then laid out certain behavioral, moral, and legal conditions to which I agreed. We were married in 1966. Over the years, I have had to come to terms with my role as father to Kay's two racially mixed children, whom I adopted, plus the two children Kay and I had together, a role in which, at the time, I felt reliably lame and not entirely game. Although I did love Kay and did feel the time was right to have children, I entered the marriage as a savior on a white horse: *Save the poor ones, the disenfranchised, save them, do!* That is a big mistake, Dear Reader, as I'm sure you know. After much infidelity on my part, in-fighting on everyone's part, and the ongoing paradox of my marital *decision*, we divorced in 1982.

In 1971, with sanguine intentions, we decided to go on a grand camping trip for as long, and as far north into Canada, as we could manage. I outfitted our Dodge van with a rickety platform bed that the kids had to survive the thousands of miles on—this during pre-seat belt days. Yet everyone did survive the perils and joys of the trip. Reading the journal now, fifty years on, provides a dusty window into what it must have been like for a wife to navigate the shallows between her four children with disparate needs and her sexually ravenous husband.

When writers write confessionally, their confessions often serve as mirrors for their readers. Whether or not that is the case here, these vignettes are my movie of what happened over a span of forty-three days in a van with four kids, a wife, and a husband. It's a writerly step toward my eventual acceptance of each one of us for who we were then and for who we have become. Over time, the real subject becomes forgiveness for others and for oneself.

I have edited these entries for clarity and sensitivity toward those I have loved and love still. For what is unspoken, let silence be the record. I will attest to this one thing, however, and more than once: feminine nature possesses the ascendant creative power. This is and has always been true for me—it just takes decades for the outer layer of flint to wear away from your average male human for him to recognize it.

๛

Mathieu Dramatis Personae:
Kay, age 31, mother of four, wife
Allaudin, age 33, turning 34, conflicted father, husband, wannabe *serious* composer
Athena, age 10 going on 11, eldest born to Kay, in the front lines of parental bullshit
David, age 8 going on 9, sole male child, moody, creative, pugnacious, developmentally problematic
Lucy, 3 turning 4, the good girl, generous, usually escapes the wrath flowing overhead
Amy Moon, age 2, seems to absorb the family vibe, cries a lot and quickly, knows how to be happy

๛

Saturday, June 12, 1971
Between Calistoga and Middleton at a private camp run by a Mr. Wells who descends from his 1962 Dodge van coach to fix us in his bourbon eye and says in Murshid's voice, *yeah* as he took our $3—if you happen to be looking for connections this day of setting out, which I am, and not in vain. Kay and me by firelight saying as much as we can right now. And Amy, one big apricot. Auspicious beginning.

But there was an electric bulb strung above, and from 3am to dawn I sleep-weep because I don't want Murshid to have died. And I dreamed that that big apricot is some adolescent, updated to sing lead for David Crosby. Perhaps because Kay was so perfect under the bare bulb, and when one centers there, well—more days like this *one*.

Sunday, June 13
Too much driving through the north end of the Central Valley, everyone cacked out, the land cocooned on either side by mountains and Mount Shasta 70 miles away LOOMING. Flat and unending this valley, and then gentle rolling, the land begins to change, and the breath deepens, and the kids wake up, and a little chatter fills the air, and the peaks are almost as sudden as the stands of trees. Riding through this land-space *is* our emotion, if you're looking for connections, and who isn't?

Wednesday, June 16
Exhausted, rewarded. Campaign to get the kids to clean up after selfs. Working at being here. Saw Crater Lake; snow tunnels on either side of the road. Breathing with the land. Mom and Pop are together. Family lurches toward unity. So far so good. Into the rhythm of days.

Thursday, June 17
Oregon scenery today wonderful when it was boring and wonderful when it was wonderful. Buttes and mesas in Indian land. Fluorescent forests. Now it's raining over nicey-warm tent. Nary a leak. Thinking, on the road, *but I SEE this good—it goes through me: that's what I do, so why should I be attached or angry?* and then feeling that goodness and *still* failing, toward evening, with David over and over...and *still* feeling it will get better, it will get better, etc. repeat, repeat....

What if I were actually creative about my *family*?

Sunday, June 20, Father's Day
Nature helps but it doesn't make it all okay for you. A truly scenic drive through Chinook Pass through all snow tunnels and the air crisp like winter Kansas, great glaciers all around; then a long time through Washington evergreens to the coast, and then along the coast. 'These aren't campsites,' says Kay, 'they're stalls.' This particular link in the inevitable chain of disastrous Father's Days is commemorated by the beautiful blue sunset mist, the near Pacific Islands of Chuckanut Bay, the water like hand-blown

glass, and David's beloved beach ball, which he *just now* has been singing to, floating with surprising swiftness out on the tide, farther and deeper, me ambling over along the sandy beach, heart sinking as the precious ball is receding, knowing all was and is forever lost, then Kay shouting, 'Aren't you going to *get* it for him?' and me dreading every depth, and angry at her for wanting me to drown myself to save the boy's ball: 'Terrific!' I yell, turning my back on receding ball and weeping boy, and that's it for mucho hours.

Monday, June 21
Hot showers in the morning get us going. Then slouching on toward Canada the resolve ever renewed not to die in our own traps. Finally, after dreadful paranoiac anticipation of the Border Judgment (which actually materialized in the form of a schmuck) we give a Hip-Hip-Hooray three, nay six, nay nine times and Canada thus receives us. On to Cultus Lake and a good campsite with interesting friends, good water, trees and birds, flirtatious relations with my wife, a can of beer, three joints shared, and the awakening around 3:30 AM with a migraine manifesto of the uncertainty, inconstancy, forgetfulness and finally the antipathy, guilt and repression of the last few days. Fortunately dawn was just breaking at this Northern Birthday of Summer, and with pills, bird song, and the gentle love of the lake, I'm born again, again.

Oh dear, I heard the birds.

Wednesday, June 23
Most of today bipped along okay, but here in Victoria we found a real Conservatory with real pianos and I really wanted to play, to rediscover myself musically and I couldn't, and I felt alien and tired until finally Kay and me broke date we maybe didn't have and she went to bed and I made a mess of making coffee, and fuck it anyway, what is this anger? Why are hearts closed?
I am very anxious to make music, to carve the old name, but how? And which name? I feel very dumb to Allah.

Thursday, June 24
Waking up with the old headache, staring straight into nothing and hearing four kids purring and laughing. Breaking of camp climaxed by Kay's finger-pointing analysis that I was repining for lack of her sweet favors, and ending with her white-capped peak of fury, which suddenly revealed and relieved frustrations on all sides. I drove us straight to a mall where we all had pancakes with real whipped cream, then on to the Nanaimo Ferry and a *good*

ferry ride by all mates sustaining happy times, by Atha and David running off by themselves, by me and Lucy and Amy hanging in, and a little bit by Kay and me seeing we were doing it right on, even through the gray waters.

Friday, June 25
The beauty of Highway 1 here is how many different things you see at one glance: mist hanging on the foothills, immense towering clouds over snow capped mountains, green chubby farms and flat valleys fed by water falling from cliffs, rushing rivers with log rafts and bridges while the sun shines brightly through the showers.

Multiple variations on this landscape. Everything is perfect, all we need is love.

Saturday, June 26
A remarkably dispassionate day wherein my energy was channeled in a laser to keep the family together. By 10 am we seemed to be drifting upward toward the inevitable plateau, but what I know is that these rolling ups and downs are just what scenery is but what the spiritual life precisely is not. What black certainty today, what horrible fantasies. But we keep driving north. It is God's country. Tonight we are camping by a waterfall and a huge bonfire, and the future is azure, unsure.

What I really want to do is write better and better music.

Sunday, June 27
Yep: Talked it all out last night over the bonfire. Words like fuel, maybe low-grade speed. Something for nothing? But here we are with our BEST FEET forward. Today is Lucy's fourth birthday, she the angel child doing splendidly under most adverse circumstances. David made her a beautiful Totem Pole Bird, Kay a macramé belt, Atha a collage of natural-found things, and Amy two sweet collages, one of Tiger flowers, another of tin foil and red crayon. And we ate cake and went into Clearwater and got ice cream, and watched a long time the mama and her baby horse stand in place, and went to brother Ray's health food store where a murshid, in lower orbit to be sure, lies waiting to be The Murshid. And we had dinner and more cakes and Daddy practiced flute a lot and Mom and him took turns looking hard at the 200-foot Spabats Creek Falls there by experiencing formal transformation, and Mom and Dad got along real good, that best foot stickin' right out there, hoping not to trip wobbling onward.

Monday, June 28
A day of beautiful, sparsely settled land, and without domestic crisis! From Clearwater almost to Jasper via Lake Lucerne, the mountains are sheer walls of rectangular thickness, white on top. Hard driving through two hundred miles of these, rushing streams and many bridges, and sun and rain, and little mysterious towns of people who know or do not know how strong they are. One imagines—just to make sure not to be tempted—the countryside perpetually under six feet of snow. This lake has a gentle breeze and a clear reflection but too many mosquitoes. Now Kay stands before the fire watching for the wash water to heat, and by the dying sun at 10:20pm I feel very peaceful. Today Atha had a good long music lesson, Daddy practiced his high flute tonguing, Daddy and David threw sixty balls without a miss—both very proud—and David made a marvelous chipmunk trap, and Amy's fort got pinned under a seesaw, she was brave and very real, and Lucy got through the anti-climax as did Mama too.

Wednesday, June 30
At Miette Hot Springs, our most northern destination. A refreshing flash of knowing we've gotten us here. It is a camper's ghetto, it has everything: scenery, hot pools, wild mountain sheep wandering through, a store for snacks, hot water, and a wood stove, all on the eve of Dominion Day with Canadians placidly and correctly becoming neighbors on all sides. Hot baths, like the lead cure, make you heavy.

Today David chopped wood proudly while I anxiously predicted my failure as a teacher—but he came through. With her finger, Lucy helps me to write. Atha met Samantha, ten-and-a-half and straight as an arrow. She and Sam and David are swimming alone now. Amy took a long piggyback ride. The ranger spoke French. Daddy went to sleep in the sunshines. Woodstove dinner with biscuits and popcorn and marshmallows.

Thursday, July 1, Dominion Day
What a rest. Big breakfast in a cozy wood kitchen. Bacon. US News and World Bullshit. Flashed last night about how precious this time is with the children. Easy to make resolves from comfy internal place, but to be out there with four monkeys, something else again.

Friday, July 2
The snow sufficeth, it sufficeth us. Big fat snow was at first sight a surprise and a pleasure. But as the day wore on and the discomfort grew, and the thresholds became apparent, I had eventually to see my fear of the cold and wet. But the two long swims in the pool

Horsie

with the rising steam blowing in my face and a long twisty ride
to the far shore through the mist and little waterfalls, and Kay's
patience and calm and coherent trying made it all okay even
though the snow turned to slush. I *see* that all the kids here are
products of homes together enough to go camping and they are
all okay: if you can go camping you can raise kids. I *see* all the
middle-class men, with whom I identify as having consciousness
very like my own—the insights of similarity are being confirmed
moment to moment. And I *see* how my gifts are unusual and my
responsibilities are simple facts. Do these men see me?

Saturday, July 3

Birthdays are fucking hard work, this one, thirty-four, threaded through by the not very calm resolve to produce more music from now till I'm thirty-five. There now, I've written that number. All of this is pretty silly knowing that death (according to John Cage) is like any other part of a piece it just comes at a special place. It is the fulfillment of the promise and we are preparing for that mysterious moment, yes, and it's a good movie I thought today, which began with a long walk up the mountain with Atha to a place where the stream came out of the rock and someone had built a waterwheel. It was Daddy's day, and except for the struggling with the unquiet inner necessity to become quiet, I was Daddy all day. Kay did so very well, she made it my day with popcorn balls and candles stuck into ten-cent jelly rolls. I got:

> some lovely drawings of our trip (Atha)
> a plastic moose (David)
> pipe cleaners (Lucy)
> a rock with ballpoint hieroglyphics (Amy)
> wood-smoked leather moccasins and neat wool socks (Kay)

Tuesday, July 6

Driving south to Athabasca Falls, then through the spectacular river valley always between two ranges, and watching the glaciers die inch by inch. Fleeing the rain. It dries. After the endless ridge we approach the glaciers themselves. Blue crevices. Deceptive distances. Immensities. We camp; we take our snowmobile ride. The snowmobile is the purple monster. We learn about moraines and melts, and walk on glacial ice. Says Kay, 'Too far out, *Al-al-u-deen.*' Then we go to the toe of Athabasca Glacier and walk on it and gather stones, and this is really neat: kids get chipped glacier and eat it. The toe is really the toe of a giant.

Gemütlich kitchen camp: three male teachers (medicine, biochemistry, music, all clever) and their supportive wives and, miraculously, happy children. Amy in delight, other three highly social. All happy: good dinner, warm kitchen, a meeting of folks, and it *snows*. Far out again. Many jokes; nothing ruined by the Jewish biochemist and the Jewish composer being slightly threatened by each other. We have our positions after all. I asked him about the crossover between consciousness and inert matter. He diverts it, but asking the question clarifies it for me. Now Kay and I are reading the geological description of where we are. It's 30° outside the tent and inside we can see our breath.

Wednesday, July 7
The Canadian Rockies gave me this: the mountains are symbols of ancient birth in the state of decay. Their shape is time. My death is puny and lonely in the face of their immense death. They gave me also: if I can hold in my hand a rock 500 million years old, *then* and *now* are connected for me. That's one-eighth the age of the earth, on the same order of magnitude as the age of the universe; it is also twenty-five million human generations away, a number I can conceive as not timeless. The origins of the universe, the rocks in these mountains, and this present moment are thereby conjoined. From here the step to other universes is easy. Good trip. Our campsite is lovely but the wood is hard to chop—needs a long axe.

Thursday, July 8
After dinner much singing. Little girls filling Amy Moon's new boots with gravel and presenting them in duet first to me, then to Atha, and then to Mom, singing fortissimo altissimo happy birthday with their eyes clenched, laying the boots down and running away and then doing it all again. Later, Atha and Kay and me sang Sufi songs in the kitchen where a retarded, disturbed little boy overheard. Kay and I had a long talk with him and then we took him off and sang Sufi songs to him and he was delighted, he was Jesus, we were wasted, we were Mother and Father.
Okay, I see: it's taken a month but I'm into family now—I see what that absorption can be, and we are all so much more content.

Friday, July 9
Took a long hike with David, including: following along a disappointing trail in the woods, which became other trails, then all trails; discovering an abandoned motel for tobogganers; discovering an inexplicable rope, pulley and pole device, then making groovy sine wave patterns with the ropes; climbing up a 600 foot hill and peering out from the top and seeing in all directions and loving it; not finding a bow and arrow branch; finding each other coming down another way having been real high; digging rocks on the way down; finding the way home; telling about it; feeling good.

Saturday, July 10
Up early in the rain to drive to Field, B.C., where we waited happily for the train, and the train came, and it was good. We sat in the dome all together, spiral tunnels, everything a first train ride should be. We picnicked in Banff in the rain and Amy was good, and we walked and got treats, and bought stuff and got more

treats, and suddenly Lucy and Amy were gone and the internal life of the parents became quite active. We raced from one end of the block to the other in and out of stores like a labyrinth montage, and there were twenty pairs of little girls screaming *Mama!* and the kidnappers receded into the future, and Atha and David were scared. Then suddenly they were discovered in Hudson's Bay store where this too-kind lady had led them for safety. Exhaustion! Went to the playground. Daddy napped. Walked back a mile to the train. Amy did good—waited interminably but happily for the train, which was three hours late. Daddy took movies, the choo-choo came in the setting sun, and this time Daddy got to watch out the window, and feel his bones sink into childhood safety and flying happiness with all the green, and the rocks and the odd structures fleeting by. At Field, hamburgers and beer.

Tuesday, July 13
Kay re-caps the day, I write it down:
"We lay around in bed, ate and we all went to the bathroom I think; potato chips for breakfast: um-m-m; kids got money for being quiet; Lucy was naughty, said no and had to go in the tent, and then we all said oh I don't know whadda you wannna do and I said okay you're done eating? Well stand up turn around and sit down and eat *lunch*—and that was funny. Well, I got in the car and did the laundry. We read dirty magazines. We had lunch and it was good. Then we drove around Invermere and looked it over (yawn) and we came back to rip-off city. Then we went swimming. The guys did the diving. Then we looked down into Red Streak Canyon. Then we had yucky spaghetti and Atha had to wash the noodle pan, which was very hard but she got fifteen cents; and Atha and David made a pup tent, and we went to bed but we couldn't find the book so we read Chinese Stories instead, and we had the giggles a little while, and I lit the light all by myself ho-ho-ho. And Daddy brought me my pen and my tissue and my drink with my coat on himself all backwards and (giggles) then some kind of subjective intellectual horseshit to end it all—and I'm sure glad we're leaving tomorrow. And—and—and thank you all for listening, friends, and good night, and tune in tomorrow."

Friday July 16
South through Oregon today. We had a good dinner: bacon and Spam and peas and potatoes and lemonade. Early to bed. Preparing for home in much the same way we are preparing for our kids to become pubescent: there's a hard road ahead. Moths give us the creeps as I write. The forest has strange echoes— mysterious callings of animals that captivate the whole family: forest puzzles.

Thursday, July 22
It's okay here at the relative comfort of Gold Lake Lodge in the Sierras. Atha and David prepared all morning, then gave a play wherein a prop man was caught and eaten by the witch and the vampire, a lady visitor was scared off, and mysterious relatives were met outside. All this in the ghost-story-monster vein; all deeply symbolic and indecipherable.

Kay and me had three hours to ourselves, and so had our day at Horse Lake, totally nice, during which my conniving, manipulating, calculating, father-ish, busily aesthetic self tuned in unison quite nicely with the crickets, birds, dragonflies, water, trees, rocks and snow. Later, Kay found a hook and some line and some eggs and almost went to sleep with her shirt off and her front to the sun and her line dangling over, brain quiet and our boat idling in gentle circles around our dragging anchor. We rowed; we watched the bottom; we listened, and almost didn't waste that perfect setting. Then to dinner for seventeen at the Lodge—nice enough if you're human, I imagine.

Friday, July 23
Getting very itchy to leave, or rather to arrive at my only being, or so it seems from here.

Saturday, July 24
With relief I write that this is our last day out. Tomorrow I will see my piano, our telephone, call my students, Sufi friends, etc. Well, next time will be shorter; it was cuckoo to allow six weeks. In the afternoon we got a sitter and a company of six of adult friends hiked a mile to Deer Lake where we swam and talked and threw rocks and had a pleasant afternoon. Fell asleep after a feast of a lunch, the leftovers from last night's dinner feast. Woke up just now very out of sorts, knowing that knowledge which comes when the line between Kay and me is broken, or at least sags— that the difference between us is like the seed

(The Canada Journal ends abruptly here.)

In 2017, for my eightieth birthday, I asked the kids each to write me something. Amy Moon, forty-eight at the time, wrote several "micro-memoirs," this among them.

Brotherhood

It was record cold in Chicago the night my mom called to tell me my brother David died. I had had a dream the night before that I was Isis and my husband Osiris. After I hung up the phone I had the feeling of falling from a great height. It is said that a death in the immediate family will bring you closer together or tear you apart. Oddly, my family vacillated between the two with no rhyme or reason.

I used to sneak my brother's *Easy Rider* magazines out to the old tire swing in the back yard. I'm pretty sure this is how I learned about blowjobs and how I developed a fierce commitment to feathered bangs. I was always careful to put them back exactly as I found them, in the cardboard box under his bed, and I'm 100% sure he knew whenever I had taken them.

One day, David came home from school with a tiny black kitten in his jacket. He had saved it from the other boys at school, who were using it as a football. Our mom said he could keep it and he named him Zeppelin after his favorite band. David was considered the black sheep of the family, but that label was unjust; more accurately, Lucy-the-middle-child was the white sheep, and we all just trickled down from her. My brother was half black, cross-eyed and shy, and wore braces in the years of his life when it humiliated him the most. My father had adopted David and my oldest sister Atha after marrying my mom because it was the right thing to do. He also loved them. I don't remember the moment that this sweet shy boy turned into a broken lonely drug addict, but I fiercely and blindly held on to the belief that it was not the fault of my parents. My brother never stole from me, but he cleaned out Mom and Dad a few times. A couple of months after he died we began to tuck our memories in and seal our feelings, not discussing them, not expressing them. I tried to vacuum up the horrific grief that had flooded our house, sweeping my own feelings tight into a corner to make room for what was far worse: two parents outliving a child.

About a year later I had the same dream, but instead of my husband as Osiris it was my brother.

David at Fifteen

13

The Holy Ones:
Message and Messenger

In the early 1970s, in the apartment of the poet and lyricist for the Sufi Choir, Richard Tillinghast, I noticed a dog-eared book titled *Cutting Through Spiritual Materialism* by Chögyam Trungpa.

"What's this?" I asked.

"Just open it," he said.

"But what *is* it?" I insisted.

"Just open it to any page," he insisted back.

I've never been able to find the exact passage again—maybe I'm just remembering an amalgam of sentences—but the gist was just what I'd been waiting to hear: *There is no Holy Book, no Dharma, no high or profound teaching, or illuminating commentary that is not fully available in the present moment. Everything you need is given to you whole in the now.*

I wanted so to believe this. One learns, however, not to *believe* such high-sounding statements but, with perspicacious practice, to live them. I never much liked Trungpa's style of in-person, live teaching. Through reports from friends who were involved and well-circulated videos, I recognized his rascality early on. His self-abuse was legendary. He was a serious alcoholic, and his self-proclaimed clarity in the transmission of the dharma while blotto was definitely arguable. Yet his book, one among many, is one of the clearest explications of Buddhism in English.

What took a while to emerge was the extent of his abuse of others, often his disciples and closest allies. Skilled in his many facets as he was, and brilliant as was the clarity he brought to his Buddhist lineage, Trungpa did a lot of harm to a lot of people before he finally did terminal harm to himself in 1987, at the age of forty-seven. His books still sell well, his institutions thrive, and I hope the people he wounded have somehow managed to heal.

In religious or moral teaching, is the message inseparable from the messenger? If a teacher is not living a creed meant to be lived, is the message valid? Who could preach loving kindness and practice meanness? My answer is that message and messenger are ideally inseparable, but you can judiciously separate them in your own mind. Each person has to work this out according to their own purposes. By far, the most valuable teachers model what they teach. We learn not from ideas but from experience, and experience can be advantageously contagious. Ideas point to but do not transmit experience. A teacher's authentic joy can be transmitted directly in the moment. "It can't be taught, it has to be caught," said Buddhist Joe Miller.

So I carried Trungpa's teaching about everything being *given to you whole in the now* to and fro with me for a thousand years until I found myself beginning to catch it from living master teachers.

ود

Along with the hippies, Holy Men of every stripe, from highly credentialed to self-proclaimed, flocked to the City of Love to seek followers, found a movement, populate a commune, or make a living, or a bundle, teaching. It seemed like the Bay Area was one big spiritual campus, and I was thirsty to learn more. Idealized spiritual talk and brilliant insight hung low from trees and peeked out from under loose rocks. But where were the guidelines for how to live these ideas in quotidian life? Where were the guides to demonstrate these ideas in the everyday? I found the Sufis and my true teacher in Samuel Lewis. Numerous useful practices were given that formed the body of his teaching. But the search for a variety of holy ones with a variety of views also seemed part of the requisite education. Murshid Lewis himself drew from numerous sources. He delineates three kinds of monks in zendos: (a) rice bags, who have come to escape the turmoil of life and have a place to stay, (b) sutra reciters, whose delight is in the intellect, and (c) those with the real insight into Dharma. It turned out there were these kinds and more in the Holy Zoo.

ود

Back in Chicago, when I'd first read *The Joyous Cosmology* by Alan Watts, it was as if a prophetic, enlightened author was pointing his finger west to California. I thought of Watts as a true Holy Man, one who had fled religion to seek a more expanded view. Then someone told me he lived in Sausalito. By 1973, he had heard the Sufi Choir, loved it, invited us all out to his houseboat to sing and party, and wrote a rave review of our first album for *Rolling Stone*. He was a sweet, gentle, generous man, but to my amazed disappointment, he was also a practiced alcoholic.

Why does one need alcohol in their Joyous Cosmology? I do. I split a bottle of wine with Devi each evening in our living-room corner bistro. Over my life span, if I'd judged the addicted too harshly I wouldn't have read many, if not most of, the writers I love or listened to many of the musicians who shaped my musical voice. Isn't one mark of a realized person the acceptance of another *as they are*? Show me the perfect human. But I must confess, Understanding Reader, that dear Alan was one more pedestaled father to bite the dust, one more Holy One mainly in mind.

৯

I am five. Dad and I have a little leaping game we play. The four back porch steps are neither steep nor deep. They end at a narrow sidewalk, beyond which lies the thick grass of the lawn. I would stand on the second or third step and jump with all my might into the waiting arms of Dad, who stood ready at the edge of the grass. It was a little dangerous but, since he would always catch me, a lot of fun. On this day, he doesn't catch me—he sees that I will land without injury, steps aside, and I land on the grass unhurt but shocked and angry. Frowning, I look up from the green. With arched eyebrows he looks down and says, "Never trust your father."

That seems mean-spirited, yes? Or did Dad know human nature well enough to warn me against the dangers of setting up fathers, or surrogate fathers, on pedestals? Spiritual lore is stuffed with stories of high teachers disabusing their disciples of idealized devotion by similar acts of seeming meanness, or even cruelty.

৯

Every Sunday morning, from the age of nine, I attended Rockdale Avenue Temple School. Even at that young age I knew that the preaching, the Bible stories, and the wretched hymns were nothing I ever wanted to be alive in. With the help of bossy, bored, faith-propped teachers, not to mention the self-righteous Rabbi Shyst and the absent-minded Rabbi Schmegegge, I learned over the many Sundays that rejection of what you know to be deceiving is a crucial form of wisdom recognition. Most of the kids in my class leaned in this same direction, and my parents also, but rebellion against our cultural norms was unthinkable except, of course, as a test of bravery. We had some brave boys in our Sunday school, ever braver as they were shamed. But those years of glazing over at moralizing prayers and wrathful writ had an unexpected denouement thirty years later, as will soon be told.

৯

In 1981, the Mount Madonna Choir invited the Sufi Choir to give a performance at their spiritual center near Santa Cruz, California. The resident yoga master was Hari Dass Baba (1923-2018), a smallish playful man with an aura of sunlight. At age twenty-nine Hari Dass had taken a vow of silence and, for the next sixty-six years, carried with him a small chalkboard, which was all he needed to speak with the world. The Sufi Choir performed, we all had a refined party afterwards and we slept overnight in the homes of our new friends. The next morning, there was a brief yoga presentation, after which questions for Hari Dass Baba were invited. Baba-ji listened intently to each question and answered with only a few words written quickly in white chalk on his little board. I concocted a pride-of-knowledge query about the nature of music. I forget the content, but the idea was to make me sound brilliantly knowledgeable. Without hesitation, Hari Dass Baba wrote on his board, WHAT IS SOUND?

We so often say, "That was a moment that changed my life." Well, this one really did. The Yogi's reply unbound all my conditions and shot an arrow directly to Source. All pretense evaporated, my question disappeared, and the sun-limned present became all I needed. Many have loved Hari Dass Baba and cherished the many moments he has given us. He died during the writing of this book, but his light is in my being as I write.

৯

From a 1984 birthday letter to my seventy-four-year-old Dad:

> The Wise Ones say that life should begin anew with every breath. Half my brain understands what they say; the other half says *show me one who can do it.* From time to time I've thought I've met a really bona fide one. True, I may have met the Wise One many

times and not known it. Maybe it was the cab driver I found myself drawn to.

Ten years ago, when the Sufi Choir was at the height of its popularity, we often performed benefits for some worthy cause featuring other bands and choirs and at least one big-name guru, who was the big draw. On one such evening, we were billed with a celebrated north Indian mystic named Swami Muktananda, who, within a few years of residence in the United States, had collected a hundred thousand disciples. Perhaps because I was beginning to sense my own power, I was extremely cynical about his. So I made a point of seeking him out backstage.

I was reminded of the old Stan Kenton days. Amid the sandbags, the flys, the Klieg lights, and the union stagehands, there sat the Great Man. But this time was different. The incense was sweet. The rose petals were everywhere, and from Swami Muktananda, seated on a velvet throne, there issued a radiant sphere that lit up your insides. I tried to see the frayed stitch, the hidden mole, the fatal secret, but there was only this gentle middle-aged man with light around his body. He took my hands in his and gave me a *darshan* of bright, quiet joy. "Okay," I said to myself, "I've seen it once."

Now it's 1984. In the February issue of *CoEvolution Quarterly*, there is a merciless exposé of this same Muktananda who, it appears, collected five million in Swiss accounts, did in one virgin per night, and violently abused those who threatened to squeal. "Next time," he said to one young lassie who, among others, did eventually speak out, "don't wear underpants." He died suddenly a few months after he confided to his successor, "I thought they'd hang me first."

So who can you believe? I was illuminated twice by Swami Muktananda. Once in his lifetime, before he had succumbed to his own power. And once again thanks to posthumous revelations. The answer is, you can't believe anybody, really. You have to be born on your own breath.

The Swami perfectly modeled a fundamental contradiction implicit in the profession of inner guidance: on the one hand, his perfect darshan; on the other, a scoundrel, or worse. So once again, how can a seeker separate the message from the messenger?

The judicious aspect of wisdom is the discernment between what is of benefit and what is dross. Maybe wisdom itself consists in that very recognition—having the experience to know that a thing that looks bad looks good in another light, and vice versa. Maybe Trungpa's alcoholism is the devil to the angel of his realization. Maybe my father really *was* loving his son by stepping aside. Maybe we really *did* have to hang Muktananda before appreciating his gentle clarity. Truth, fiction; meat, poison—wisdom cannot be pinned down. Authentic wise ones have to be on their toes, ready for the counter-spin, the bad hop. Maybe the mind of God changes every time a crow caws. Kabir has warned us: *Don't go back to sleep!*

❧

So, what was the "unexpected" denouement from thirty years ago in Sunday school? Zalman Schachter-Shalomi (1924-2014) was a Hasidic rabbi trained in the Lubavitch Orthodox tradition. He had wide interests, great curiosity, and a great heart. In his late thirties, he encountered LSD, the hippies, and the Sufis. Immersed in the born-again Aquarian consciousness of Berkeley and San Francisco, he attracted many followers in sympathy with his cross-cultural and mystical ideas and founded what was known as the Aquarian Minyan. Pir Vilayat Khan, son and successor of Inayat Khan, initiated him as a Sufi Sheikh. And he was drawn to the music of The Sufi Choir, especially my musical setting of the seminal Jewish prayer, the *Shema*. Zalman and I had never met until one evening when we shared a gig on the UC Berkeley campus. Afterward, we sat on the floor in a quiet corner of the ballroom and settled down for a schmooze with some good old California Red.

Considering all my youthful resistance to Judaism as a religion, I was delighted to meet this large, loving, highly articulate seeker. An Orthodox rabbi wide open to the sky? I told Zalman about my early Jewish religious and cultural experiences, my refusal at age thirteen to go through with my bar mitzvah under the guidance of our hypocritical and narrow-spirited rabbi, and how, despite my continual disregard for Jewish prayer and practice, this omission continued, at age thirty-seven, to haunt me. Zalman was leaning in.

"And so, Zalman," I said recklessly, "why don't *you* bar mitzvah me?"

"*Now?*" he asked, leaning back with his bushy eyebrows raised.

"No, not now," I answered giddily. "I want to go through the whole megillah—learn to sing the chants in Hebrew, wear the robe, pass the test."

He said it would take the good part of a year.

I said okay.

He said I could tutor with one of his students.

I said okay.

My tutor turned out to be a pleasant young woman, herself on a Rabbinical path, whom I had known from my Sufi circle. A course of lessons was set up. Zalman gifted me his own musical anthology of ancient songs and chants filtered through centuries of European Jews—I think he had hopes I would find a new American style for them, so the whole project felt collaborative. I did my homework and every other week showed up at my tutor's house. We grew fond of each other, I took my lesson, and I went home. The next week, I would come back with more Hebrew and more songs learned. Zalman gathered a minyan of ten men. When the bar mitzvah date came, I donned the elaborate robe, shawl, and yarmulke Kay had sewn for me and performed my lessons successfully. As was evidently the custom, at the victorious conclusion of the ceremony, the minyan delighted in throwing candy, *very hard candy*, at the bar mitzvah boy. There were many direct hits. Having never been to a bar mitzvah (!), I was unaware of this ritual and painfully stunned: a rabbit snared, a pond frog tortured by mean boys. Repeatedly stung by millennia of cellophane-wrapped, crystalized Jewish shame, I wanted to cry and crawl under the table. Although I showed nothing then, a boiling rage settled into the belly of this newly born adult and lasted for months until one day, I understood it.

A bar mitzvah is a direct transmission of Jewish wisdom given to boys at puberty as a vow to carry on their lineage through their generation. It marks adulthood; it says, "Today I am a man." I had chosen to bypass this rite when I was thirteen, but now that I was in the driver's seat, I had permission to speak and feel as an adult feels. What I felt, to my astonishment, was my fury at my early inculturation of a self-righteous, provincial, superficial interpretation of Judaism, one that reduced it to the cult of a vengeful God and a Chosen People. But now, having been initiated through a power-conferring religious rite by a rabbi I fondly trusted, I carried the authority to reject forever the arrogant and woefully incomplete religious education I had received. I felt free at last of an unwanted identity.

In later years, unsurprisingly, my view and my heart softened. Religion is, after all, what we make of it; observance is up to whomever, and we all get to choose. It was pointless to be angry. I never mentioned any of this to Zalman, of course. But the truly odd thing is how his deeply loving guidance resulted in *permission*, and the permission led to rage, and the rage atomized, finally, into full acceptance. Open sky!

Zalman was a unifier, a resolver of seeming opposites, a compassionate force for peace, a genuine Wise One. In this case, the message and the messenger were dancing cheek to cheek.

❧

Pir-o-Murshid Inayat Khan (1882-1927) is the teacher credited with pioneering Sufism in the Western world in the early years of the 20th century. He founded the Sufi Order (now the Inayati Order) with centers all over the world. His writings are famous and influential. *The Mysticism of Sound* has become a link between music and Source for many thousands of practicing musicians, including myself. Inayat Khan died at age forty-five. He was a very young Wise One, full of grace.

His youngest son, Vilayat, was named his successor at an early age. It is often difficult to be the son of a great man, and Valayat had a difficult early life. Samuel Lewis died when Pir Valiyat was in his fifties; since Murshid Lewis was a direct disciple of Inayat Khan, it was assumed that Pir Vilayat would take over the guidance of Lewis's disciples, which was fine with some of us and not so fine with others. Vilayat was emboldened to institute constraints within our community that many of us felt were manifestations of a subterranean homophobia and misogyny, antithetical to our rainbow acceptance. Also, drugs were forbidden, a deal breaker. An inner circle of his strong women disciples disabused him of these tendencies and, to his great credit, Pir Vilayat developed a more accepting spirit. He had a loquacious intellectual side but it was mixed with a certain tenderness, and with a sincere longing to articulate the Sufi message of his father and his lineage. He also had powerful *siddhis*, a deep connection with the inner world that allowed him to guide meaningful meditations and discerning guidance.

I have always held Mozart as my secret musical father but had never confessed that to Pir. Once, deep inside a cave in the mountains above Chamonix, he interrupted our darshan by saying, "Allaudin, why do I always see the spirit of Mozart in a blue light around you?" That was an astonishing corroboration of two secret truths of mine (Mozart, blue). In a subsequent conversation, he referred to the fractious rift between him and Lewis' followers. "Before *the break*," he was saying, but I interrupted him, asking innocently, "What break?" He examined me quizzically, then said, "Oh well, *you*, Allaudin, you don't have to worry about such things." This was an important validation for me: that musicians are exempt from political, administrative, religious, and social factions, that we fly above the radar and are justified in thinking of our music as teaching that transcends such earth-bound concerns.

Pir Vilayat played the cello. He also loved to conduct Bach choirs—the larger, the better. He had briefly studied to be a composer and was as deeply affected by music as anyone I have known. You could tell when he played or when he conducted that the music was coming down to him from the angels. In the earthly execution of that music, however, he was a most challenged cellist, and when he conducted, few could follow his ecstatic facial expressions or wild gesticulations. Yet whenever he played the cello for his disciples, adulation arose in the room because people heard the sincerity of his heart.

Pir considered me to be his accompanist and musical supporter, available upon request. Seated at the piano, however, I was in musical purgatory. Pir had the metric sense of fog, a vibrato Ganges-wide, and a quasi-accurate sense of pitch. To avoid chaos, I became bold enough to correct him in public. To my appreciative surprise he took my suggestions with great seriousness—as though, sitting among those upturned faces, I was his music teacher. "There is a dot after the G, Pir, and don't forget the flat in front of the E." Such became our performances. Honoring the lineage, I did this for years. I wanted to keep the peace. I collected and rehearsed choirs so Pir could conduct them. I was the musical director of a wild extravaganza of his called *The Cosmic Mass*, his chef-d'oeuvre involving local casts of hundreds in half a dozen different cities. *Time* magazine reviewed a Manhattan performance at the Church of St. John the Divine, headlining it "Cosmic Mish-Mash." But the piece was not without merit—it was a sincere theatrical panorama attempting to display experientially the unity of religious ideals, and was instructive and illuminating to many of its hundreds of participants.

One of Pir Vilayat's life desires was to conduct Bach's B Minor Mass. On a day in his mid-seventies, he called me from France asking me to travel to various centers around Europe to train choirs so that on his eightieth birthday, he could conduct the assembled singers and have his wish come true. I replied, "Pir, I'm sure we could find some venture more truly collaborative." There ensued a long pause. I could hear the ocean between us. "Well, Allaudin," he cleared his throat, "I see you've gone beyond our orbit."

This felt too sharply cut. I wrote Pir a letter explaining how my life as a composer, author, and private teacher had become my calling. I was gratified to receive this reply:

"I feel and have echoes of the fact that I may have offended you in inviting you to coach my choirs. It was an excuse to draw you into our work because I felt your participation was so very important. But it is clear that you are placing all your energy into composing and are orbiting outside the kind of involvement you have helped us with so much in the past. I realize that it would have been better to ask you to simply teach people music and encourage their creative abilities."

Subsequently I composed a setting of one of his father's prayers, called *Pir*, and sent the score to his man in Europe, Ophiel, an excellent and amenable musician who played, with considerably more devotion, a role similar to mine. He rehearsed the piece assiduously with his own choir and it was sung beautifully on the occasion of Pir Vilayat's eightieth birthday. Ophiel sent me a tape. Well done!

A magnificent wisdom from the east passed through Pir Vilayat Khan to a waiting Western world. His teaching has benefited millions of us. The relationship between message and messenger always needs discernment, and this case is no exception. Pir Vilayat Khan was the struggling son of a great man, and he deserved everything he could get. As with all my adopted fathers, time has humanized Pir for me. He was the second to last of my Holy Ones. My real father is the last. After that, no more. I'll get to those ashes someday and then, next after his, mine.

We all take our turn alternating between being holy and being selfish; it is the intrinsic reciprocity between Self and self. A narrow ledge seems to be set in place awaiting the Holy Ones; there will always be those who choose to stand there, and whose stance we choose to recognize. Ultimately, the need for the distinction between them and us falls away as we teach one another what we need to know: to be born on each breath.

Pir Triumphant

14

The Izness Bizness

"It is wise to agree that all things are one."
-Heraclitus (fl. 500 BC)

"There remains but one word to express the true road: IS.
IS has no beginning, and never will be destroyed. It is whole, still, and
without end.
It neither was nor will be.
It simply is NOW, altogether, one, continuous."
-Parmenides (putative founder of ontology, fl. 475 BC)

"All in One, One in All, All in All."
-Plotinus (205-270 AD)

"In math one jumps from numbers to the infinite—suddenly—and the same
is true in spiritual experience."
-Murshid Samuel Lewis (1896-1971)

"Seems like we're just put down here, don't nobody know why."
-A West Virginia woman as quoted by Annie Dillard

"You were always frowning when you were a child...you always looked as
though you were thinking about something."
-Rosella Mathieu to her son

"What is this?"
-Leonard Bernstein, reportedly, at the moment of his death

Opening my eyes as if for the first time, I'm looking at a surrounding globe of abundance. Wonder first: the green of trees and the motion of wind in them; a toy fire truck casually upside down on the brown and blue carpet. And here, behold! I am a living creature with a name, with dancing fingers. They are so beautiful. And look! So are you!

When the wonder settles, the wide world seems whole. Then the question occurs to your mind: What IS this?

Ontology is the field concerned with nature of Being. I call this inquiry, along with all its professional purveyors, the Izness Bizness. What sort of field of study is that? Does it involve hypothetical first principles? Is it a path of strutting reason? Or lurking faith? Will it tell me if existence is static Being or emergent Becoming? Or if I can transcend into Oneness? Or that I am already there and need only to realize it? Will it tell me if, from my realization of the nature of Being, I will become wise? Or compassionate?

I find philosophy in general and ontology in particular a drag, but a necessary drag. Drag is the price paid to obtain lift, like the drag that holds an airplane aloft. What if, however, looking as if for the first time at the surrounding globe of abundance, I *don't* pop the question? What if I realize that I *am* IS, no questions asked? That precious state is called Wonderstanding, and Wonderstanding has no language. I have observed that this abiding sense of wholeness, well conditioned by life's buffeting, does generate a sharpened sense of what is just and kind. That seems to me like a working definition of wisdom, but where is the ontology there?

These days, there are times I do look like I'm thinking about something, except when I don't look like that, because those times I'm not thinking about anything. This chapter traces my windmillian jousting with the concerns of ontology and their evaporative ways, beginning at age two and continuing to the present.

A Brief Ontological History of the Author

At age two, the Dew God, Billius, was merging with the woods. This is a particularly abiding memory, but the mystery is that in the *feeling* of the memory there is no room for a witness. Yet the feeling of that memory is still very much with me.

At age five, standing alone in the Kindergarten cloakroom, I experienced an intense moment of merge in an unremarkable setting. Through the window of the long, narrow room where all the coats were hung and the boots lined up, there was a street of apartment buildings; at my feet were some yellow boots; and throughout my body, there was a flushed sense that mine was a complete life. I needed nothing else. The impression of this moment is still bright.

In the second grade, I found that the girls playing hopscotch and jump rope on their side of the playground were far more companionable than the boys playing war on our side, so I started to play on the girls' side. I was happy and whole there, and learned the games, and how to be fair, and the girls let me in. After a few months, the grown-ups thought I was learning to be queer, so one day, *both* second-grade teachers interrupted our hopscotch game by marching me off from the girls' side, saying this was no place for boys, and if I were caught playing there again, I would be sent home.

For the six years of walks to and from grade school, I took a shortcut that led me over the vast lawn of the Saint Theresa Retirement Home, through back yards, between the hedges separating houses, avoiding the mean dogs and befriending the dear ones. On the way I lost myself completely in sensate experience; the details sank so deep into memory that I can now recall every step of the fifteen-minute journey. The distant voices of the kids on the playground, the close hum of bees, the flying cries of birds, the beauty waving from the littlest blossoms in the growing green, and the dew, or the snow, or the play of shadows on the grass—each and all were entire worlds. The merge was the best part of most days. If others had similar experiences, I never heard about them.

This sense of merging was never articulated in either the Christian working-class environment of my grade school or the striving upper-middle-class Jewish culture of my high-school crowd. If I tried to speak of it I was made fun of, so by age seven or so I stopped trying. And I was afraid to share such states with my parents because I had never heard them speak of anything close to what I was feeling.

Precociously, Jacqueline and I fell in love when we were eight. For the two years of third and fourth grades, we were constantly getting in trouble for passing love notes to each other. Near her house, in hilly Afton Woods, a gracefully curved wall built up from thin flat stones protected a small elm tree from the steep hill beside it. Between the tree and the wall was just enough room for two kids to stand facing one another. At Jacqueline's suggestion, we slipped between the elm tree and the rock wall and, hands to our sides, touched slightly lingering lips. A week later, sitting on the floor next to her kitchen stove, we kissed again, quicker. I asked Mom if people who fell in love in the third grade ever got married. "Only in the movies," she replied.

With Jackie as my girlfriend, I went into euphoric states quite distinct from those of young kids playing tag on the lawn or rolling around in the grass. This was disappearance of self into feeling for Jackie as a loved yet separate person, my first real Other. Sometimes we seemed telepathically connected, and when that happened, she was my world, a world with a higher altitude of aliveness and knowing.

❧

When I was nine, my father acquired an oil painting called *Blue Boy*, painted by a family friend. The canvas was divided into quadrants, each showing some different aspect of a young boy. The left upper quadrant showed the top part of his face, with solemn, staring, expressionless eyes. The other three quadrants were Mondrian-like forms of deep blue to gray-blue color. The fragmentation of the quadrants, the solemnity, and the dark understatement was a disturbing corroboration of the isolation of my own inner life. *Blue Boy* was placed on the wall directly above our spinet piano, three feet from my nose as I played the instrument. For many years, practicing every day, I subliminally became Blue Boy, and have been ever since. I still strongly identify with the color, which seems to connect me to the deep ego-loss experiences of childhood. I have an extensive collection of cobalt glass that adorns my studio and is everywhere in our house. It is also the color of the Healing Buddha.

❧

Suspecting that I would not follow in his footsteps in the publishing business, my father decreed I should be an astrophysicist, so he hired Dr. Hanford, Physics professor at the University of Cincinnati, as a private tutor for his ten-year-old boy. Dr. Hanford, then in his late twenties, had been a polio victim as a child. He used a wheelchair most of the time but got around on crutches fairly well. He was extremely bright, had a playful smile, and immediately accepted me as his student. What we did in our lessons was play.

During the first lesson, we played with some ping-pong balls lifted by compressed air coming out of jets. The game was about how many balls you could balance in the air stream for how long. I began to see and sense the air, which was real and could form sensate shapes. The game gave me a lasting understanding of gas as rarefied mass. During another lesson, we pondered the long, heavy pendulum suspended from the huge dome of the physics building as it slowly swept out a large circle three inches above the floor. After a patient hour, I had made the connection between the circling pendulum at my feet and the rotation of the earth, a scale of gravity far different from what I could feel directly.

At another lesson, we put on thin rubber gloves and swooshed our hands around in Mason jars full of mercury. How could metal be a liquid? Well, here it was, streaming through my fingers. And we spent one memorable session playing an elaborate game of tag involving a blacked-out lecture hall and a flashlight. The hunter had no flashlight, and the hunted did. He had the choice of turning the flashlight on or off, moving or staying stationary, and if moving, carrying the flashlight with him or laying it down, lit or unlit, on one of the desks. It was an archetypical lesson in empirical science. The inductive evidence was whatever you could contrive to see and hear; on the basis of this, you needed to deduce where your prey was. Dr. Hanford may have been a Full Professor, but he was also a Full Puer, and surprisingly spry at that. The Doctor and I were kids again, playing in obscure shadows of dangerous woods. The game, which ended in a tie, was a core demonstration of the scientific mind at full bore combined with pure ecstatic experience, and it gave me a lasting affection for science.

The next year, my professor friend moved away. His replacement, Dr. Schwart, tried to teach me algebra. "But if *a* stands for a certain number of apples," I whined, "why not just let it be *that* number of apples?" No matter his mounting impatience, I couldn't leap to the algebraic abstraction. "If he's going to be a physicist," Dr. Schwart told my father, "he will have to learn mathematics, and he doesn't seem to have the knack for it." Goodbye, physics career. Music seemed a better way to spend my time anyway.

In the sixth grade, Diane Peckinpaugh, a green-eyed, freckled, quick-witted southern girl; Pat Hand, a soft, subtle, and loving girl; and I would take walks after school, arms around each other, laughing, counting to a hundred, not stepping on any cracks in the sidewalk. I am swirling in a heaven of youthful becoming, and our trio is the entirety of what can be known.

All of the stories above involve some form of ego-loss, some aspect of the merging of self with what is felt beyond self. As I approached puberty, however, relationships with my female classmates became circumscribed by my testosterone-fortified projections. I had more meaningful connections with my male musician friends. As is chronicled in *A Young Voice* (Chapter 4), *The Old Man* (Chapter 5), and *The Journalist* (Chapter 9), from the age of thirteen, music and orgasm had become my primary channels for ego transcendence. However mixed with ambition and aggression these may have been, when I was immersed in either, I could sense the pulse of the world's vastness beyond my individual knowing of it.

Sexual Union

There are dozens of ways of being assured that your partner is sharing some communal experience with you, and millions of ways of getting it wrong. So what follows is about me and my own perceptions. I have only an inkling of what others think or feel, then, now, ever, unless they tell me and then, by definition, only partially. Isn't that a primary condition of the Other?

The sixties were licentious days for most males and many females in my theater culture. At the Second City, we had a sort of dance card attitude about matchups, so there were always two or three waitresses or actresses to choose from, or who would choose me. I was the flashy pianist on his nightly perch at a famous cabaret theater; that I could easily consort with willing women was a simple given.

I will spare you those stories, but there was one long affair that did wake me up quite unexpectedly. Ann, a Second City waitress in her early thirties, was preternaturally quiet. When she did speak a few syllables, they usually bespoke three pages' worth of comprehension and response. I could feel her receptive aspect, even if only as a passing nod in the lobby. We began to go home together quite often. I'd play for her—practice, since late night is when Bill practiced—and I had the feeling she was internalizing every note. Then on to the bedroom, weed, nakedness, Mozart on the stereo, and sexual union that expanded, over the many months of training, into a most complete model of female/male bonding. This time it wasn't the passion of possession; it was calm abiding in the heaven of One Body. We seldom had actual conversations, but when she would say some words, I would really listen and hear. When we would just lie quietly touching, I could roam around in the stillness of her gardens, be quickened by the *permission* to enter the bright room of her mind, and feel the warmth of her heart. She gave me her expanded Self with scarcely a word to wreck it, just this quiet, gratifying sensuality.

Of course, the limits soon became apparent. The edges of our proto-linguistic mosaic began to fray, the sex gradually became routine, and my intellect was restless. One night I found myself unconsciously counting left-right thrusts up to sixty-four—sixteen bars' worth. Uh-oh. The next night, when Ann came to work, I found a quiet corner and said gently, "Thanks for showing me what it is and what it isn't." She nodded with a little smile, and after that night I never saw her again.

Increasingly I felt the harshness of this. Eventually I came to recognize the profound loneliness, the silent longing that had produced such meticulously manicured repression in such a magnificently capacious woman. I wanted to hold her again and reassure her that life has meaning and is good. I tried to find her many times, but she was gone, gone for good, and here I sit writing.

స

During those years of sexual freedom, there were a few mutually generous times when the ego was atomized and a larger truth emerged. Murshid Lewis says, "When love is linked to eternity, the heart has no time or place, the body is safe there, and one carries the world as its child. When the heart has no time or place, being becomes empty of a needy self, and personal history evaporates."

Sex with unselfish love and mutual desire is a direct line to an original state—from the first vibrations of the Big Bang, to the subsequent oscillations between potential and manifestation, to the biochemistry of meiosis and beyond. All are in a state of eternal Becoming or, in the language of science, "emergent reality." We feel most good, most close to what is real, when we are most reminded of this eternal transformation. We are graced with a sense of total union, the mutuality of the merge—one body, then one no-body. During a fully realized, mutually loving human orgasm—a good come—we are in close resonance with eternal Becoming, Everyman and Everywoman conflated into Pure Being.

Let me add a quote from Judith Viorst in her classic book, *Necessary Losses*:

> The physical merging that sexual union may bring takes us
> back to the oneness of our infancy. Orgasm can be the means

by which we repair the separation of mother and child through the momentary extinction of the self. It is true that few of us consciously climb into the lover's bed in the hope of finding our mommy between the sheets. But the sexual loss of our separateness brings us pleasure, in part, because it unconsciously repeats our first connection.

The wisdom here, the saving grace, is that if sexualized dominion develops into unselfish love, there is an odds-on chance of love being "linked to eternity." Kicking and screaming, you are flown off by the Verities. You bow to a new feeling of rightness. A light that has no gender seeks you. An expansive intention occurs in your love. You can be a true friend to anyone. And you can take no more credit for this than you could for being struck by lightning.

Murshid Lewis: "Real love is a universal communication that runs in all directions. In a spider web, each ring is connected not only with the center but also with each of the others. The love and the community go together."

Now Rumi weighs in:

> Essence is emptiness.
> Everything else, accidental.
>
> Emptiness brings peace to your loving.
> Everything else, disease.
>
> In this world of trickery, emptiness
> Is what your soul wants.

When we begin to learn music, we hear the surface of the sound first without hearing the deeper and ever-deeper meaning. Just as in person-to-person relationships, there is always more listening to be done, and more than one can ever do. And no two listenings are ever the same. Practicing the same fugue over and over is like loving the same person over and over. When we are really listening, the loving is always new.

As earnest beginners, we are concerned with how well we are doing—the mistakes, the little triumphs—but over time, that concern evolves into an appreciation of the beauty of the music itself and how such beauty drives the music-making. It takes more than a life to learn this, so there is no end to the learning. There is, however, a chronology of how the high lusts of the young years pass over into long dinners over wine and reminiscence. You and your lover become an old couple on the porch swing saying *yup* and *way it is* a lot. All that's missing is the cigarette after.

Vocabulary Break

I can write no more words until I speak of a particular word, a vexing word, a word that seems stuck to us like a scrap of double-sided tape. I think that everything in this world is "sacred," or "holy," or "spiritual," or that nothing is. I can usually shake off those terms and find others less exclusive. The especially sticky word, however, is "spiritual." I guess folks use it to describe some aspect of refinement, but I find the term divisive. I cannot find a meaningful boundary between what is spiritual and what is not. Isn't everything both high and low, depending on the view and the lens? Or am I a bleeding-liberal linguist?

A century ago, Inayat Khan wrote, "The whole of life in all of its aspects is one single music; the real spiritual attainment is to tune oneself to the harmony of this perfect music." This lets me feel a little more comfortable using the word.

A Spiritual Path

In 1967, simply being alive in San Francisco was a shift in perception: everything appeared a little loose and transient, more emergent. When I first arrived I knew I was walking in earthquake country. I could feel the geological instability through my feet. My cabaret theater work at the Committee, the Summer of Love, meeting Murshid Lewis and the Sufis, my new job at the San Francisco Conservatory, and the arrival of Lucy Amadea, my first-born, all added up to a larger life. The East Coast and the Midwest began to seem provincial. The present tense became immense. Hello everybody, bring your Truth to San Francisco!

The influence of Inayat Khan and the teachings and presence of Murshid Lewis were my guides. When Murshid died in 1971, we

Me and Poke

all became our own teachers under our gentle, loving, spiritually strong guide, Moinnuddin Jablonski, whose classes taught me how to teach. In 1978, I was initiated as a Sheik, which meant that I could take on disciples, and had the responsibility of continuing both the esoteric and the exoteric teachings of the Chishti Sufi lineage as it passed through Inayat Khan and Murshid Sam Lewis. The methods were heart- and breath-centered, a path of tolerance, inclusion, and spiritual love. I taught music to the Sufi Choir, and the singers taught me a deeper meaning of music than Chicago Bill could ever have imagined.

After about twenty-five years of active teaching and music-making within the Sufi community and the international spiritual community at large, I began to consider my Sufi lineage as my Alma Mater. I had chosen to stay loosely within its disciplines and protocols and teach through its lineage. But I was not seeking the responsibilities of a higher initiation, and slowly separated myself from its activities. I felt I'd learned what I could from chanting the names of God and from heart-centered circle dancing, strong and sweet as those always proved to be. I found that integrating the tropes and practices of the world's religions, despite the idealistic intent, constrained my own experience.

Buddhism

A substantial thread in our Sufi lineage is Buddhist, especially the Mahamudra training of mindfulness, or "watchfulness," and the Dzogchen practice of "falling into awareness." I found the central tenet of Buddhism increasingly attractive: it points toward "emptiness," a state of equanimous, balanced, unformed energy from which both compassion and dispassion arise. I resonated with its focus on the present tense, and the ultimate disappearance of the witness. What is "now"? it continuously asks.

The teachings can be repetitive, it is true, always the same old same old, and all of them would, like Rumi's books, be eventually tossed down the well. But the insights of the Buddha and the centuries of instructional, metaphorical, and poetic commentary seemed beneficial, even necessary at the time.

From the early 2000s to 2021, Devi and I were in a bright and loving Mahamudra sangha guided by Donna McLaughlin. The class was a turning point for me—Donna would bring me from head-bound thought straight to feeling in the moment. The core instruction was to look directly at the mind and *rest right there*. The danger was getting all-too-easily lost spelunking in the enticing crevices and hypnotic caves of dharma—lost, trapped, swallowed whole. But in our sangha, there was much direct looking and resting-right-there. For our mutual benefit, we tried to describe our experiences. When we ran out of words, we started using our hands and body language to say what cannot be said, and laughing, and saying: "Here we are again."

For what I'm calling IZ (because IZ buzzes) there are various words in Sanskrit, Tibetan, and Hindi. In English, it is sometimes called "Buddha nature." I might say "the nature of nature," but I try not to hang on to names; rather, I look directly at what I am given in the present, just like Chögyam Trungpa said I could in a book I'd read many years previously. There's no denying that concepts of Sufi gatha and Buddhist dharma have helped me along—most certainly they have—but ultimately one's education has to be utterly absorbed into the present tense. What has been learned becomes transparent, empty in the moment.

The Ontology of Music

In our Mahamudra sangha, I learned something about being transparent, and began to practice making the music of transparency. It is a rarefied feeling, a sense of being *carried*, but not carried away— carried forward with a breeze at your back. What is called "program music" is avowedly *about* something—think of a ballet, a film score, or Holst's *The Planets*. "Absolute music," on the other hand, is instrumental music, like a Bach fugue or a Mozart string quartet, that is not *about* anything except itself and your listening to it. It is its own story, its own narrative, unscrolling its own meaning in present time, its own non-linguistic description. Unless we distractedly happen to be ruminating about the historical, cultural, or personal contexts of the music, it does not tell us about anything other than its intrinsic sound. So, as an ontological descriptor, it is in a special category— it's about you. When one is playing or listening to such music with complete attention, it seems to approach pure Being. Received as such, absolute music is the ontology I can live most comfortably with.

The Number One Lie

Sometimes, Sympathic Friend, you just have to talk about what's bothering you. Numbers, an indispensable tool for knowing our world, much perturb and sometimes grieve me. They require a mighty leap of abstraction and, shockingly, we have come to rely too heavily on their concepts. And their innocuous ringleader lives incognito among us, closer than our underclothes.

Numbers began with a single slash drawn in the dirt, the stroke of flint against sandstone, a notched stick, a single cow now counted. But the big secret here, the most hidden of all secrets, is that there is no such thing as a single thing. No single thing is entirely detached from every other thing. Any single thing is inseparable from its evolution, from its kind, from its environment, and from its porous boundaries of matter, energy, and time. Not to mention such quantum mysteries as entanglement.

Consider some countable noun: one pencil, this very pencil I am holding in my hand. It is just a pencil, right? I know its shape and purpose, even if I use it for a bookmark, or as a shim, or as a backscratcher. My pencil has a history. Each step of its present form came from growth and assembly; it grew from living wood, and the minerals and chemicals in it were mined and manufactured.

It exists also at the molecular and atomic scales. If I make myself small enough to be inside the molecular structure at the polished wood surface, I would find a gallery of gaseous exchanges, acids from human skin in a celebration with acids in paint, and I would sense the wood fibers losing electrons to oxidization. A trillionth of a second, called a picosecond, is how long it takes light to travel less than a millimeter; an electron could have a lovely courtship and respectable wedding in that amount of time. So, when is *now* for my pencil? It appears that *now* is just as fuzzy as *forever*, and what was, what is, and what will become of my pencil, whatever it is, is subsisting through an infinite-ring circus of uncountable events.

The phrase "one pencil" abstracts us away from the pencil's living choreography and turns it into a concept, the idea of pencil. *Abstract* is from the Latin *abstractus,* meaning pulled away, detached, stolen from: the *idea* of something stolen away from its complex reality. Is idea reality? I'm asking you. We leave out living nature when we say *one thing* and settle for its ghost. The price of numeration is the loss of wholeness. It has transformed our aboriginal-forest mind into a civilized-computational mind. The more evolved the modern brain, the more it uses abstraction to navigate the world. But there is hidden loss with the advance of conceptual thought, including not only numbers but also words, symbols, memes, money, icons, mobbed celebrities, charismatic dictators, computer algorithms, and indeed every form of abstraction under the bright heavens. We all get snookered behind ideas.

I spend half my life elaborately describing music to people and the other half trying to get them to listen to it as pure sensation. What ancient knowledge have we had to abandon in order to become older and supposedly wiser? I am forever hunting down the modern incubus in our innocence, the invisible thief of sensual purity.

The danger of numbers is in their radicalism: of all the concepts we use, theirs is the greatest theft from essence. And yet...no math, no civilized life. Which would you rather have, flying or cross-country walking? Internet or essence? Fresh veggies or turnips from the root cellar? These are questions you might ask. We need to listen to the barking Toto. He is warning us to draw back the red curtain so we can see for ourselves how the Wizard of Number One is dressed in such plain, everyday clothes.

Sister Sue and First Grandchild

The View From The Middle

For me, physics is not separate from love; it's just another way of playing out the dance of connectivity and unity, the non-duality of apparent opposites. Thanks to the modeling of Dr. Hanford, I've always sought a more subjective view of physics that begins with an inner sensate knowing and proceeds outward toward theory and empirical corroboration. David Bohm, in the early 1960s, was the first to catch my attention. "The notion of a separate organism," he said, "is clearly an abstraction, as is also its boundary. Underlying all is unbroken wholeness. Mind and matter are not separate, they are different aspects of whole and unbroken movement."

From the point of view of both quantum mechanics and cosmology, we humans seem to be smack dab in the middle of everything. The total size of it all, the unfathomable scale, stuns the mind. At the large end of the scale is the cosmic event horizon, defined as the distance that light has traveled from the Big Bang over 13 billion years ago in order to meet the eye. Now we would also have to make some sense of the six *trillion* miles light travels in a single year.

The opposite end of the scale is even more challenging to imagine. The smallest distance we can measure is called the Planck length: in meters, 16^{-34}. That distance is about a 10 trillion trillionth of the diameter of a hydrogen atom, and there are about 12^{24} hydrogen atoms in an amoeba. This is difficult to imagine even for those theoretical physicists for whom these numbers are everyday tools. But it's instructive to put yourself through it to see how far our limited mind is from the enormity of IZ. You can stand with half of yourself expanded into the cosmos, the other half mute with amazement at the intricacy of the ground beneath your shoes.

A dynamic canvas is presented in *The Order of Time* by Carlo Rovelli, a lucidly articulate theoretical physicist. "Physicists," he writes, "call 'fields' the substances that to the best of our knowledge constitute the weave of the physical reality of the world. The world is like a superimposition of strata, of fields that flex, stretch, and jostle with each other. Equations describe the reciprocal influences that all fields have on each other; spacetime is one of those fields." This is hardly a static picture; it is an animated, interwoven world, not unlike the fields of LSD-modulated mandalas that Beethoven's String Quartet in C-sharp Minor allowed me to see while on the lip of insanity.

All I have in my body prison are my mirrors and how I translate their sensory barrage—no more than that, especially if I'm convinced otherwise. There is no place to stand, and I'll enjoy my moving place in the moving maze, mistrust the brainstorm, and trust the breath, which, as Murshid Sam Lewis says, "is more refined and carries vibrations that are undertones from the hidden spheres of the unseen world...the connecting link between the above and the below, between the below and the above."

Central to Buddhism is The Middle Way, the path of the included middle. The most beneficial aspects of experience are drawn from all sides and forged over time and practice into an ideal balance. I sense a crucial need for the empirical sciences to honor and include the subjective point of view, by which is meant *your* view and mine. The subjective view is perforce limited, but its limits are reciprocal to those of the empirical method, along with the math crucial for the measurement and organization of what we observe. We need to calculate what we cannot feel and feel what we cannot calculate. Both must be in our view to keep our balance on the high wire of the middle way.

I have come to believe that consciousness, according to the conditions of wherever it finds itself in the universal skein, is everywhere, and, given the entire maze at once, there is no distinct boundary between life and death. Death in the human octave is life in the octave of a water molecule. There is intrinsic, embodied intelligence, however strange it may look from our scale, wherever one can imagine to look. Obliquely we can know being and Being at once because they are not separate but interrelated, merging and reemerging fields. The analytical neo-cortex is bravely doing what it has evolved to do by separating them. So we shall stage an intervention and say, *The analytical mind leads us so close to the truth because it is what led us away from it in the first place.* Again, there are no paradoxes in nature. They are in your head. We need the middle way between mind and Mind.

A Middling Practice

Close your eyes.

Take a deep breath all the way *in* to a dot in the center of your forehead, your "third eye."

Breathe all the way *out* to the horizon.

Repeat *in* to the dot, *out* to the horizon.

Repeat once more.

With a normal breath, rest in the middle.

Emptiness and Form

Emptiness, a slippery word used in Buddhism, refers to an alert mind with no organized content, no thought, no story. *Entropy* in physics generally refers to "disorder." More and more scientists, however, believe that what appears to us as disorder from our scale of observation is actually our blurred vision—we just don't know how to see what is there. The blur is in us, not in nature. Nature is neither blurred nor non-blurred.

Form is the complimentary term referring to something appearing in a fixed state. The *less* solid the form—think of swirling gas in space—the *more* potential for transformation into something else, like a planet, to occur. The *more* solid the form—think of a diamond—the *less* potential for transformation into something else, like a firefly, to occur. Emptiness allows the greatest potential for transformation into form.

In meditation, when the mind comes to a place where no thought is held, the potential for the "nature of nature" to manifest as form is at a maximum. You might notice a feeling associated with this potential to manifest, to express. In Chinese medicine it is called *chi*, the invisible, activating source of energy. To me it feels like a continual surge, infinitely collaborative. But the feeling of this potential is yours to discover and is there for the looking.

"Space is not empty," David Bohm writes. "It is full, a plenum as opposed to a vacuum, and is the ground for the existence of everything, including ourselves." The radiant-hearted Sufi Murshida Asha Greer used to say, "I like to fill the full with empty in order to make more room."

Projective Ontology

My experience tells me that the most fundamental aspect of Being, what is beneath the littlest toe of the last turtle down, is a quality that is sometimes called Purpose, or Impulse, but that I like to call Intention. Intention, as a substrate of what is, has no dimension, is everywhere, and has no where. My realization is that Intention cannot be measured as a quantity but can be *felt* as a quality. Not measured. *Felt.*

Intention, then, is what is *felt* to be done: It is full of potential, of possibility, and occurs to Form (us, for instance) as a knowing at the appropriate scale. At my human scale, I feel Intention as my hunger, my sexual desire, my anger and confusion, my loving kindness. Intention is seated inside the next brush stroke, the next grace note, the next poetic metaphor, any step I take, whatever I am feeling is to be done right now. It is a continuous present Being inside me, ready to ignite the next happening in time.

Now, how could I possibly know that whatever I happen to feel is fundamental to anything? Well, I don't, Dear Reader, I do not. I'm just suggesting that we say this and see what happens. That is what some philosophers do with their intuitions, and then they think. And that's what scientists do, and then they experiment, then think some more. For any of us to have the slightest notion of Intention in any octave other than our own, we have to feel it in our own octave first and surmise how it might be elsewhere.

We could call this Projective Ontology. It asks if an action I feel arising from the wholeness of my alert, empty mind is a key to the most fundamental energy to be known, and could be mapped micro to macro with coordinates appropriately adjusted for scale.

Intention is connective; it is a quality that exists everywhere but is experienced differently on different scales (photon, human, solar system). Intention occurs and becomes experience according to the prevailing conditions of its place in the maze, harmonizing with form across the shapes of time and space. Imagine you are a quark: what is next to be done? Mitochondria ask their version of the same. A grasshopper waits for its cue to hop, a neutron star to implode. There is no way we can know everything that could happen in the whole story, but it could be revealing to project our deepest sensate feeling of something-about-to-happen, appropriately adjusted in unknowable ways onto all orders of magnitude from quarks to communities of galaxies, and bring that back home as cosmic wisdom to ourselves.

Feeling Intention

Here is a three-minute practice:

Sit quietly for a few moments. Settle inward.

At the deepest inward point, feel what is to be done but do nothing.

If there are thoughts, feelings, or physical movements, let those happen if they need to, but keep focusing on the impulses to do something, not the doings. Untangle Intention from any action.

Even involuntary actions, like breathing or salivating, or sweating, are part of this looking, but at a deeper level. So keep looking.

Look ever more *directly* at Intention and its various entertaining forms and flavors.

Stop after about three minutes.
Repeat whenever you feel like it.

੭

Wisdom entails going back to Source. More fully, wisdom entails the *recognition*, in our octave, of the active agency of Intention, and using it to balance the hours of our lives. The key to your unique knowing of Source is not only within you; it is the most fundamental feeling *of* you. That is the solution to every koan, and the very jewel of Dzogchen: You are looking for what is already there.

Rumi says, "When you look for God, God is in the look of your eye." Intention is what you *feel* as you seek; it occurs to the heart of your mind. Wisdom is not only the recognition of Intention, but its judicious playing out in this worldly abundance of greening trees, dancing fingers, and your lovely eyes meeting these hungry words.

These nets that we cast wide, mend, and cast again in the companionship of precious others, along with our reading, writing, and maybe a little frownish thinking, bring *The Ontological History of the Author* up to date.

An Ontology of Ontology

At the top of these verses are four traditional lines of Kagyu teachings. The last five lines are modern additions.

So Close you can't see it
So Simple you can't believe it
So Profound you can't grasp it
So Good you can't accept it

So Natural you can't contrive it
So Pervasive you can't isolate it
So Here you can't find it
So Clear you go right past it
So Now you can't remember it

Lady Bug and White Moth

I am rebelling against civilization, against
reading and writing, so here I sit
clothed, warm, well fed, and reading my writing.

Have you ever noticed how the weeds
and the grasses, tall and leaning, have such majesty?
Still, the sky-blued air is what I long for,
and the flying things in it.

The intelligence embodied in a flying beetle amounts to more
than the difference in intelligence between a mongoose and a man.
Between a mongoose and a man is a hair's breadth.
Between a clean slate, a no-clues-at-first beginning and
this ladybug is—well,
once you've gotten that far, if you're God,
you might as well retire and let the animal fly.

Right now as I'm writing this, and for a long time,
she's been hovering about seven inches in front of my third eye.

And now a tiny white moth is perched on my paper
taking over this poem.
I hold the paper edgewise to my eyes
looking downfield at her resolute squat
her wiggling antennae. "Anything you can do," she says,
"I can do. Anything important, that is."

The Voice

You may live long enough to hear it
as a cry through your bones,
or a Siren song over the storm,
as a keening at the back of your mind,
or a calm music well beyond your own devising.

The Voice calls when the leaping mind
takes a deep breath inside the supine body.

One plain day you'll hear yourself
speaking with that Voice as your own—
you the mother, the mathematician, the madman,
you the lonesome lover the oboe d'amore's story
has suddenly ravished.
The Voice is yours now.

You keep going.
Then the future comes in. Nameless and on fire,
The Voice speaks on its own. You listen.

Your old world is compliant with this new one,
you walk a long way while your Voice speaks and speaks.
When your body gets tired, your mind becomes simple
and you sleep dreamless until morning.

Soon you will hear others talking abut your Voice as a cry
in their own bones, a wind from behind, a heavenly music
they will presently claim as their own.

Very good.
What seemed forgotten shows up on the road in another form.
You keep going. There is no need to look back.

15

End Game

Wisdom comes to us from all sides in every order of time. I try to sort these impressions out, to be discriminating and judicious. I want transparency, but how difficult does that prove when the impressions are about one's *parents* and—as happens—they keep merging with and reemerging from one's own identity?

Lucy Turns Thirteen

In 1980, when my daughter, Lucy, turned thirteen, my Dad, at age seventy-three, thought to write her a letter:

> I was resting in bed for an hour thinking about when I was a boy of thirteen. If there was a difference between boys and girls, no one had yet explained it to me. My folks were good, solid Germans, very down to earth and much minded to end their days "without going to the poorhouse" or "getting into trouble." They believed in work and more work, and family. They didn't read or write except as necessary, or draw, or play a musical instrument. When I started to write, they appeared startled and to my surprise, and I expect to theirs, they bought me a typewriter. Your great-great grandmother Bertha spoke slightly illiterate German for, although she was born here she really never tried to learn English, being of the opinion "Deutschland Uber Alles." She and my grandfather would take me to a beer garden on a Saturday night where my grandfather outraged my grandmother by tipping the waiter a nickel every time he bought a glass of beer.
>
> One night my father took my mother and myself by interurban streetcar into the country to a fun place called Chester Park where

they had free vaudeville. My father had worked all day—he earned $45 a week—which supported us in 1920—and had no rest or change of clothes or bath, and was giving of himself to the family. The venture may have cost $2 all told and in those days that was an item. As my family figured it, if you did this every day that was $700 a year, so you'd better not get into bad habits.

In the evening vaudeville show there was a chorus line where a group of girls came on stage in crinolines that were not too well pressed and one was wearing a wristwatch. I noted the dowdy clothes and the anachronism in a voice that was carping and too audible. My father went into a temper, we got into a quarrel and we never made it up. How can things like this be? Was it because I had no one with whom to discuss such matters?

We look forward to the day we will see you. My days are spent in gardening, writing, tennis, reading, and being with friends. Retirement is a sweetheart way to live.

Best to your family,

A

✎

During that same year, 1980, Dad recalled to me something that had happened more than fifty years previous, when he was twenty-nine and just breaking into the upper echelons of the publishing business. He had presented a risky but inventive way to double the circulation of *Writer's Digest*, the company's key magazine. He made his pitch to the curmudgeonly founder of the company, Ed Rosenthal, who surprisingly embraced the plan, adding, "Don't worry, once we get the show on the road, it will get easier as we go along."

"I had to go into the men's room," Dad told me, "and sit in a toilet stall where I could be alone and cry because Ed was understanding and didn't yell at me."

Your Delight

Jump ahead eight years; now it is Dad's eighty-first birthday. Already there is a long-held tradition of birthday letters to and from; this is from a suite of mini-essays about my daily walks called *Walking Papers* and dated April 7, 1988.

Sailor Boy: Dad at Six

There's a lot of water in the air today, and I'm inside my head. An umbrella is tucked into my belt like a scabbard, leaving my arms free to swing—the same reason the dog's leash is looped through my belt. As I begin the rhythm of the road's long ascent, I'm loving you.

You and I are similar in many ways; I have taken on aspects of your personality. Perhaps the greatest likeness is that though we both had magnificent creative energy as young men, our sense of being whole men was slow to mature. For you, I think, because your Dad died on you before you could work out your relationship with him. Sons rage against fathers; this rage fuels them, like it or not, and limits them whether they know it or not, until one day they let it go, like a kite is let go.

I've known about my piece of rage for thirty-five years, but I could never quite get the dynamics of how it slowed me down. Lately I've been getting hold of this and today the wheel clicks another notch, but through feeling, not thinking.

THE SHRINE THIEF

Uphill we work, downhill we glide. The work begins sweetly. I am four and showing how well I can read. I remember your delight, the smile on the forehead of your happiness. You love me to pieces. You are the father to me you never had for yourself. Our play is crisp joy. I am your child of light, affirming that existence is good news.

I'm at the first switch back now, my sweat evaporating into the heavy, damp air, the vast gray light from the sky blending the generations. Now my thoughts easily turn to my own delight in Amy and Lucy when they were young. I am recalling the swimming ecstasy of laughing with my girls, of playing riddles with them, taking walks, telling stories. Now I slip back again to your delight in me, then mine in my girls, then back and forth and on and up the rising country road. At the top, I realize I have been able to let go of Amy and Lucy with hardly a lurch because I gave as I had been given.

But as a son, you had scarcely known a father's joy; no wonder you had a hard time letting me grow past our magic bonding age into the individuation of pubescence and adulthood. And no wonder I've interpreted this glowing part of your heart as a constraint to my growth, a meanness in the channel of my rites of passage. When, in my forties, you would introduce me to strangers as "my six-year-old son," for half a crazy moment, I could be six for you, gnalking gnecret Gnu-gnanguage, and absorbing your love. As for me, my piece of rage would flap like a banner in a storm. I'll never get your permission to grow up. Look, Dad, this is "J." Two times seven is fourteen. This is my new recording. This is my happy wife.

Standing in the late misty morning, I see clearly that you didn't intend to deny my manhood by replenishing your own underground spring. I turn and float down the hill, thinking about your Dad again, the missing member of the cast. Maybe you can get to know him better, have some little chats with him, tell him your son needs him, too. It feels warm to make out a pattern in your life that modulates mine. Sure, I can be six for you, and fifty too—we can love each other at any age. Down at the driveway, I look up to see the image of a kite disappearing into the gray light.

Explaining-Myself-to-Dad Day

In 1989, I am fifty-two. Devi is visiting her folks in Texas and I am visiting mine in Cincinnati. Mom is out with a friend tonight, so Dad invites me to dinner at Charlie's Crabs up the street. Earlier this afternoon, Mom had asked me, "Why are you so reactive to Dad?" I must have been railing against him. Now, sitting at Charlie's Crabs, I feel the old depression, a subterranean catatonia fueled by repressed anger. The anger comes from my overpowering need for paternal approval coupled with my inability to see my way through it, to rise above it.

Instead of being driven home by Dad, I ask permission to walk myself home. I jog up Camden Street, walk across Montgomery Avenue, turn right on Belkenton, and cross Grace Avenue. The unchanged look of the old houses, the dark aura, Carol Crowe's house exactly the same as forty years ago. Then at last the woods, the spirit of my childhood. Under these trees, along the old school route, I can feel the arc of my whole life. The lawn of St. Theresa's Retirement Home glistens with upscale Catholic survival: the air conditioning is ON in every room. In the wooded strip before our house I pee, marking *my territory* in the orange sunset. Our 1920s wood-and-brick house seems unlike any other house anywhere because I see it in the context of my personal history. Although I know I might return, I am sensing this visit home as my last, my parents as having moved away, or as dead, and I open to the preciousness, the diminishing hours of it. The eye of my heart is open.

Earlier in the day, Dad said he felt "defeated" that he couldn't understand my music. So all day, he has harbored a plan. He wants to know if I'll "give him a few minutes." I'd heard him say to a friend, "I'll see if I learn anything." He wants me to explain my music so he can *name* it, to have at it that way so he might at least approach it but not fear it. Now we are in the dining room, me sitting at the tired old spinet, Mom seated at the table in back of us, listening.

I begin, but when I get to Buddy Hiles, he interrupts and starts to tell stories. He wants to talk about himself. I am hard-hearted. I ask if he wants to talk about himself and tell stories or to listen. He says he wants to listen, he'll shut up.

But a little later, when I say that I chose music over physics because it seems to me on a higher plane, he says, "Cocksucker."

I say, "I'm *your* son, get serious, give me a break."

He says, "I take it back."

Then I play for him Bach's F major Little Prelude and identify the motifs. Then I play his favorite piece, Mozart's C major Sonata, K. 545, explicating the formal structure of the first movement.

He says, "This is very complicated."

His face is drawn to a point of concentration as though he has heard something familiar for the first time. He is actually trying to understand—he's eighty-two, it's now or never.

I say, "You're slow but deep," tapping my head, but he just draws himself deeper.

Then on to jazz, framing it as music that has triumphantly emerged from suppressed African sensibility ("They were much better off in Africa," he interjects) and the physically present tense of jazz time. Then on to Third Stream music: angry black and effete white. Then on to raga. He keeps getting North Indian and American Indian mixed up. Then on to the sophistication of indigenous African cross-rhythms. Then the negative rigors of commercial composing. And then, finally, my own music. I point out that I am not deliberately eclectic but am influenced over time and then I compose what I hear. He understands and is moved. There is intensity in his open face. He has heard.

And now my parents are tired; it's bedtime. A little later, I hear his voice from the bedroom, "What a wonderful son we got."

The next day, Dad says, "You would have made a wonderful physicist."

I say, "Coming from a musician like yourself, that's high praise."

He finds this very funny, but in his too-high laugh, I feel trepidation. His own creative—and especially musical—inadequacy has cut him off from his son's expressive life. Although he can appreciate my success, will he ever be able to acknowledge who I am?

෯

Of course, I did visit home again. The next summer, I went looking for him one late, quiet afternoon and heard soft whistling. I found him lying on his back on his bed, looking out the window, whistling a song I had never heard, a song he must have learned in childhood. It is extremely difficult to whistle in tune, yet to my absolute amazement my father, who as a singer could scarcely match pitch, was whistling a sophisticated melody dead in tune. I froze, hid behind the door. He came to the last phrase—flawless. Then, after a pause, he began again, then stopped after a phrase. Dead. In. Tune. I stole away so he could lie there until he was ready to get up from his nap.

Birthday Rosey

In 1988, when Dad was eighty-one, he had already been trying for three decades to dream up publishing projects that would both interest him and convince the four grandsons of Ed Rosenthal, who had been his colleagues and bosses for sixty years, that he was still a vital creative force for the F&W Publishing Company. The "F" in the name refers to a magazine Dad founded and published for a decade mid-century called *Farm Quarterly*. The "W" stood for *Writer's Digest*, the magazine he edited (under the fictitious "house" name of Richard K. Abbott) for 30 years. But the Rosenthal brothers became increasingly wan toward my father's risky, half-realized ideas, and Dad felt more and more marginalized. When he heard that the company was up for sale, he thought up a scheme: He would write an authoritative history of the company. If the history proved significantly persuasive in the eventual success of the sale, he would get a percentage of the profit. When I asked him what that would amount to, he held up six fingers, meaning at least $100,000. I realized the fuzziness of the bargain, and my heart sank for him, but I wished him luck.

༖

The title of his historical account, *Birthday Rosey*, came from the name of a horse whose long-shot win provided capital for the founding of the company in 1913. Dad dove into his project and, during the four years that the company's sale was in protracted negotiation, produced an amazingly well-written manuscript, rich with the details of the 20th-century publishing business and the part his boss's company had played in it. The title page looked like this:

Birthday Rosey
The History of F & W Publishing Company
Its Birth, Youth, Growth, and Recent Market Explosion

But the title was not an accurate description of the contents, which were, first and foremost, the passionate autobiography of Aron M. Mathieu. The actual events and dialogue had been imaginatively reconstructed out of a combination of Dad's memory, his considerable editorial savvy, and his over-the-top self-aggrandizement.

The finished first half of the manuscript was largely about Dad himself, his evolving vision of the company, and the editorial and marketing knowledge he had acquired over the years. Every page showed his devotion in detailing the frail line between success and failure. The narrative ended with Dad's semi-retirement in 1953, came to ninety thousand words, and was a terrific read. At this point, Dad decided to show *Birthday Rosey* to his boss, who read it, recognized it for what it was, and wrote FICTION across the title page, adding a note to his partners: "It looks like Aron just dreamed this up. Sorry, I can't do anything for him." So the deal, which was at best a pipe dream from the start and was never really on, was clearly off, and the manuscript was returned to Dad. He became silent and withdrawn. He hadn't been valued, he was now eighty-four, and there was nowhere to go. *Birthday Rosey* broke him, and thus began a five-year mental and physical decline. He increasingly talked about himself and his successes in stories that were repeated, fragmented, tangled together, and eventually forgotten. By age eighty-nine he was in deep dementia, and he had to be strapped down and carried feet first and raging out of his own house.

Just after *Birthday Rosey* was rejected, my first book, *The Listening Book*, was published by Shambhala. During my very next visit home, I read Dad's half-book and loved it, thought it was masterful (though I didn't say why), and told him so.

He said, "You're the real writer in the family."

Stunned and saddened, I protested, but Dad just shook his head.

Leopold and Wolfgang

In a phone conversation with his son a month before he died, Dad said out of the blue, "We're just looking for what we lost. One of us has to find it, and it isn't gonna be me."

The night before he died, I knew I couldn't make it back to Cincinnati from San Francisco in time. Dad was almost gone. I asked the nurse on duty to hold the phone up to his ear, and I played the same Mozart sonata for him (K. 545) that I'd played in a recital when I was ten, and that Dad had asked me to play a few years later for a dying friend as Dad held the phone up to *his* ear. Now, for my dying father, I'd played a page when the nurse came back on. I asked if he'd said anything, and she said "I think he groaned a little bit." When Mom called the next morning to say in an even voice, "Dad died last night," I felt a lurch as though a train, long stuck on the tracks, had begun to move forward. Saddened and relieved, the writer I was learning to become said to himself, "You gotta remember how that felt." Okay, so now I am sitting here writing *I felt saddened, relieved, jolted forward by the inevitable.*

The Evening

About four years after Dad died, I found myself counting all the pluses and minuses of my life with my father, a *Counting the Ways*, as it were. I'm thinking how the house Devi and I now live in is painted just-right white with country-blue trim and all paid for thanks to Dad's rare photographs we sold, about how our grounds and garden are beautiful, and my wife and I are safe. I'm thinking, too, about Dad's prescient educational choices for his son, his own patient teaching. Then I'm thinking about his seamless infantilizing of me, his fear-generated ego, his temper, and his blind prejudice. And then there is his occasional turning toward some inner light, and the lovely quiet conversations we so enjoyed. And I'm thinking that all told, everything pretty much evens out. Now, although he's dead four years, here we are together, lying on the bed during some resting time at sunset and saying, "All told, everything pretty much evens out," and laughing, good-times laughing, like two men as one man.

"Pretty much everything evens out except for one thing," I say.

"What's that?" he says.

"This laughing," I say.

"That's extra," he says.

As I age, I am reminded more and more how I resemble Dad so variously—in body language, in humor, in my capacity for social expansiveness, in my volubility and—not at all least—in how I clean underneath my thumbnail with an upper front tooth while I'm thinking. I often interrupt people before they finish speaking when I know how their sentence will end—is it not my privilege to do so? I also know how different we are: my inner life, my artistic range, my retreat from the world of business and marketing. But most of all, I am struck by how I have had to struggle *so much less* than my father for whatever success I have come to because I was given so much more than he was, and primarily by his very self.

The Loose Finial

After Dad died, I would check in periodically on Mother's grief. "I don't miss him," she would say, and in fact, her life had become simpler and much happier. She decided to sell the house and move into a retirement community owned and managed by the Episcopalians, who kept a tidy ship. She did have to learn to cease admonishing strangers to stand up straight. After the five years of her residence there, her daughter Sue predeceased her. Mom had no nuclear family left in Cincinnati, so she decided to move to California, closer to Bill and Devi. For seven years, from age ninety-five until her death at one hundred and two, Rosella Feher Mathieu lived in a retirement community near us. Instead of having to care for an old lady who happened to be my mother, I discovered during those seven years that I had as a mother an old lady who became a dear and deep friend.

I became fascinated with her history, which I frequently asked her to recount. Rosella Feher's ancestors lived in Transylvanian Hungary. They owned vineyards there, and the "gypsies," the migrant workers of Europe, worked the harvest. Mom's father, Moritz Feher, was the boss's son: he got away with cutting school to hang out with the Roma musicians, who taught him how to play the violin. Just before the turn of the century, Moritz's first wife died in childbirth, together with their baby daughter. In grief as the century turned, Moritz decided to come to America and build a new life.

The family of Therése Rosenwasser, my mother's mother, was highly educated, but Therése never received a dowry because college for her brothers took precedence. The families of Moritz and Therése knew each other, and it was arranged that she would come to America and that Moritz, now Morris, would marry her, and she would bear his children. Therése arrived in 1905, and within six years they had six children together. Rózika ("rose" in Hungarian, "Rosella" in American) was the eldest.

Morris Feher was in the buy-and-sell business, the junk business, the antique business. He bought a two-story house on the edge of Cleveland's Hungarian neighborhood. Downstairs was the store, packed to the walls with desirables. Morris Feher knew what people wanted to discard and what they wanted to buy; his business was very successful. The family lived upstairs. All the children of Morris and Therése (now Theresa) slept in one bedroom. Rosella slept on a foldout bed with the next eldest sister, Adrian. The bed had brass fittings, including, at the foot, a rail six inches above the floor that a child could stand on. From the rail, she could reach up to the top of the bedpost and grasp a brass finial so loose that when twirled it made a rough, percussive sound. The sound of the loose finial was a perfect drum to keep time to her singing. "I was always singing," Mom told me, "all through childhood, always singing." The image fills my eyes and ears. Standing tall on the rail and reaching skyward is my mother on a morning in her sixth year. The other children, aged five, four, three, two, and one, are tucked in their beds. The eldest is singing full out and twirling her finial drum, twirling and singing to keep the family whole for another new day.

My Friend in Assisted Living

As the chaos of the move to California leveled off, a quietness and a trust began to develop between Mom and me. We shared deeper confidences, more memories. She loved to talk about botany and herbs and the plantings she nurtured on her porch. By then she was nationally recognized as an expert on herbs and potpourri; her nose for fragrance was as acute as ever and she knew the Latin names for everything. Because of macular degeneration she was functionally blind, and she was becoming increasingly deaf. Her love of herbs and potpourri sustained her.

Mom found a devoted secretary, Ivy, who cared for my mother as if my mother were her own. Devi too was continuously generous, making sure Mom had whatever she needed. Aside from the occasional mid-week phone call and other communications via Ivy, she made herself satisfied with the Sunday afternoons we spent with her. Our friendship grew in the warmth and respect of mutual acceptance.

Mother took some bad falls, had some scary hallucinatory periods, had such an intense love of doctors that the staff at her HMO had to rotate her from one to another—she would have been in a physician's office every day if she'd had her druthers. But through all the hardships, pain, and discomfort, Mom survived with grace until she was well past 100. My niece, Elizabeth, was on deathwatch on the June night Mom died and called at dawn to say, "Your mother seems to have stopped breathing." Devi and I went into wide-eyed, get-it-done emergency mode until the funeral-home drivers in torn black coats and crooked black ties carted her away at nine in the morning. She had willed her body to science, which I suspect made good use of her remains. Ten days later, via UPS, there appeared the ring retrievable only by cutting off a finger. That's when it hit home that she was gone. And there appeared an emptiness, a quiet place where my mother, my Highly-Honored-by-the-Herb-Society-of-America Mother, once had lived.

Do I miss her? A little. Her life was a full rainbow, ground to zenith and back to ground. It came and went as rainbows do.

Dad and Mom

Mom As Teacher

As the eldest of six, it is a sure bet that Mom never missed a chance to guide those around her. We who were around her could find this edifying or exasperating or anywhere in between, but one learned to navigate one's responses, to paddle around the rapids. With Ivy's help, Mom was writing well until very nearly the end. For the Sunrise Community Weekly she wrote a monthly advice column; here is a sample from November 30, 2005, when she was ninety-nine.

How To Practice Not Falling

One of the greatest fears is the fear of falling. It is a fear shared by all of us on the geriatric playground. How does one learn not to fall? One needs to practice eternal vigilance to be a non-faller. Eternal vigilance means constantly thinking about not falling. It means not getting up without some means of support, and not moving without your walker. It means remembering to seek your balance every second of the time you are mobile. Lift your feet. When moving, don't carry things that can drag on the floor. Have your hands free whenever possible.

These ideas are presented by someone who has practiced not falling for a long time. If you can practice being a non-faller for six months, you become a novice non-faller. That's a long time to concentrate on one thing, but it's also a long time not to fall. In another six months you can become a freshman non-faller, and after yet another six months you are a full-fledged senior non-faller! This is not only a great personal triumph, but avoids a host of unpleasant things, like a surfeit of hospital visits, doctor bills, and costly medications.

None of this is easy. The most difficult thing is to keep your attention in one area, even while you are thinking about something else, or talking with someone. But this effort is its own reward, one of the greatest rewards a person approaching the century mark can earn. –RFM

With her beloved musical son, Mom was gently encouraging, always sympathetic with his music-making, never pushy. I think she had a deep longing for her own lost music, for the child on the rail twirling her finial drum, singing and singing, always singing. Could that be a hidden transmission to me without name or form, a feeling only, the feeling of longing, of reclamation behind my music? It does feel like music comes *through* me from somewhere, some half-forgotten joy.

Transmission of Wisdom Through Parents
Living and Dying

I'm not sure I'll ever be able to define what I've received from my folks. I was relatively close to my parents and lucky in that way; dead or alive, I'm still not sure where they end and I begin. I suspect one never quite knows, or needs to know, but the older I get to my parents' ages when they died, the more clarity there seems to be. My mom was creaky of body but sound of mind at eighty-five, my current age. Dad at eighty-five was showing signs of decline, and so am I. In the little crevices of the day I empathize with them both.

Whatever wisdom I might have, whatever ability to discriminate what is of benefit to others, compassion for my parents helps me sort it all out. Age mellows the wounds and leavens the heart. If all is well, I'll be a day older tomorrow. So we'll see how it goes for my wife and my children, and their children, and my friends and my students, and for you, Treasured Reader, for you.

PART FOUR

16

Bali Journal

In 1989, Devi and I had been together for seven years, married for two. I had just received good money from a commercial album (*Available Light*), so we decided to spend two months in Asia: two weeks in Thailand and six weeks in Bali. By that time, I'd known for years that I understood something about the way music behaves that needed to be put into a book, and I thought I knew what kind of book that would be. But Bali profoundly influenced my feelings about books, and about me writing books.

I spent a lot of time writing in Bali, half of it writing in my journal and the other half writing the new book, which I soon realized needed to be more than a single book. The original plan was to explicate what I had discovered about modern tuning and tonal music. In Bali, I came to realize that folks should really learn to listen before being told what they were listening for. So the book, outlined and half-written during those six weeks in Bali, became *The Listening Book*. It marks a fundamental change in the relationship of my ears to the world.

We flew from Thailand to Bali and hired a car and driver to Ubud, the much-touted cultural center of the island. Ubud was still a village in 1989, albeit a large one, but already past its paradise-for-hippies days and well on its way to being a primary tourist destination. It was, nonetheless, a viable stepping-stone to the rice paddies and the ancient villages of the interior. After a twenty-minute walk from Ubud we found and rented a two-story thatched cottage, one of a half-dozen that lined the rice paddies stretching to the horizon. From the balcony, we could see volcanoes rising in the far distance and soak up the equatorial sun smiling down through the island air. Below are some excerpts from the journal I began our first morning.

The Bali Journal

Thursday, February 9
A young man brings breakfast: fruit salad, white bread, butter, jam, tea. His name is Made (Mha-day). He wants to practice English and is super friendly and sincere.

Twenty-three, married, but no kids yet. He sits only tentatively with us, half ready to jump up and perform some menial task. I manage to ask him (over many attempts) if the tourists have hurt Bali and the Balinese. "I fear for you," I say. He seems to hear this, though even as I, the fox, deny my foxiness by inquiry after the health of the chickens, he, as chicken, claims health. "Bali is Bali," he says with innocent belief, "and tourists are tourists." There is so much evidence to support him: the political and societal and religious foundation seems solid; but also so much evidence around us, even in the eyes and glances of the people, that shows the erosion of the cultural soil.

Made tries repeatedly to convince me that the elaborate stonework on our temple-style house façade has been hand carved, not poured from a mold. "You don't believe me," he says reproachfully, but I am honestly incredulous. But when I look more carefully I see that what he says is true, and the image that has become strong over the last few days—of millions of hands in patient labor—grows even more vivid.

Much of the morning is spent sleeping, or half-sleeping; later I realize that here at the equator there is less difference than one might have thought between sleeping and waking.

Tuesday, February 14
Devi greets me in the early light: Happy Valentine's Day. And it's true synchronicity: today the village of Penestanan, hidden in the forest a few paddies from our balcony, has begun to harvest the rice. And this morning I am starting my book with the wash of good energy that has always felt reliable to me. I will write for thirty days and see what happens; I know I've been writing this book in the back of my mind for years. I look at the Muse then quickly look away lest our glances meet straight on.

Meanwhile, twenty women and a dozen men from the village are doing serious agriculture beneath our balcony. The sounds are from the soundtrack of the dream we are dreaming, and absolutely in real time. It does take some getting used to. By dusk at 6 PM, the women have taken the bags of harvested rice back to the village on their heads; the men have followed, and the duck herders have penned the flock; I have read and written my heart out, and my book has begun. After a little foray through the neighborhood, we decide to commit ourselves to this holy spot for an entire month.

Wednesday, February 15
The harvest energy coming up from the rice fields is a miracle, the plane where earth and humans meet, the tangent where their transformations touch and join. The sounds are joyous and serious, gentle, deliberate, random, and metered. The slapping of the thrashers and monster music of the cries to scare the birds are the foreground. Then, softly embracing those, the calls and exclamations and plain talk of the women, the foraging quackery of two hundred ducks, the swishing of the winnowers, the rich white noise of the infinite grains. The wind. Everyday conversations along the path to Penestanan. And now the rain comes, with its infinite drops. Everything is muted but nothing is changed. Protecting the rice against the moisture appears to be the same action as winnowing the rice in the sun, different sides of the same gesture. Cloth is folded up, people drift to shelter. The rain lets up, the cloth is spread again, people drift back. The sun comes, goes. I am sitting on the balcony writing my first book, and the rice harvesters are my gods, my helpers from a lost world, my passport to Source. They say, "You're not just jiving. Do your work in the rain and sun like we do. Don't think about your thinking so much. It's work much like ours. And it gives people nourishing grains to eat."

Wednesday, March 1
While writing on the balcony this morning I spend a far out five minutes watching a woman from a neighboring village drop her load of kindling from her head because the packet was coming undone, then re-pack it and move on. Every move is both precise and psychologically revealing. She is one-hundred per cent absorbed. No part of her isn't doing it. Only at the beginning, when the load first slipped, did she look around with an expression of annoyance, that others might have seen her pack come undone. But the eyes of the villagers were not upon her; no one except me, unseen, sees her, and no one passes her on the path. She unties the strong vine bindings, lays the sticks out in parallel on the ground, and reconstructs the pile stick by stick. There are four kinds of wood: discarded building scraps, tree branches, bamboo, and brittle, hollow sticks. She picks them up from the old pile, builds them in that order into four new ones

and then, with considerable strength, ties each binding tight. It is the most immaculate bundle of kindling ever seen—balanced, secure, handcrafted, a world classic! She raises it to her head, flicks away the butt of the Clovie she's been smoking all along and with immense, raw dignity continues down the path toward her village. I know my writing constitutes the same work as her stick carrying, but I have to shake my head in admiration as I watch her load bob down to the river. At the time our two activities seem far apart.

This morning I write two chapters: *Walking* and *Now Time*, and these feel good. This book is something I can do, and it will make my way for me as well. I was thinking while writing—it's okay for me to write a popular book just like it would be okay for Coleman Barks to write a popular song.

Friday, March 3
Wyon Tunas, son of Pak Sadri the landlord, has come to stock the fridge. As he is working, there comes a musical calling from paddy to paddy—I see some men running as well. I hear the Balinese singing "Nan-Non-O-Nan-Non," at intervals of melodic minor thirds, with many delicious variations from near and far, man to woman, register to register. I ask what's happening. He says it is the monthly five kilometer run organized by some Australians with participation by Europeans and Americans. I see a line of silent white flesh jogging and jiggling up the road from Campuhan. To the Balinese this is highly amusing, like a circus. But their mellifluous response is far from ridicule. They see it as a kind of ceremony by white people, a parade, a specially energized processional. As their own ceremonial proclivities are awakened they scurry for a vantage point. "What is the meaning of the words?" I ask. He answers, "They are singing 'on and on.' We call this The On-and-On." It is no surprise they are so gently amused. Nothing would seem more absurd than jogging Balinese.

Saturday, March 5
From our balcony I am watching a Balinese rice farmer with a scythe manicure a wall between two rice paddies of different levels. The upper paddy is about four feet higher than the lower one. He is working from a path on the lower paddy; the wall is as high as his sternum. Along the top of the wall is a path bordering the higher paddy. His work is to clip the grass at the roots that grow out from the wall, turning the long, unbroken curve of it from lush green to a greenish brown. His tool has the classic sickle-moon shape, smallish, sharp. His motions are accurate, slow, efficient. As I watch, he wipes the sweat from his face in the same andante tempo as he works. No wonder we can't

conceive of the connectedness the Balinese feel with each other and with their holy island-gift: because we haven't done their work, singly or together. Work the land for a generation, or forty generations, manicure the little embankments that demarcate the rice-fortunes, dredge the irrigation canals, herd the ducks, place your muddy feet on the muddy earth over and over again to prepare it for your children's children's muddy feet, and then it will not seem too strange that Weyon Tunas, Sadri's son, has never been to the other side of his own island.

Tuesday, March 7
Devi and I decide to hike the high ridge that connects the villages. We have a sense of adventure—some wild place we've never been. As we climb to the ridge we see endless fields of new rice and hear the late afternoon silence of the young crop. After an hour we sit down to rest by the side of the path. At our left is a small stone altar. The water rushing through the irrigation canals is *piano* under the insects. Everywhere the baby green is glowing in the cloudy sunset. Above, dozens of darting swallows in the frenzy of the evening feed. We sit quietly. Three breaths.

Along the path comes a smallish man, darker than most, on his shoulders a pole with empty fodder baskets at either end. We nod. He smiles sweetly, then sits on the other side of the altar, a respectful meter to my left. "Where you from?" We say where. "Where going?" We say *jalan jalan* (just walking). We ask, "You live here?" He thinks, nods. His English is exhausted. He tries a few phrases in Indonesian, we smile and shrug. His earnest love fills the air and for a moment we sit inside it, a presence beyond language or sound. His is the feeling of new rice, the swooping of birds. I offer him our water bottle to finish, he does, and throws the empty plastic into one of his baskets. I notice his bristly little mustache, jet-black, and how it becomes the gentle innocence of his face. In some language he says he'll be walking on, and from our seats we bow the bow of travelers well met. He walks off with the empty blue bottle catching the indirect light. I turn to Devi and our eyes are clear. We've just met an angel person, a nature god.

Thursday, March 9
This morning we go to the gamelan maker, the patriarch of a family who for generations has made Bali's gamelans, one of two primary such hereditary lines, I think. In his compound there are the usual generational layers of inhabitants, but also a foundry, surprisingly efficient, where the bronze (70% copper, 30% tin imported in ingots from Java) is heated, hammered, filed, sculpted, beat, and filed more into gamelan chimes and various

gongs. Huge gongs and smaller ones are everywhere. The primary position in the compound is given to the shaping of the metal, the continuance of the ancient blessing.

He sings pitches well in a clear falsetto; I think he's gotten his tonal knowledge from several ancient bars in his possession, some of them hanging from the walls of his shop. We manage to have a conversation about tuning. He can tell I'm for real, and also that I'm not going to be a big customer. Nonetheless he busies himself finding me precisely what I want: an old low-pitch bar chime, its matching bamboo resonator, and a hammer. Part of the deal: I offer to play a concert on the blowpipe Yamaha mini-keyboard I've discovered half-under something. The offer is immediately accepted and I play a little dance impromptu, making much of C sharp equal to D flat, plus some Jegog-like repetitions and a little IV-I moxie. Much appreciation from the family and genuine recognition from both our guide and the master builder. I feel confirmed as a world musician, no problem. This is a high point to be sure, though it isn't at all emotional. Just a nod from above, as if Murshid were saying *of course.*

Saturday, March 11
Devi and I have dinner at the Warung tonight, with disconcerting company. We are sitting at the counter. On the porch at one table, a party of four women: a 55-year-old writer with a truly bright and uprooted mind whose last address was LA; a petite flutist with glasses who rarely practices her classical music and has spent the last three years in Japan; a New York paintress whose mind is still on West 87th; and a woman from Pennsylvania who has just disembarked from her flight and is sleeping with her chin on her wrist on her elbow on her knee. At the other table sits a silent old hippie drinking beer.

As conversation progresses, origins and professions emerge. I mention Windham Hill and the hippie chimes in that he knows Scott Cossu and Michael Hedges, would we like to hear him play spoons, on which he has performed with both musicians. Of course we would. The master un-towels his instruments—it is choice table cutlery from thirty years of collecting—and plays three minutes of ecstatic, highly musical, skillful *utensil.* Also expressed are his disconnect and sad wanderlust.

The upshot: we are in Berkeley in Bali; the feeling is special and high, but also artificial and intrusive *to ourselves.* How could we be so well met and yet so destructive of each other's paradise? I say "Where am I?" and it gets a big laugh. *The American Corner.* Crud! Rats, Batman! Once again our anonymity has eroded into fame and privilege.

Ibu, Owner of the Warung

Monday, March 13

We are taken by our guide, Godé, to Tinganaan, a Bali Ayn, 'original' Balinese village. The village does seem old enough, the vibe of the place is veritably ancient. If we'd thought we'd seen the collective primal innocence before, we are reintroduced here to a new purity: sweeter smiles, deeper peace, greater wholeness in each motion. Yet virtually every house is a shop, and each shop has a mixture of local craft and imported goods. The big thing is the 'double ikat,' a fabric woven in the ancient way they seem in no hurry to sell. It's highly priced (hundreds of dollars for small pieces) and not very beautiful from our point of view. Nevertheless it is made with a complex technique by primitive means, and seems to be a genuine tie to their past. If the populace must be tourist-i-fied, at least it can happen on their own terms, by which I mean real dollars for real value. The sense of village hangs in the air undisturbed like an elevated lake. There is almost no indication that the basic paradox of shops in the ancient village is even a ripple on the surface of life, which does simply go on, tourists and all.

A lovely thing happens. A lady is trying to sell me wooden cow bells carved especially for tourists, but then I spy some old used ones, the real thing, retired from the fields of buffalo. She offers each one dirt cheap, but then in a sudden inspiration says all four for 10,000, and I instantly say yes. Godé groans. I realize I've agreed to a sum far greater then her original offer but I have to pay her. She laughs and laughs as does everyone else.

Several times during the next hour she sees us and laughs, and so do we. The lady can't believe her good fortune.

But by now we are tired of looking at tchotchkes and making choices, so we decide to leave. I am just then leaning against stacked sacks of pig chow. An old man appears. I offer to buy: "What price?" "One million," he says. "Two million!" This whole part of the village is laughing. "I take to USA." Ha-ha-ha-ha. "For American pigs." Ha-ha-ha-haha-ha.

When I get home and I see these four gorgeous wooden carvings as a gentle musical reminder of the fields and animals, I can't believe my good fortune either: all mine for $5.75. I laugh with my own delight. A Balinese win-win.

Wednesday, March 15
"Beware the Ides of March," I said to Devi upon arising. At 8AM I am sitting on the balcony. Cloudy sunshine fills the fields with silver blue sky. A few paddies to my right, a man is plowing, but not with a wooden plow submerged beneath flooded mud. He is walking behind a hand-guided tractor, clambering through the mud with both arms stuck to his machine, rassling it upright. The sound is like a motorcycle standing stationary with its engine racing. A few fields farther away there's a second tractor. The combined noise is like living on a drag strip: fucking loud. The sound of the ducks, which are still all around our house, is totally drowned out. I am certain that we must move away instantly and that the Balinese are damned. The sudden change in the countryside, the leap of centuries so devastating, that I can't believe how the natives, who have absorbed migration after migration including the Dutch, the Japanese, and tourism, will tolerate it. I feel powerless, evicted from Paradise. The little two-stroke motors that will (as it turns out) be whining and throbbing from 7 AM to 6 PM provoke me beyond savoring my own cynicism. There is no joke here. I've been double-crossed. I'm leaving.

After dinner, for some quiet company, we go to the house of our friends Mark and Constance. Now we can hear all the way into the horizon, but not for long. There's a Balinese catch: Frogs! At night they are deafened with them.

Friday, March 17
In the morning Tunas comes to visit and we speak our unhappiness to him. He is sympathetic of course, but says, "It's the farmer's work." I try to explain the real evil, the mechanization of the ancient. But it's like explaining chicken divinity to a fox. The Balinese want progress. "The tractors make the farmer's work easier," he says. I'm sure that's true, but I'm also beginning to understand just how such problems in modernization worm their way from the civilization without to the soul within.

We are on the road for hours today with our guide, Godé, driving through the life of Bali. During those hours I realize that the time of my being a tourist here, a watcher, an outsider looking at and in, has to be coming to a close. To stay here longer, or to meaningfully return, would mean participating in the work of the people, being part of the commerce, being connected to the land, the wave of the land. There is no way to continue to objectify the place—it can no longer be my paradise or my vacation, I can no longer see the countryside or the people as beautiful or irritating objects. No more pretty scenery. No more gifts for friends. No more experience of the timeless, no more shots of ancient patience. The only way to continue to be here is to work here, and pray here, and work some more. Adding my dollars to their economy is only adding work I've done somewhere else in another world. My feet would have to be muddy with Balinese mud to be part of the Balinese fabric—there could be no other way. That's why the Balinese gods sent tractors. If you don't like them, leave.

Wednesday, March 22
A few days ago I gave one of the familiar workers a cold Coke as he was hoeing, for the seventh consecutive hour, the paddy below our balcony. This morning he appears with a huge coconut he has picked. He cuts two triangles from the green husk, shaves a bit from each, replaces them and pours a quart and a half of warm pungent coconut juice into small paper cups he has brought for the three of us. He drinks off his as we gingerly sip ours. Then, as if to show the full progression of friendship, he takes out one of the plugs, hoists the huge fruit to arms length above his head, which he throws back, and in a series of astonishing, coordinated gulping swallows, takes in the full stream of coconut milk, about a half pint in all. The sun glistens on the cascade. We are in an unbreakable circle: Coke to coconut.

I give him a postcard of Mount Shasta and a cigarette. We sit and smoke. Devi looks up words in Indonesian (he speaks zero English). Very Balinese moment. Reciprocity is real here, active and intentional, not mere karma. We sit for twenty minutes of respect and good feeling, then he excuses himself and goes off to work.

Sunday, March 26
Tomorrow is get-away day. At the Balina Beach Hotel we secure a good room, unpack, and settle down on the balcony. I am not writing a book, not repaying the intentions of my many friends with gifts. I am sitting listening to the ocean, watching it. I am listening to the birds, and to the quiet tendrils of Balinese language. I am not composing, I am sitting. I am resting. I am finished.

We walk down to the beach where we procure the first of our three evening gin and tonics. Directly in front of us, fifteen boys are playing soccer in the sand. I recognize how immersed they are in the play of what they are doing, in the joy of activity—not in the competition, but in the movement and structure. They seem uniformly happy. The scene is unadulterated: native boys in the sunset, white folks drinking gin. The match goes on for twenty minutes without a point for either team. The sky goes through every painting style from naïve to abstract in five continents. Then, as a point is scored, hardly a cry goes up, just a kind of exclamation that the game is over. Some of the boys run into the ocean and the rest evaporate up the beach.

At dinner, just beyond a large, clear pool adorned with colorful carp, two blind musicians are seated facing one another. Each plays a jegog, a bamboo gamelan, spread before him. They look like twins, thin, straight-backed, symmetrical. We thought we'd seen sweet, but this is a sweetness reserved for last. Shy, soft, sightless, introverted and masterful, they are so tuned to each other they redefine love. And what music! The One-in-All and the All-in-One, all at once in one's ears.

Monday, March 27
We take an early jet from Bali. Balina Beach is now a small indentation in the receding haze. Then below us comes the pattern of the green rice fields, brown villages, and sparkling rivers in their gorges of the central uplands. The land that has shown us its life force through our feet is spread out below us like an ornamental quilt. Brown village, green velvet, brown, green, village, velvet, on and on. The moment of rising and leaving has come.

End of Bali Journal

Transparent Wisdom

Bali changed me forever as a musician, as a writer, and as a person. The Balinese showed me a certain way of being alive in the world. On their part, there seemed to be little or no effort in transmitting anything—they were simply living their lives in my presence, tourist or no. Devi and I knew enough not to objectify our new friends, and so more or less real relationships were able to be established up to a point. I learned most by being a quiet and, when possible, responsive witness. What I witnessed was new: I had never been in a society so willingly bound in collective mind. Not to idealize the Balinese— families are families, and people are people, so there was anger, and discontent, and fractious behaviors. But there was a leavening, a softness, and a nearly continuous loving kindness, hard even now to imagine. For a little while, Devi and I lived within a high wisdom, maintained for generations, of self-sustaining everyday life.

The tradition of gamelan music is a microcosm of this. Nothing is written down, everything is learned and taught by ear. There is a master player in each village who oversees the passing of the complex repertoire from player to player, generation to generation. Yet even he might not fully know all of the compositions. It is the village itself that has memorized the body of music, and it takes a village to learn it, perform it, and pass it on. The individual gamelan parts are so intertwined with one another that only the players themselves can be sure of who is playing what. There are typically daily gatherings of musicians where all are welcome, and the whole of the music is thus kept alive continuously.

One day, when I was discussing the techniques of gamelan music with Ubud's master player, I asked innocently if there were ever gamelan soloists, since I'd never heard a particular player stand out, much less stand up and take a bow. The master was greatly amused at the question. He said if any gamelan player ever stood up and took a bow for, say, some well-executed passage, the village would think he was acting crazy on purpose, and everyone would be laughing as we would at a circus clown. From that day on, I have tried to consider my own musical culture back home as the gamelan of my village, and my music hocketed forever with my fellow musicians, our listeners, and every societal connection down to the last soul.

Standing up and taking a bow is madman's work, a denial of the collective nature of music. Applause is a hideous sound to my ears. I wish Westerners would sit silently after the music is over, then go about their business, like the Balinese. Often when I perform, I ask audiences to keep the silence after the music is finished because then the blessing of music will bloom. I wish making music were like prayer for us, or a blessing ceremony, which it is in Bali.

Something similar has become true for my writing. *The Listening Book*, shaped on the balcony above the rice paddies, was written as if by a member of a village gamelan—my home village, that is: a gamelan of readers, including myself, interested in discovering our own music. My view had changed. My writing voice had changed. I wasn't writing for self-clarification or self-validation, like the voice with which I had talked to myself in my early journals. I wasn't writing for approval from my many invisible fathers like I was in *Counting the Ways* and the birthday letters to my actual father, pages written to distinguish what was him and what was real in myself. The book-to-be about listening is a new creature: I'm writing for the reader, for all readers who may be of like mind and who might benefit from my words. I've joined a community of writers and readers of which I am a part. I'm writing as a living person in the band of living persons. I am the woman on the path rearranging her sticks, the rice worker manicuring the wall between paddies with his sickle-shaped scythe. I am the new arrival in my village gamelan of readers, learning my part by ear and daily practice.

Looking back, I realize how definitively the Balinese sense of community surrounding me as I wrote longhand on our balcony above rice paddies shaped my coming out as a writer. However my voice may have developed over these intervening years is due in large part to the exquisite transparency of everyday Balinese wisdom, bless its dying heart.

ॐ

I'm afraid I'll have to end this account on a sad note. The Bali described here was the Bali of 1989, well over thirty years ago, and, loath as I am to say it, a Bali that no longer exists. It seems very difficult at present to find much of anything in Bali untouched by the sweep toward the big bad bucks of tourism. Bali is no longer Bali, and tourists are no longer tourists. Bali, as a tourist destination, is among the world's most expansive: over five million tourists in 2019 on an "island paradise" of two million inhabitants. Once-quiet villages are now ghastly tourist malls frequently selling imported tchotchkes. Lavish hotels border the rice paddies. The problem? Bali is the cash cow of Indonesia, and the Indonesian government, besides its own influx of developmental capital, actively encourages foreign investment. So what was once the Balinese skein of spiritually connected villages is now The Balinese Tourist Zoo. Unless that's what you crave, or unless you are willing to seek the villages far apart in the higher elevations where tourists rarely go, stay away. You and I, Patient Reader, you and I, right here at home, you and I will have to make the best Bali we can out of what we are heir to.

17

Writing It

I have never taken a writing class except by accident. What I have done is mine the minds of the editors, authors, and poets I have worked with. I have been an inquisitive, persistent pest. I am chary of books on writing and instead have read writers I like. I read for pleasure, to learn, to admire, and to trash. I agonize and celebrate with authors as I read, but I don't consider myself a real writer. What I am is a real musician. I know real writers, and I'm not one. So I feel I can give sympathetic, as opposed to lofty, advice about writing. Although it's not advice, exactly, more like just telling my own stories; not instructing so much as saying what I like and what makes me peevish.

The stories in the last chapter were about the Balinese who, as a people, showed me a place to write *from*, by which I don't mean the balcony of our rented cottage. I mean the rice fields, the village gamelan, and the silence on the path between villages. It is not easy for artists to climb down from our balconies. As a musician it has taken me decades to climb down, and I'm still descending. As a maven of musical craft, I know some things that others do not. The difficulty is in recognizing that no matter how hard I have labored to gain my knowledge, every last human alive can claim to know *some things that others do not*. Directly upon that realization, my balcony transforms into a plow pulled by a water buffalo with a wooden bell around its neck. You are guiding the plow because that is what you happen to know how to do.

A Word About Words

There is a notion I've heard attributed to Goethe (though I have yet to find it in his works in so many words): *The reason words take us so close to the truth is that they are what has led us away from it in the first place.*

Words carve out, from an infinity of possibilities, a bounded space. They are terms, limits. A word says: not everything but *something*, some *thing*. Words reify the world. They lead us down from the paradise of infinite connectivity to the hard furniture of earth, where we must walk cautiously lest we stub our toes.

On the sixth day, God commanded Adam to name the animals; forthwith, Adam said, "Ox." In that moment, the seamlessness is undone, the oneness is rent. "I am Adam, you are ox. I have colonized you by naming you." From then on, we are forever struck and stuck with language. We try to look back, but there are too many corners to see around. We're just here, talking to our friends, reading to our children, and writing out our lives.

Maybe it was on the Sabbath that God reconsidered the task of naming he'd given Adam and henceforth gave him the additional notion of analogy—*this* could now be *like* that; maybe Adam might make a discovery or two on his own. And Adam did. When Eve came along, he said, "Oh, your kisses are like honey." Then, cutting straight to metaphor, he called *her* Honey. Thus God gave us indirection, ambiguity, and, finally, poetry so we can leap about inside our minds. We can savor the mysterious mid-air spaces between *this* and *that*, recognize skeins of interconnections, and feel, at least momentarily, released from the limits of language.

Coleman Barks, in the first sentence of his preface to *The Hand of Poetry*, writes, "What language does so spectacularly is lie, that silver-tongued protector of illusions." That's a good way to begin a book, an early warning.

"Words flirt," Barks continues. "They tease and imitate and come close, but they are not the experience they point to."

He quotes Rumi:

Listen to the presences inside poems.
Let them take you where they will.

A century ago, Archibald MacLeish took a bold step beyond this when he concluded his poem "Ars Poetica" with the lines:

A poem should not mean
But be.

Now didn't we just declare that language cannot translate Being? Yes, we did say that. So what about this? Well, I guess we just have to make a choreographic leap between *that* and *this* and, for one floating moment, be mercifully released from the gravity of words.

Meaninglessness

To comprehend cold, one needs to comprehend hot. Light has no meaning unless there are shades of light leading into darkness. Stupidity is not intelligence and vice versa. The meaning of meaning is that there are two ends of a taught string the mind continually moves somewhere along. Since each end of the string defines the other, it is good to know what lies at both ends. If one end is "full of words," the other end is "empty of words." The other end of "meaning" is "meaninglessness."

When the mind is utterly at rest, its language, ideas, and even its images disappear. The mirror of the mind becomes the surface of a lake so smooth that the reflections of the stars become clear as the stars themselves. What remains is an existential presence cleansed of meaning. All experience is given to us in the moment; nothing needs to be added in. There arise no questions to be answered. This is what Buddhist dharma is pointing to with the term "emptiness." To "mean," on the other hand, is to translate from infinite essence to limited particularity. It satisfies our need to know. Meaning calms our ravenous hunger for stabilization in a wildly moving world, and it is, of course, crucial for living human life. Everyone has to find their own blend of meaning and meaningless.

When MacLeish tells us, "A poem should not mean / But be," he is pointing beyond the poem. Writers and teachers commonly use oh-so-meaningful words in order to spark transcendence beyond language. We think thoughts about not thinking, talk about not talking, and write words about writing beyond the words. Can't help laughing. But by candlelight, and far, far into the night, that is what we are given to do.

For very young children, gibberish is the path toward language. We learn to speak by the evolutionary process of combining phonemes together until something functional happens. In theatrical training, when scenes are played out in gibberish, the opposite process occurs— meaning is intentionally drained from language in order to uncover what is beyond words, in order more clearly to see into the actors' vocal inflections, body language, and spontaneous choreography. Poems that flirt with randomness can be studies in the mind's deep resources of connectivity. Such meaninglessness can be artful, but not when you have to call the doctor, or pay the bills, or order dinner from a menu. We'd be lost without both ends of the string.

For writers, providing we never lose sight of its limits, language can be not only functional but beautiful, and create streams of good authorship, good journalism, good holy writ, good history, and (say a little prayer here) a good world. As a writer, I can't trust a single syllable unless I'm remembering Goethe's caution: *Words are what have led us away in the first place.* As long as I consciously recognize that I live deep inside an unknowable, ever-moving, and *indescribable* multi-dimensional mandala, permission to write is given. As long as I remember that I am a guide toward the reader's personal experiences, not a peddler of concepts, I am free to spin my words into sentences, sentences into pages, and pages into books.

Word Hunger

One of my favorite cartoons is from a strip called *Rose is Rose.* Rose is a Northwestern housewife, optimistic in her family life with a working-guy husband, a charming son, and wild woods she can walk in. The strip, signed by Pat Brady, is in three panels on this particular day. The view in the first panel is from above; below us, Rose is peering up adoringly at two cute birdies on the limb just above her head. Rose is smiling and singing to them. In her caption balloon is drawn, *:PEEP::PEEP::PEEEP::PEEP:,* and floating about are some eighth notes as they would appear in music notation. The view in the second panel is from ground level; we see a very pleased Rose striding away from us and her interspecies moment. Above and behind her, the birdies are looking at her receding figure. In the last panel, we are at the level of the birdies' tree limb, facing them as they converse in musical chirps. One birdie says to the other, "What was THAT all about?" The other replies, "The bigger the brain, the more things that go wrong!"

Language lets us navigate civilization at a steep price, and it is difficult to climb out of debt. Even when we try, says the cartoon, it's all too easy to be incomplete: Rose isn't a bird even when she tries, at least not from the bird's point of view. I've held the cartoon dear for so many years because it reminds me that I am in the middle of worlds very much smaller, very much larger, and way more diverse than I can know or imagine. All it takes is a little bird-snark to get me to laugh at myself.

Meanwhile, words are alive inside us, and they get hungry for more words. They especially love to feast on themselves and then reproduce like mad, rendering their users fatally prolix. With all these parts of speech lurking about inside and out, I have to sniff out pure experience, lay for it, *long* for it, long for the light of sentience empty of ideas. In writing prose, and especially in writing poems, language itself has given me the courage to leap beyond the page.

Reading good writing takes me into a realm of pure knowing, a feeling of wholeness unconfined by words. A good paragraph is pulsing flesh risen from the noisy skeleton of language. Poetic prosody can be sonorous and soothing as music heard while falling asleep. Instead of admonishing God for giving Adam the burden of naming animals, I should be thankful for the opportunity to un-name the ox, to know ox as self, and thence be fit to write. Rumi says there is a field of knowing beyond ideas of *this* and *that* where you and I can meet:

> When the soul lies down in that grass,
> the world is too full to talk about.

In music, I've come to trust such states; musical transparency has become my closest buddy. It is less obvious for me to recognize such transparency in writing. I try to let the authorial epaulet drop from my shoulder and devote myself entirely to the wordless essence of what I'm writing. Whenever that does happen, and occasionally it does, I know that permission to go ahead has been granted. In a state of wonderstanding, the miracle follows. Clear words flow out from wordless wonder, and sentences, flush with meaning, write themselves.

Teachers Living and Dead

My first writing teacher was my father. He was chiefly an editor, secondarily a writer. His edits of my writing were typically concerned with message and clarity: having something to say and saying it well. I learned from him to construct clear sentences and paragraphs and to punctuate correctly, but the potential beauty of language was not yet in my sights.

My first serious encounter with poetry was when, at sixteen, I audited my big sister's Humanities III class. Under discussion was

"The Love Song of J. Alfred Prufrock." The professor pointed out how the poem's crucial tension was reflected in the two ways the name Prufrock could be construed: the weak image of Prew Frock, and the strong one of Proof Rock. He also pointed out that Eliot rhymes *tea and ices* with *bring the matter to a crisis*. My relationship with language broadened and colored. I could no longer see to the bottom of it, and that was compelling. The subject was words, mind you, not the lustrous tones in my musical noggin, but compelling nonetheless.

At eighteen I became entranced by the elegant sentences of the young nobleman James Boswell, who was himself entranced by the elegant severity of Samuel Johnson's wit. That happened, unsurprisingly, in my sophomore year at the University of Chicago, and the trance soon faded. But others ensued. The seductive voice of Truman Capote's *Other Voices, Other Rooms* led to a self-awareness new to me, dark but alluring. Capote brought me closer to the person inside.

The real deal happened ten years later when, in 1970, I collaborated with Richard Tillinghast, my first live poet. A recent graduate of Harvard, Richard went on to become a well-known voice in American letters, but at that time, we were engaged in writing songs for the Sufi Choir. I found that if I sought the music in his words, their poetic core was revealed to my critical eye and ear. I began to notice how, just as in musical composition, small changes could effect large differences. I discovered how to translate the wisdom of a leaping metaphor into the uplift of a musical phrase. Richard believed in "getting it right," a mantra I'd already honored—and pontificated upon daily—in musical composition, but jousting with Richard in real time allowed one clarity to illuminate another. Music had always been an arm-around-my-shoulder writing guide, but now I was working things out with a knowledgeable craftsman note by word, word by note. The real prize: our collaboration produced a cluster of songs as moving to me now as when they were first heard fifty years ago.

Burning Poetry

By the mid-1970s, I was teaching music full-time at Mills College, also teaching privately, continuing to turn out Sufi Choir albums, had moved north from Marin County to a run-down farmhouse on six acres in Sonoma County, built a music studio complete with a home recording system, begun to release a series of solo piano albums, and was trying to raise a house full of kids. Except for occasional letters home to family, there was scant writing in my life. No time, little interest, and a swan dive into music-making.

By the mid-1980s, however, everything had changed. Divorced. Kids gone their ways. Living at the old farmhouse with Devi—she of the angelic mezzo tessitura—and searching for poems to set for her to sing. Someone lent me a copy of *Open Secret*, the first of many volumes of Rumi poems rendered into English by Coleman Barks. "Eureka! I've found it!" cried I. Well, actually, Coleman had found it and, I thought, I'd found Coleman. I procured his phone number, dialed him up, and in an unforced display of hubris, said, "This is Allaudin Mathieu, and you are my brother." Coleman, who is not just a little bit outrageous himself, went along with the conceit. Despite this introduction we did become friends, and he did confer his blessing on my subsequent settings of his versions of Rumi poems, a total of seven song cycles in various combinations of mezzo-soprano, piano, violin, flute, tenor voice, and full choir, comprising over fifty songs in all.

When he was performing near San Francisco, Coleman was often our overnight guest. Notwithstanding my awe of The Poet, those times were rich with delicious food, red wine, and immoderate laughter. I didn't try to pick his poetry brain, we didn't talk shop, we just hung out. But when he invited me to visit him for a few days in Athens, Georgia, where he lived and taught English literature, I said sure and might I bring some of my poems, and he said sure.

We enjoyed walking the university campus, visiting his haunts, drinking, eating, lauding, dissing, plain-talking. I shot an hour-long video, *Barksiana*, not for public viewing. I audited his Friday classes and admired his generosity in the face of his students' languorous unconcern. At night we got drunker than skunks (that's in the movie). He shot me playing a Bach prelude from *The Well-Tempered Clavier* on his ancient upright that hadn't been tuned since the Civil War, which I considered a perfect tribute to the glory of a decadent South besparkled with jewels. He devoted Saturday afternoon to editing my poems.

We looked at three. The first, meant as a birthday gift for Devi, was actually (I realize thirty birthdays later) a self-serving exercise. The premise: giving Devi gifts she already had because she already had everything. Meant to be positive reinforcement, it also opportunely crowned me Prince of Giving. Coleman recognized this, I think, but was too tactful a friend to directly expose it. What he did was refine the sentiment, alter the line breaks, and cut out about two-thirds.

Here is a passage from my original, which comes about halfway into a three-page poem. (Calico was our cat.)

I give you your sweet harmony in toasts and your calm
talking with women who are yourself.
I give you the deep pink constellations of your freckles,
your whole and perfect in-the-skin transparent
Self.
I give you the child who lives when the children in us
meet.

[I am mercifully not showing here thirteen additional
lines Coleman cut.]

Just the thought of giving you these gifts
turns me into rich cream
into magic coins
into the laughing sequins on a gown into our Calico,
grown enormous, leaping the Atlantic.

To come into one's own being is to rise from uncertainty
like the red-shouldered hawk we saw yesterday
to form as a brilliant cloud from the nothing of air.

I know these gifts are not mine to give. I know this is just
a way of talking.

Leaning back in his chair in front of burning logs in his cozy
living room, Coleman took his time editing while patiently answering
my questions. He pared down thirty-one of the original lines (227
words) to nine lines (64 words). I've studied his changes many times
over the years, and discovered something new each time. Here is
what he ended up with:

I give you the deep pink constellations
of your freckles, your whole and perfect-in-the-skin
transparency.

I give you the child who, like our Calico, grown
enormous, leaps the Atlantic.

To come to one's own is to rise
like the red-shouldered hawk we saw yesterday.

I know these gifts are not mine to give. This is just
a way of talking.

֍

The other two poems, eventually published in *The Musical Life*, were stronger, less self-serving. Coleman's changes were more like line edits—little fixes with big effect. For instance, in "Erased Music," a poem portraying the physical and mental dynamics of writing musical notation as one is composing, I was saying that false beginnings and mistakes erased in your score should balance out with the good parts you keep. The verse went like this:

> The two ends of the pencil are Shakti and Shiva.
> Writing and rubbing out, we want
> balanced lives. Show me the nub of a pencil
> with the eraser still fresh and I'll show you false confidence.

Coleman replaced *false confidence* with *mindless charm*. It sounded to me like a Southernism, but after a while I liked it, and left it in.

"Bach Dying" is an imaginary narrative of the composer's last hours. After he suffers a final small stroke, Bach hallucinates himself at his own bedside as the passionate adolescent he once was. Lute on lap as he is composing a love ballad, he inadvertently plucks an open string...

> ...an offhand twang that rides out the window
> and up into the bright sky.

Coleman changed *up into the bright sky* to *up into white glare*. There are so many reasons his is a better line of poetry, I can't think of them all at once. For starters, *the* is omitted, so five words are now four. *White* is a more visual descriptor than *bright*; also, *glare* adds a more specific—and affective—quality to *sky*. So far, two better descriptors and one less word.

From time to time, the fire burns low and needs replenishing. Proper tinder is secured: some aging pages from his trash. Toss onto the pyre, toss, toss, toss—but hold! What's this? The Poet spies a thick sheaf of poems from an unsolicited source, scans it for a moment, tosses it onto the flames, watches it burn, snatches it back, and reads a few lines from the burning page. With his right hand, he holds the page so the flames crawl from left to right. As words disappear, Coleman reads what remains with increasing delight. The poem is getting better and better. Concision by fire! Now The Poet, reading louder and louder, is proclaiming single-word masterpieces in triumphant baritone. The poetic remnants are finally consigned to the flames, and fresh logs placed over them. It is smoky, it is funny, and the point is made. "Poor poet," says Coleman.

When the editing is over, Coleman says he likes my poems and encourages me to write more. I can scarcely believe this, as Coleman is not lavish with praise. Yet he is sincere. I will have to think long about this. I do seem to have learned that concision is the essence of good writing. Concision is not minimalism, which reduces the word count until the ideal is reached: the empty page. Concision is economy of means. A poem is best when it is zaftig with meaning, svelte in word count. It is a rare poem or paragraph that cannot be improved by omission. A single extra word, I have found to my absolute delight, can ruin a perfectly good poem.

Where Is the Light?

A few years before the visit to Athens, I had set a song cycle for the Sufi Choir of Robert Bly's translations of Kabir poems. When I met him at a summer seminar where we were both teaching classes, I secured his reluctant permission to release the album. In the late '80s we met again, same environment and circumstances, but this time his manner was warmer. Could I teach him to tune his balalaika? Sure. Would he look at a poem or two of mine? Okay.

I showed him a poem about my guru, raga singer Pandit Pran Nath, referring to *the light in the larynx*. When Robert read the line, his head drew back.

"Why not *the light in the throat*? Larynx sounds medical."

"But what about my alliteration? My precious all-American, allergy-alleviating alliteration?" is what I did not ask. I did not ask because *throat* was so obviously better, made the line better, made the poem better, and made the poet better. The lesson was to not sacrifice meaning or clarity for the sake of a poetic or literary device.

Zen Music

In 1976, I found myself on the California Arts Council, sitting next to chairman Gary Snyder. He was a model leader, drawing us all out and then bringing us to consensus. A year later, Gary helped me choose some of his poems for a song cycle I would compose; we had a lively correspondence about them. But the project lost steam because, try as I might, I couldn't find the music in Gary's poetry.

Robert Bly and Balalaika

He uses words in a beautifully precise way, his thoughts are sound, and his lines have the diamond's gleam but, at the time, his music was hidden from me.

Thirty years later, the Galax String Quartet, with contralto Karen Clark, recorded an album of Gary's poems set by four different composers, of which I was one. This time was different. With Gary's help, the right poems were chosen and the music poured out—a whole half-hour of it.

The album came off well, and our live performances with Gary were high times. All through was the blessing of Gary's presence, his simple humanity mixed with his complex poetic aesthetic.

Gary taught me precision—that poetry could still be poetry even if not especially musical—or if the music is the content itself, expressed *just so*. I realized also that poetry silently read from the page can make silent music.

Hyper Hafez

A few years ago, I was swept away by Daniel Ladinsky's English versions of the Persian poet Hafez. I set a cycle of eight of his Hafez versions for Devi to sing that I titled *Café Hafez*. Daniel, who had already heard the Sufi Choir, bestowed his blessing and encouragement for the recording of the album. There commenced a barrage of literary emails and, I do believe, for a time we were each other's high amusement. Hafez can be an over-the-top poet with profound transmission disguised as egoist displays. Daniel Ladinsky has that extreme gene as well, and the marriage has produced a Hafez/Ladinsky oeuvre of great value for readers of English. For me, the music of Daniel's poems can be Ella at full throttle, Janis belting her truth, Itzhak Perlman at full vibrato. Nothing is wasted, wall-to-wall euphony, boundless, if tough, love. The music composed itself, and on the album, Devi sings at the top of her form.

A Pearl From Our Bard

I met Bob Dylan briefly, once, in the lobby of the Second City. Although I never had the impulse to meet Bobby Zimmerman—for that is surely whom I would have seen—whoever he actually is, he is a great lyricist bordering on a great poet. In an interview published long ago, he advised lyricists and poets: *Put your strongest line at the end.* That is hardly an infallible guideline, but it is undeniably useful for all writers; it can save the line, or the stanza, or the paragraph, even possibly the chapter. It is your stern schoolmistress, posture drawn straight, looking down through rimless glasses over your shoulder as you write. Every so often, she points to a line on your paper. Really, you say, *really? That* line? Oh. Yeah. Right.

The Music of the Leap

In *Leaping Poetry*, Robert Bly speaks of "riding on dragons" between conscious and unconscious thought. The leap typically is a metaphor that connects two unlike things into a single savored experience. The gap gets filled in. Two strangers shake hands, maybe share a kiss that turns the air red. Zen poetry and koans encourage the serious reader to be fearless of the ultimate leap conjoining opposites, the leap beyond polarity, the leap opening into an empty field of endless possibility.

The Persian poets Rumi, Kabir, and Hafez are primary teachers. Their metaphors for the inner life of longing and transcendence are a poet's catechism. It is no surprise I have sought out their English translators, Barks, Bly, and Ladinsky, for musical settings. Like attracts like. I'm after that leap beyond language, the leap into musical stanzas that light the mind. There is a wisdom in that leap that comes to rest in you. May you soon land next to me, Gentle Leaper, and far from here.

In music, there is an energetic engine called a cadence that creates a harmonic gap and then fills it in. Most of the clock time of tonal music is taken up with this device: expanding the harmonic field to include tones increasingly disparate, then collapsing the field to a single tone from which all were originally generated. A cadence takes you out on a refined breath to a mysterious orbit, then brings you back home to the black earth of meaning. In the choreography between literary metaphor and musical cadence, you go out on the dragon and return in both realms. Kansas and Oz are the same girl, but new.

Writer's Gym

Keep writing everybody says, and I say it to myself. It's the writer's mantra, the composer's too. When I'd returned from Bali and was finishing *The Listening Book*, and shouted to my wife in her office across the hall, "This is the sixteenth fucking draft of this fucking chapter," she sweetly called back, "Sounds about right."

Writing offers a curriculum for what wisdom is and what wisdom is not. Deciding what to keep and what to toss is like a writer's wisdom gym. Will anyone read this a hundred years from now? A year from now, a week, ever? Who cares about my vision of a spiritual democracy or my lousy date in eighth grade? When does my heart join with the heart of the anonymous world, and when does it belong on the messy floor of my closet?

You winnow and you edit. The winnowing never ends, or the editing, or the walking away or the racing back. Sometimes frivolous details are the perfect fit; other times I have to leave out something so crucial that I'm certain I'll die without it. The truth is that I'll die with or without it, so I have to think down the line: *There is only the generations.* I wrote that in my journal when I was in my mid-twenties, adding that, insightful as my thoughts may have been at the time, I knew they weren't being *lived out*. Well, now I have lived long, and I am writing autobiographically, and I am confronted with life and death in all their graceful pliés and clumsy stumbles. So many trillions of stories are lost, and who cares? Who actually cares?

The act of discernment is forced into consciousness. I have to think who could benefit, who could be made whole? Wait! I know! I'll write *the bottle is corked and sitting on the table*! It might be recognized eight hundred years downstream by a reader who, sensing the presence of an old friend, sighs. Wise poet, Rumi.

Books and Editors

My three books for general readers, *The Listening Book*, *The Musical Life*, and *Bridge of Waves*, try to frame sound generally, and music specifically, by focusing various lenses on the reader's life. I had, for many years, felt the call to articulate my understanding of music. I soon realized, however, that I first needed to write about the primal act of listening, so readers could learn to hear before I discussed what they were hearing. I began with sounds surrounding the reader in the present, and moved on and out from there.

By the time I began writing *The Listening Book* on a balcony in Bali, years of teaching had given me empathy for people convinced they were tone deaf (no one is) or who wanted to know how to listen more deeply. Beginning with that connection, a writing voice appeared. All my students, all the poets and writers in my life, all my Sufi and Buddhist training, all the improvisational theater and musical work, plus a love of clear talk and clear talkers—all were steady winds from behind urging me on. When I raised my head, I was looking out over an immense expanse of Balinese rice in a uniquely gentle, cooperative environment. Not without its birth pains, my first book squeezed itself out, the easiest (as it turns out) of five babies. I'm still surprised at the sharp focus of the voice. Loving listening as I do, it was actually a lark to draw others into my sound world. And all the sounds around me, including the infernal combustion engines of tractors plowing the fields, modeled and shaped the flow.

When the manuscript was done, I sent it around. One of the rejection letters reminded me sternly that "our company publishes only works of literature." Fuck 'em. I sent the manuscript to a friend at Shambhala on a Friday. The following Tuesday, veteran editor Dave O'Neal called and said, "I love your book. We want to publish it."

Carol Sill edited *The Listening Book* very lightly, giving me the same encouragement that Murshid Lewis had by giving me a predictably green light. Ms. Sills did suggest a chapter on silence, and I wrote it, and she was right. *The Listening Book* got rave reviews when it was first published in 1991 and is still selling well. One year later, Dave O'Neal said he wanted another book from me, which he would edit. *The Musical Life* was, to some extent, leftovers from the first book; it was the perilous second album that musicians fear. It takes thirty years to produce your first album or write your first book, and the second is supposed to arrive shortly thereafter. But as the new book went along, surprising new things occurred. My writing voice became a little richer, more complex. Dave O'Neal edited it closely, and it was great to work in tandem with him.

I'm especially proud of the last seventy-five pages of *The Musical Life*, a section called "Sound is the Teacher," an anthropomorphic view of the overtone series. To help edit that part, Dave brought in Larry Hamberlin, an excellent composer and freelance editor, and we forged a mutually welcome composer/writer bond. *The Musical Life* was less successful in the marketplace than *The Listening Book*, but it is, in my opinion, a deeper book.

Harmonic Experience, edited by Larry Hamberlin and published by Inner Traditions in 1997, finally said, just as I turned sixty, what I had to say about what I knew best; the writing of it was half music and half language. It has become a definitive book about the theory and practice of tonal harmony. Since I wanted amateurs to be encouraged, serious musicians to be taken as far as they could or would go, and academic theorists to be impressed by its invention, its range and, above all, the *rigor* of its presentation, I had expected that finding the book's proper voice would be especially challenging. But those very constraints guided me toward a voice that sounded friendly and inviting to a wide spectrum of readers. Over a quarter century, it has sold consistently well. I'll say quite a bit more about *Harmonic Experience* in Chapter 19.

A decade later, Dave O'Neal called again. He said he liked my writing and wanted another book. *Bridge of Waves*, published in 2010, completes a trilogy for the general reader. It assumes a reader more committed to musical understanding than the first two, is longer (too long), is more wide ranging, is my favorite of the three, and has sold least well.

An objective, discerning editor is crucial for both the writing and the writer. This writing voyage of mine would have stalled early on were it not for the editors provided by the publishers, or for the many readers who have read chapters, or for reading out loud to patient friends, often students during their lesson time. But there would have been little headway without my editor-wife, her smile, her gleaming axe, her eagle eyes, and a brain grounded in syntactical clarity.

Devi has been the first reader and editorial guide for all five books. She knows me like none other and can tell before I can when the writing has gone off the rails, or belongs somewhere else in the book, or in another book, or is fair tinder for The Writer's Pyre.

ॐ

An underlying motivation for writing books on music has been to make the writing musical, to reflect the euphony and flow, the expansion and contraction, the dynamic range of music itself. That has served me well for four books. This one, *The Shrine Thief*, does cover the music of my life, but it is about my life, not about music. The challenge has been to keep intact the musical writing while not talking directly about music. What is musical writing? Well, I thought I knew, but it turns out it is a lot easier to write musically about the qualities of various musical cadences than it is to write musically about an argument with my father, or about the ambiguities of ontology, or about moving from this to that city. Discovering the music of a mundane life is one thing. Discovering the music of writing about a mundane life is another.

Even when it feels like I'm balancing sentences like a trained seal on the end of my nose, finding the prosody of the mundane clarifies as it unfolds. I never thought *The Shrine Thief* would be an easy book, and it hasn't been. Its voice will still be cooking until the final edit, until I get my fingers caught in the printing press snatching away pages for revision, until you read it, until after you've forgotten most of it. This book tries to frame the whole of my own life beyond its particulars into a practical philosophy. The big lesson has been to stop writing for my father. The next lesson is to write for you. The music books were easy. But autobiography mixed with philosophy, that's a different story, and finding the true voice for it has been, well, let's say *emergent*, which brings us up to the present.

Currently, writing for me isn't so much about content as it is about refined experience. It is the flow of IZ, ever-morphing momentary engagement. I move the pen over the lined page; my line of words connects pen to heart, heart to language. I resist nothing; experience thaws from the deep freeze, stories dissipate into space. Atoms disappear or reconstruct back onto the page, showing up as fancy molecules, which I rearrange until a paragraph appears.

After I have written, my eyes close. But now yours are open.

We need both of us. Let's take turns.

Taking Turns

Among the "micro-memoirs" Amy Moon wrote for my eightieth birthday was this one, which I am pleased to share here.

Twelwe

Pat Martinez committed suicide. He was 13. They found him in a creek bed not far from where we lived. We were born on the same day. The year before, we decided to meet in secret at midnight, each of us with our group of birthday friends in the meadow across from the Oliver's. It was understood we would play truth or dare even though no one spoke of it. One of the boys brought a 40oz of something malt. None of my friends took it as it was passed around, nor the flimsy joint already smoked halfway down. I half expected people to wait for him and I to kiss, a birthday rite or some such thing. Pat glanced at me once with his hooded starlit eyes, but David De Santos took over and started the game. It was a particularly cold November, and our tweenage angst made us colder. Nothing could thaw out the raw fear I had of what would happen if my mother found out. I could be grounded for weeks, months, years.

We did finally kiss. He smelled like weed and tasted like beer. It felt good and dangerous, and I knew I would love him in the future.

We rushed back down the hill, full of kisses and horrible truths; we were older and unstoppable. Sneaking back in we made more noise than a chicken coop and there you were in the hallway: a half-dressed sleepy sheepherder sent out to check the flock. "All here? No one eaten by wolves?" (Not yet, anyway) "All right, back to sleep then all of you." You ambled back down the hallway and I loved you fiercely for not giving away our secret, even though I knew you could smell the wet meadow in our hair and hear the crackling of our young bodies.

❧

Amy herself turned fifty the year after I turned eighty, and I wrote this for her:

Moon at Fifty

At the kitchen table, tea between us, maybe wine,
while all around us a bright field of understanding, a wordless sky,
our words running free as ground squirrels—travel words,
sibling words, what's-up-with-so-and-so words,
work and friends words—our lives spill out in random detail,
our sky open and still, enveloping, invisible.

Did I ever expect daughters and dads could have this?
By what kindness are we allowed to gaze through one another,
to call each other out, to have no fear? I love you, Amy Moon, and have
ever since the first light caught your face.

In that clear moment my thought was
so beautiful an infant female will teach me to be an adult male,
a true guide and guardian
and, in a way I hadn't seen at the time, you did.

What I've learned over life is to trust you.
This sky-blue field has arisen and abided even when you were angered
or submerged by sadness, or were tied up by some intransigent
awkwardness. What has grown is the knowing that you would emerge
whole at the end of every story, even the tragic ones,
especially those.

I've never felt the need to steer you toward some goodness
or turn your head toward some invisible light
—well, maybe some of that—but you're a self-floating boat
and know full well how to navigate by the stars,
as knows every True Moon.

At each turn of our half-century, memory places us
in some age-appropriate version of sitting so lightly, sharing a glass
at the corner table, enjoying what folks call *Being,*
but what we know simply to be ever-ripening human being, as in
happy fiftieth, dear heart of mine.

May your deep sea gleam
and the hills, moist with dew and new growth,
resound.

18

Music at the Core

No Answer

We listen, we babble, we mimic, we try to get what we want. When we are first learning to speak, we give no thought to why air is pulsing through our lungs, our tongues rising and falling, our lips shaping the stream. We know only that everyone else around us is doing something similar, that some sounds work better than others, and that it seems essential.

Learning music was that way for me. I heard music on the radio and on records, in kindergarten everyone sang as the teacher accompanied on the classroom piano, Sue practiced piano every day, and I was picking out notes on the keyboard that I heard her play. She was reading from pages that were above my eye level, so the connection between page and music did not occur to me. But by the time I was six I was the one learning to read music, and the proper technique to play it. Music was less of a separate activity than a language I could speak and read whenever I wanted.

My first piano teacher, Charles Keuhner, was a well-groomed, heavyset gentleman of thirty-five prone to profuse sweating. He was stern but patient with his numberless pupils, who viewed him as a necessary accessory to childhood. Mr. Keuhner taught small elective classes in a basement room of our grade school. Most of his students were girls; only three or four boys in the school of six hundred "took piano." According to the working-class ethic of our school, boys played football and fought. In endlessly inventive ways, boy pianists were reminded of that by their peers.

By the second grade, I was taking private lessons at home. A year later, the teachers had me routinely playing for my classroom. Although this felt good when I was doing it, it was made to hurt afterward. So my musical language became ever more private, and I felt a little superior to those who couldn't understand my attraction to it.

Mr. Keuhner, a graduate of the Cincinnati Conservatory, was most incurious as to why music behaves the way it does. He taught from the page only: at first, the wretched pieces sold by the millions to children. But by third grade, I was playing real pieces, simple Mozart and Schumann in collections. The Mozart K. 545 Sonata with which I wooed Jacqueline Keller (and her mother) was my first real piece.

When I was nine, I attended Rockdale Avenue Temple Sunday School, where most of the Jewish kids were taking music lessons, so my musical language became more social, more alive. During that year, our house was a way station for Jewish refugees flowing from Europe. One day Hildegard, a petite pale woman in her twenties, arrived, and I played for her. She was happy to hear me and, as a kind of test, snuck up behind me, put her small hands over my eyes, and said, "Now play." I kept going, and when she took away her hands, her face was beaming. "See, he can play with his eyes closed!" Something fluttered. My music and the touch of female flesh: forever linked.

I was a slow learner. I needed a grammar for the music I was learning, but none was forthcoming. Mr. Kuehner toggled between encouragement and dire prediction. But I was enjoying the music around me. Sue and I were both enamored of pop radio, and especially, on Saturday nights, in her room, on her bed, as she pretended to do her homework, *The Hit Parade*. I loved this music, and I wanted to better understand it, but I could not, not from there.

My dad, noticing my interest in jazz, and noticing that colored people play jazz, asked our colored maid if she had any colored friends who could teach his young son to play jazz like colored people. A few evenings later, Mr. Sheffield, a solid, tall man, and Mr. Banks, a slight, short man, appeared in our living room, distinguished, polite, and dressed for performance. Mr. Sheffield showed me how to play twelve bars of boogie-woogie. Mr. Banks showed me the chord progression for "On the Sunny Side of the Street." In the ensuing weeks, I practiced hard, and the boogie-woogie turned out to be the hit of the Rockdale Avenue Temple Seventh Grade Dance. But what interested me to the point of obsession was the chord progression to "On the Sunny Side of the Street." Why this excruciatingly good feeling in my body? When I had asked Mr. Sheffield and Mr. Banks, they said because each song goes a certain way, and this was the way this one goes.

Buddy Hiles

As recounted earlier (in Chapter 5), Buddy Hiles, my first major teacher, appeared a few weeks later. Same living room, but Buddy and I felt a friendship immediately and he wanted to share his best friend, music, with me. Sitting at the piano he showed me a single jazz chord, and a voicing of that chord meant to be spread over the range of five saxophones. Then he showed me how to move that voicing up and down the scale.

Then he had me play it. Then, as he played it again on the piano, he whistled "Ol' Man River" along with it—familiar but strangely, beautifully new. Then he had me play it on the piano as he played along, with simple virtuosity, on his alto saxophone. Then he showed me how to write a transposed five-stave score of the chord progression for the five saxophones. Then he said to write it out with no mistakes for my next lesson.

At last! Somebody could show me some grammar to the music I heard but could not imitate, much less notate. The floodgates opened. Within a year, I was writing music for Buddy's big band, The Buddy Hiles Jazz Orchestra, which rehearsed and often performed at Cincinnati's Cotton Club in the middle of the toughest black streets in town. Dad entrusted Buddy with his son, and without a single raised eyebrow the Black musicians accepted me as Buddy's boy. I was quiet and absorbed in everything. I was learning as much from the cultural vibe as I was from its musical language. I learned that they were inseparable.

As one decade folded into the next, I realized with increasing sobriety that jazz, like most other means of communication among Blacks in white America, was a form of protective code against the ever-present constraints of white subjugation. Jazz is the music of slavery married serendipitously to the song forms and harmonies of Europe. To even listen to it, let alone learn to play or compose it, a white American must learn to honor its innate joy as a transmutation of pain. What is possibly the 20th century's most expressive language arose generation by generation from the enslaved people of 17th-century America. For the cruelties our white ancestors visited on Blacks in order to build our proud nation, there is perhaps no more realistic version of "reparation" than *fully* hearing and honoring the voices of their descendants. At age thirteen, I could not have framed what I was learning in such terms, but that is precisely what I was learning.

After two years of intensive study with Buddy, I felt that he'd given me what he could and that I'd learned enough to study on my own. Thirty years later, Mom discovered that he had died suddenly at age fifty. Despite his turbulent private life, a statue of Walter "Buddy" Hiles should be erected in the middle of the treesy mall between the two interstate freeways where the Cincinnati Cotton Club once stood. The inscription could say: *He made his way.*

As the truth of American history becomes more widely acknowledged, I am increasingly grateful to have been given a chair at the table. I offer my bows but I know my limits. Yes, there have been great jazz musicians of every stripe. Cultures admix over time, as do gene pools and languages. The old order changeth. Even the word "jazz," which by the mid-20th century referred to the evolutionary peak of bebop, is now, in the third decade of the 21st, an almost meaningless descriptor.

R. Earl Snapp

Mr. Snapp, whose name you could scarcely contrive for a high school band-and-orchestra conductor, did not have much musical grammar to teach me, but when he wasn't admonishing me for some hidden musical mischief, he was hiring me—at five dollars a pop—to write arrangements for his weekend gig sextet. He encouraged me to write for the high school orchestra. I composed a concerto for orchestra, featuring me as soloist on trumpet and French horn, that impressed Leonard Meyer enough the following year to get me into the University of Chicago despite the poor grades I had incurred composing it.

William Russo Jr.

In 1954, immediately upon entering the University of Chicago, I began to study with Bill Russo, who was twenty-seven at the time. Russo was an iconic composer/arranger by reputation but a newbie at teaching. He knew his share of jazz grammar, much of which had passed directly from Lenny Tristano, with whom Russo had studied in New York in the late '40s. I learned a lot from Russo, enough to keep me busy, but not all of what I wanted to learn.

Bill Russo

What was missing? What was missing was the secret of those beautiful passages in Bill's writing for the Kenton band that gave me such chills and pangs. I surmised finally that he had only a surface idea of why his harmonies worked so well, although he had found a functional way of using them. We never studied his scores. He wanted, instead, to build a comprehensive jazz curriculum, which, through his books and his academic teaching at Chicago's Columbia College, he accomplished. Most disturbingly, however, as his teaching became more doctrinaire, his music became more cerebral, more tightly wound, and often overtly bombastic.

Over time, our age difference became less significant. In the 1980s, there were long telephone conversations, house visits, and discursive evenings of the student-teacher relationship transformed into two old friends circling each other for nourishment. Bill died in 2003. In 2015, I was invited to assemble a concert of his music for the Los Angeles Jazz Orchestra, and it was an honor and a coming of age to conduct it. By studying his scores, with what I now know about harmony I can say, "Oh, so that's what he was doing" (namely, adroit handling of modal flux), and I'm doubly grateful for his musical influence in my early life and collegial presence in his later years.

Music at the Club

When I returned from my life on the road with Kenton, the Second City, with its requirements for nimble scene setting, awaited me. In the cabaret environment, I wasn't trying to find a musical voice; one just crept up on me. It was perforce an eclectic language. The music was needed to set up—and often participate in—scenes ranging from a kindergarten class to a blind date to a holdup in a dark alley to a Chinese restaurant to making love in a cornfield during a thunderstorm. I drew from all the music I had ever heard and loved: from Mozart, from *Captain Marvel*, from *The Shadow*, from Dinah Shore's "Buttons and Bows," from Lenny Tristano and Cecil Taylor, from dozens upon dozens of popular standards and jazz classics I knew by heart, from Bach, Beethoven, Chopin, Stravinsky, Schoenberg, nursery rhymes, and myriad atmospheric sounds (lightning, factory machines, wind in the wheat). Everything was fodder for the onstage scene. Folks found my eclecticism remarkable, but not me. I was just using the language I knew. Eventually that became not diverse languages but simply the one I spoke.

Easley Blackwood

Although I had abandoned my MA in English literature at U of C, I still haunted the campus, including the Music Building, where I met Easley Blackwood, who would become the principal teacher of my early adult life. When we met in 1960, he was a brand-new professor at the University of Chicago and one of the great hopes for contemporary American composition. He had studied with Paul Hindemith, intensively with Nadia Boulanger, and had recently won the Koussevitzky Prize, which included a recording by the Boston Symphony Orchestra of his First Symphony. Easley and I seemed to

Easley Blackwood

get on well. I invited him to the Second City; soon after, he visited me in my nearby basement apartment. He began visiting on Sunday nights, letting himself into my apartment to practice on my Steinway so that when I got home from the theater, there was Easley playing the classical canon with great virtuosity.

We got heavily stoned first thing. Then we got silly, laughing at juvenile jokes. But for the rest of the evening, he practiced, sometimes with commentary for my benefit, and I listened. Around 5AM I prepared breakfast for two: a 12-ounce glass of freshly squeezed orange juice each and a three-egg cheddar cheese omelet with four thick-sliced pieces of bacon on the side. Then, in the Chicago dawn, Easley took a cab back to his apartment on the Southside.

During that period, I was trying to find my voice as a composer of contemporary chamber music. A *Sonata for Flute and Piano* was in progress, and I had some good ideas, but I rarely knew how to proceed convincingly or even complete a phrase. I was guessing, hunting and pecking through a language I marginally understood. I asked Easley to take a look at the piece. He took the sonata home with him, and when I called him a few days later to ask his opinion, he said, "If I were a professor of composition at Yale and this piece crossed my desk, I would recommend that the composer attend our Yale High School Summer Program as a junior." I was mighty deflated. I had imagined I could make the jump from my catch-all eclecticism to a stylistic maturity in *serious* music. The next night, stoned and depressed, I was listening to *Le Baiser de la fée*, a neoclassic ballet of Stravinsky's that I found particularly beautiful. Haunted by Easley's assessment, I took the score to the piano only to discover that the workings of the piece were a mystery to me. I knew a lot, but this I did not know. I felt like crying. All of my music now seemed superficial. And, according to professional standards, I played my instrument poorly. Where was the mastery? Maybe I did cry a little.

The next day, I called Easley and said, "I want to be your disciple." He said that there would be a little test and that if I passed the test, the fee would be one lid of grass per lesson. The lid was easy—the Second City was a hub in those days. What was the test? Learn the five-part Fugue in B-flat minor from Book One of Bach's *Well-Tempered Clavier* and play it for him from memory with no mistakes. I agreed.

The Fugue in B-flat minor is a two-pager and not pianistically difficult, but the five-part polyphony must be rendered clearly for it to be played well. It took me three weeks to learn the fingering, and another month to memorize the piece. I had never worked on anything with such concentration in my life. For the first time, I was hearing independent parts—separate melodies heard simultaneously. So this, I realized, is what the real guys can do.

A few months earlier, Easley had been recounting an exchange he'd had with a student we knew at the university. The student had not done his work well, but Easley was harsh with him, even, I thought, a little bit cruel. I called him out on it.

"That wasn't very nice," I said.

"Music students are not to be encouraged,'" he replied.

In the fiercely competitive world of Easley's career, music had better be its own reward, or no student could survive. So although my thinking was (and is) quite different from his, I understood what Easley was saying. On the other hand, it was my neck at stake here.

On the day of the test, Easley met me after hours at the theater because he wanted to simulate a concert situation. He sat in the back row. I played the Fugue in B-flat minor atrociously, inwardly groaning and outwardly sweating. When I finished, Easley said, "Okay, now that you know where you stand, I'll take you on."

In a way, we had already taken each other on. I was fully absorbed in Easley's progress as a musician, and he was fascinated with the byways of my life ill lit for him. We actually liked each other and, usually at the expense of others, we laughed a lot. We made up outrageous scenarios about people. He earnestly shared his sexual fantasies. Easley was one hundred percent gay, and I was going through my own internal explorations of gender balance, but he knew that he had a sloppy pianist and talented, ill-formed composer on his hands and he felt bound to turn him into a disciplined musician. Overt sexuality never surfaced. On the contrary, he worked me hard as a musician, and I practiced according to an elaborate schedule of technique, pieces to learn, theory, and composition—six hours a day, in fact, with scarcely a miss for four years, even while on the road with the Second City.

A linchpin of the work was a kind of musical crossword puzzle called *figured bass* that has come down through centuries of European pedagogy and performance, through the Paris Conservatory, through Nadia Boulanger, through Easley Blackwood, and now through me. I realized that these compositional puzzles constituted an encyclopedia of the language I was trying to learn, a trove of every sequence, suspension, cadence, and modulation in the European zeitgeist, all in four-part puzzles waiting for this starved student to solve. It was the pivotal language I needed in order to assimilate the classical style I so adored. Everything I have composed or authored about music is informed by this discipline, and I am one lucky musician to be in the Boulanger lineage through Easley: direct transmission from masters of their craft. And the *very best* part of this transmission has been that in later years I have been able to transcend it. By fortunate osmosis (and transcendent experience to come), the technique has been absorbed.

Easley loved to show off his rare gifts to me. On an evening in October 1961, toward the end of the Cuban missile crisis, he asked if I had a newspaper. I handed him that day's *Chicago Sun-Times*. He asked me to name one of the minor keys. I said E minor. He then commenced to transpose by ear Bach's B-flat Minor Fugue into E minor while reading aloud from the front page of the *Sun-Times* until we gave up laughing at the ironic juxtaposition of private skill and world crisis. And yet I had to ask, what sort of brain could do this?

Another trick: At that time, I happened to have two grand pianos facing one another. He had me sit at one and play five-tone chords ("not six") using absolutely random tones spread out over the entire keyboard; at the other piano, he reiterated the chords in a blink. I tried to trick him once by playing six tones. He said, "I can't do six."

Easley played with rigid hands and wrists, a not uncommon piano technique that depends on finger strength and independence. Although I benefitted somewhat from this, it took years of effort from subsequent California coaches to relax my muscles enough for me and the piano to melt into each other. This is different from conquering the piano. Easley played with great clarity, palpable ambition, and a sewed-up heart.

One thing Easley could do with his rare skills was play complex atonal music. Pierre Boulez wrote his Second Piano Sonata in 1948, at age twenty-four. Few pianists could even approach the piece, much less memorize it, but Easley did both with accuracy and verve, and I got to hear an iconic mid-century atonal composition unscroll week by week. He did perform it for audiences, most importantly in New York, and eventually had the opportunity to perform it for Boulez, whose aesthetic—he was in his mid-forties by then—had softened. Boulez pronounced Easley's rendition too rigid, too stiff. Easley was very downcast about this, about not being *chosen*. It seemed to me like a turning point in his career ambitions. Although Easley recorded and toured extensively and successfully with various chamber musicians, for the next thirty-five years he hunkered down at the University of Chicago, steering his career from there.

Easley and I kept our friendship alive after I moved with my family to San Francisco. In 1967 he came from Chicago to visit. I took him on a tour of Haight-Ashbury, set up a concert for him, and witnessed his delight as he stepped into the Pacific Ocean for the first time. Gradually, however, our friendship became strained over differences in musical, theoretical, and publishing issues. One thing must be mentioned, however. In the mid-1980s he produced an album of equal-tempered tunings from thirteen to twenty-four tones within the octave, displaying the properties unique to each tuning. The collection, widely available, is called *Micro-tonal Etudes* and is required listening for musicians everywhere who are interested in the psychoacoustic effects of equal temperament. Since the relationship of just tuning to equal temperament is the subject of my own book, *Harmonic Experience*, this has been a rare and serendipitous intersection of Easley's creative interests and my own. We do disagree about how music works, though. "Pure thirds," he once said to me, "are for people in California who like to sit around singing long tones." Well, Gentle Reader, he was right about that!

In 2013, at age eighty, Easley was admitted to an assisted living/ long-term care facility in Chicago. For eight years, taxed by physical and mental decline, he kept himself isolated but alive. From our very first meeting, I've been glad that the universe got Easley Blackwood and that I got a piece of him when we were young. For over five formative years of an intense relationship he was my mentor and my troubled, idiosyncratic friend. I listened patiently to his vitriolic screed toward his enemies, a changing list, and he nursed my musical thickness and sloppiness toward some sort of fruition. I am so glad to have known him. He passed gently away on January 22, 2023.

Improvisational Games

Theater games have long been a substrate of my musical language. Trust-based games touch on the social psychology of behavior, and it is likely that the substructure of such games mirrors the structure of animal behavior and of our capacity for change. This work was important to me not only because I resonated with it, but because it happened to be my salaried job. Initially I saw my task as trying to teach actors to be more musical; eventually, however, I realized that I could teach musicians to be more compositional with the same kind of trust in the spontaneous and the unknown.

In 1964, when I first heard the inventive playing of drummer George Marsh, the hair stood up on the back of my neck. We agreed to rehearse together, and musical games readily appeared—the very structures that were anathema to actors. One of the most telling games, Sparse as Possible, was meant to thin the musical texture down to its essentials—to make more space in order to listen more deeply. Another game, Gather Ye, asks each player to play only their version of what they hear from the others. Another game, As Much As Possible From As Little As Possible, or AMAPFALAP, is a study in aleatory motivic development. Each of these games, and of the dozens that followed, gives a new insight into a musical language that might not have appeared by any other means. As in theater, the player's language expands and deepens game by game, as if there were an intrinsic wisdom to the games themselves.

For me, there was a confluence of particular events: hearing Black free music, which was just surfacing in the early '60s, and feeling its validity; then finding a free player, George Marsh, who thought like me; then finding a likeminded bass player, Clyde Flowers, and then a fearlessly imaginative wind player, Rich Fudoli. Our quartet, though white, was much beholden to the Black school, which I felt arising from the same sense of community I had recognized when I was thirteen, walking ghetto streets with Buddy. Now it was ten years and a blooming revolution later and I thought, *These musicians aren't playing games, they're redefining their being, their relationships with one another and the world at large.*

We wanted our own kind of freedom in listening and playing but did not have the same social and psychological imperative that came from Black culture. Cecil Taylor we were not; Archie Shepp we were not; Albert Ayler we were not. But we needed to express a new freedom we felt. After over a year of rehearsals, the Chicago Improvising Players gave our first concert in 1966 at the Second City. Our quartet may have been among the first to play these trust-based games in a free-jazz context, but a lot of people were on a similar path. There was a zeitgeist of such freedom in the air.

I realized during the early rehearsals that a quality of listening was required that was different from anything I had experienced. It was faster and it was deeper. One had to hear the intention behind everything at all times. This was a new challenge, more intricate and absorbing than was possible on a cabaret stage. I realized that making up a new game and aiming for a certain musical result is a fundamentally compositional act.

Composers set boundaries and work within them, or they start composing out of thin air and the boundaries appear. Same with the games—there is as much skill in inventing them as in playing them.

The ultimate game is the disappearance of the dichotomy: *Game/ No Game* is the title of a duet album George and I recorded in 2004, after forty years of playing together. The Chicago Improvising Players did not release an album—the experiment was just too new for us at the time. The whole experience did serve as a core for the Ghost Opera Company, soon to begin (in 1969) at the San Francisco Conservatory. These were the early days in the formation of a spontaneous language for actors and musicians, a language that mirrored life in new ways. This new improvisational language spread like wildfire to artistic communities that were first recognized as avant-garde but are currently accepted as mainstream, even a tad old-guard.

A new question now arose for me: how to mix the spontaneity of improvisational games with through-composition. Ralph Shapey, a visceral American composer who held a professorship in composition at the University of Chicago, loved our improvisational quartet, featured us in a piece he composed for the Chicago Symphony, and set up a concert for us as part of the contemporary chamber music series at the university. There was a certain amount of transactional quid pro quo: I interviewed him at length for *The Downbeat Yearbook*; he commissioned me to write a piece for the Chicago Chamber Players, a blend of through-composition, improvisation, and theatrical awareness. The piece, *A Perennial Recital*, featured a mezzo-soprano and a clarinetist facing one another in a relational duet, with the chamber orchestra offering instrumental commentary on the drama. The woman sings in gibberish, she and the clarinetist soulfully goad each other on, while the percussionist George Marsh improvises in the middle of it all. The two soloists go through every manner of attraction, aversion and, finally, epiphany and reconciliation. At the end, the mezzo, finger to lips, hushes the clarinetist and then each of the players in turn. The final seconds are a conducted silence of changing time signatures. *A Perennial Recital* held the audience in close attention, was well received and well reviewed. Even Easley, who graciously made a live recording of it, was kind in his critique: "I especially liked the chime toward the end," to which I did not reply, "Yeah, that was the moment of epiphany."

Besides being held together by an improvising percussionist, the sixteen minutes of the piece contain composed passages intended to sound like improvisation; there are moments meant to have a jazz feeling, polyphony is present throughout, and it is written in a harmonic language ranging from atonal to omni-modal to tonal. I felt I had discovered a synthesis of what I had learned. Nobody said, "Your piece is so eclectic." People said, "I really liked your piece."

By the time *A Perennial Recital* was premiered in the spring of 1967, my family and I had already moved to San Francisco, so I had to fly back to hear the piece and say goodbyes. For thirteen years, from the University of Chicago to the Second City to *Downbeat* magazine to a treasured circle of weirdly gifted teachers and loving friends, Chicago had treated me well. Now I had gratefully sung my swan song.

Luciano Berio

Three months after the Chicago performance, I had the opportunity to spend some time in San Francisco with Luciano Berio, who also liked the *A Perennial Recital*. I told him then that I thought I had found *new ways of sharing*. In a letter dated July 12, 1967, Berio wrote:

> Fifteen days ago I listened again to your Perennial Recital and, again, it was very rewarding. There are things there that are more valuable than finding *new ways of sharing* it seems to me; but I understand you and I know that behind what you say there is a Big Question to which I keep answering with a special kind of loneliness. Sharing, maybe, comes after.

I am extremely interested about your theater project The Harold [which I had described to him]. Let me know something more precise from the inner side when you can.

As ever, Luciano Berio

The Ghost Opera Company

Once we were settled in San Francisco, my Chicago life ebbed like a fast tide. At the Committee Theater, my repertoire of cues and affects was refined during the development of The Harold. It was the job of the music to find motifs for recurring scenes that were variations of themselves. The music had to mark the weave. Occasionally the pianist or the piano itself was part of the scene. At our best, we were all a single being in constant transformation, and the music had to find the functional expression of that. Night after night, unexpected, extraordinary sounds came out of my instrument.

Meanwhile, at the San Francisco Conservatory, The Ghost Opera Company now included members of the Committee's improvisation workshops and was giving concerts on campus and around the city. We would string games together into Game Symphonies that tended to develop an abstract narrative. One spring afternoon in 1973, in the amphitheater of the De Young Museum in Golden Gate Park, we were fifteen minutes into a Game Symphony when we heard the scraping of ankle bells across the pavement, only to behold the queenly entrance of Janis Joplin gorgeously overdressed in her psychedelic best, along with her consort, a young blonde woman in a red T-shirt and white shorts. Amid nudges and murmurs from the audience, they found two empty chairs, and on we went. A few minutes later, the young woman leapt onto the stage, dancing wildly among the players and the actors, waving her arms, sometimes screaming, falling and getting up and falling, getting in our faces. The woman was out of her mind on acid, likely in the middle of a psychotic break. Where was our Game Symphony now? According to our high principles, we made the best of it, integrating her wildness with our protocols, welcoming her dissociation, attempting our best *Yes And*.

There was an American flag in its holder upstage that the woman grabbed up and colorfully brandished about, a tripped-out patriotic cheetah accompanied by increasingly desperate musicians. I froze like a hunter and tracked her moves. When she was close and unsuspecting, I grabbed the flagpole so that our four hands held it tightly. Centerstage now, I looked into her flushed face and flecked-green beacon eyes. Her eyes met mine, and our interlocked hands slowly raised the pole so the flag flew high. Two inches from her nose, I asked her name. *Susan*, I heard her say. I said, "Okay, Susan, you've had your turn." Her body immediately relaxed. She let go of the pole, casually walked off stage, and found her seat with Janis. I'm not sure that the audience knew if Susan and Janis were part of the act. I still don't know.

I'm telling the story because there is improvisation and there is improvisation. We all were being perfectly decent improvisers, devoted to our trust-based methods, when a little pathology dropped in. I was scared at first, then angry (*control your damn court, Janis*), but quickly realized the nature of the test. What I learned is that the language of music needs no boundary between itself and every other manifestation of harmonic vibration between and among people. The moment my eyes locked with Susan's amid the circling dancers and the wailing players was a moment of pure music for me, a moment that seeded courage for unexpected moments to come. *Now* was upended. Space contracted to a black pupil of a woman's eye and expanded to a vast green-flecked sea. In the same way that new words come into spoken language, new vibrational elements come into musical language, and you always have to begin with *Yes And*. That doesn't mean you have to use everything—you can always say, "Yes and...now you've had your turn." I'll bet Janis was amused that day. In any case, she soon exited jangling, with Susan's hand tightly held in hers.

The Sufi Choir

It's possible that the most pivotal moment in my musical education of pivotal moments occurred at the second rehearsal of the Sufi Choir one fall evening in 1969. I'd written a four-part setting of the Arabic word *Alhamdulillah*—all praise is due to God—a simple setting resembling a modern figured bass, in fact, but with a swinging rhythm section of tabla, piano, and bass. It was my first composition for the choir and I was not at all certain of the outcome. But they learned it, and soon they were singing it through. When we tried it one last time from the beginning to end, I stopped playing to see how well the choir could hold its pitch. But something happened that was not about constancy of pitch. What I heard was a choir of angels.

This music was not the atonal constructions of my twenties, nor

Guru-ji and Me

was it the clever artifice of *A Perennial Recital,* nor was it the free diving of The Ghost Opera Company, nor was it the social commentary of cabaret theater, nor did it have the devotional depth of Black gospel. What it *was* was a new kind of gospel, the best we were then able to create—*a tuning to the harmony of the one single music that is the whole of life.* The air *filled with this praising sound.* My vision went white, as if a cloud over my outer senses was needed to recognize an inner truth: the awakened praise of the singers was the music itself. Then, forthwith, I was back at the keyboard, giving cues to the singers and playing my part.

The inner truth I was experiencing was the missing link, the quality I had known was absent from my music but didn't know how to realize. Now, surrounded by these Sufi singers in the presence of our teacher, the very sound of Wonderstanding struck home. As in any epiphany worth a grain of salt, I said to myself, "Oh," and went on with the business at hand. For the next rehearsal I composed a section of ecstatic, sustained chords, harmonically complex, with the singers in their highest tessituras. I was afraid the choir could not learn it, but they nailed it, and the signature sound of the Sufi Choir was born. It was conscious union with *the one single music*, a joyous giving over.

In the coming months, as I would teach the choir, the choir would teach me, and for twelve years, seven albums, and numerous performances in numerous cities, that was the deal. Murshid died knowing that the musical part of his commission from Inayat Khan was ensured.

Pandit Pran Nath

I seem to have an obsessive need to gain cognitive understanding of musical affects. I want to know why things feel the way they do, especially the push and pull of harmony. Fascination with harmonic motion, generally known as chord progressions or "changes," has led me on. Listening deeply to harmonic motion feels as though my body, all aglow, is being shaped by unseen hands. My body is the plot of a sensual story, intelligent, cogent, and sexy. I could live there, and I do.

Up until my early thirties I assumed, like everyone else around me, that these affects were achieved by combinations of the tones in our modern tuning system, triads mostly, but other tonal combinations as well. The engine was chords, chords, and more chords arranged in sequential and cadential patterns. A chordal *sequence* enumerates the possibilities within a scale; a chordal *cadence* expands and contracts toward the one tone that *sounds like home*, teasing the ear as the phrases are lengthened and shortened before finally providing a moment of rest. But in 1972, when I was a ripe thirty-five, that perception was replaced by another more fundamental one that has guided the remainder of my musical life.

A Sufi friend happened to hear a concert by a North Indian raga singer named Pandit Pran Nath, raved about him to the choir, and set up a class and a house concert for us. Hearing Pandit Pran Nath in a raga concert allowed me to listen long and deep. I was taken by mysteriously powerful, soft hands hauling me up, up into the next phase of musical comprehension. What I heard was this: When sung in the pure, ancient tuning of sensible relationships called just intonation, the *individual tones* themselves, heard against the tonic (or home note, or generating tone, or *do* of do-re-mi), did the work of the chordal structures of Western music, and did it more purely, more powerfully, with more complexity, and with far greater speed.

What deft, sensuous hands were these pulling me up and over? How could single tones against a drone have the profundity of our Bach and our Brahms, the perfume of our Chopin, the heaven of our Duruflé? The short and only answer is: Not only do single tones against a drone do that work, but they are also the *substrate* of that work. As life went on to reveal, the reason Western music theory seemed so vague and so incomplete to so many was that no one had sufficiently connected the ancient source to the modern expression. In my role as writer and theorist, I gradually appropriated that task for myself, and the result appeared in print twenty-five years later as *Harmonic Experience.* In my role as composer and pianist, however, my language was discovering its missing existential verb. The *praising sound* of the Sufi choir is one thing; internalized mastery of the source of harmony is quite another.

By 1974, at age thirty-seven, I was teaching Music Theory on the full-time faculty of Mills College. Terry Riley and Pandit Pran Nath, whom everyone called Guru-ji, were also on the faculty, teaching composition and raga respectively. I began to study privately with Guru-ji. Our lessons were brief, intense, and intimate. As I entered his living room he would be sitting full lotus and I, following his gesture, would sit on a cushion opposite. He would ask, what *rag*? I would remind him. Then he would sing brief phrases over and over, sometimes altering the notes just enough to keep me chasing. These phrases were simple and sustained at first, but as intricacies were introduced, the phrases revealed internal lives. The music continued to grow more rewarding and mysterious until my last lesson twenty-two years and hundreds of meetings later.

Sometimes Guru-ji would stop and, in Hindi-accented English, give some historical or theoretical context. He knew of my interest in pure tuning and its reconciliation with modern tuning, and would sometimes stop the music to concentrate on the tuning of a single tone. These moments were crucial for me because I had the opportunity to check my theoretical assumptions against the acuity of his ear and the ancient dictates of his lineage. He allowed me to retune the tamboura and navigate its various harmonics in order to ascertain the exact tuning of a tone. Even though he rarely allowed others such a digression from actually singing the *rag*, he knew I was up to something and, eventually, he even encouraged my inquiries. He trusted me.

In Indian music there is a term, *svara*. Superficially, that means the degree of the scale of a given tone. More deeply, *svara* refers to "the soul of the note," as Guru-ji phrased it: its precise tuning, its particular affect, its deep particularity with which, heard against a drone, it engages, shapes, and transforms the listener. The *svaras* are a rough equivalent, in Indian music, of chords and chord progressions in Western music; they impress an affect upon the open ears and psyche of the listener. The affect moves from the ear to the heart to the soul. The soul of the singer sings the soul of the music, touching, tone for tone, the soul of the listener. These are the dark rooms of Kenton's trombone section, the transmission of a Bach Kyrie, the slow movement of the Mozart Clarinet Concerto, Miles Davis playing *Sketches of Spain*, and me—yes, me—sitting there on my cushion singing and singing and soaking it in.

During our lessons, and especially after, there might be long moments of silence. Monumentally as Guru-ji's musical training and sensibility functioned in my life, these moments of sitting were, for me, the red ruby of his transmission. We sat in simple silence, but what silence! Ears and hearts were open. The energy of merging in a single space was palpable and viscous, thick with love not separate from any other being. Guru-ji would glance out the window. I would cover the tamboura with its cloth. More sitting. Then perhaps an invitation to lunch. "I made lamb stew," he might say. "You will be perfect for three days," *perfect* referring to the next three days of the digestive cycle, and he would be right.

By the mid-1980s, Guru-ji had only three formal disciples in America: La Monte Young, Terry Riley, and Shabda Kahn; he wanted no more. La Monte, Terry, and Shabda served him long hours, taking care of his quotidian needs, setting up concerts and trips to India with students, cooking for him, massaging him, and combing out his long white hair. Not me. I kept a certain distance. Eventually, however, I wanted discipleship and asked Guru-ji to relax his three-disciple rule. He knew that four meant forty. But in 1987, he did initiate me in a ceremony that involved a woven red wristband, a silver tray, one gold Krugerrand (per year), enough highest-quality linen to make a fine three-piece suit, and (don't ask) a coconut.

In 1996, a month before he died, I paid a visit to Guru-ji with a shiny new copy of *Harmonic Experience* hot off the press. The book had been cooking for thirty years. The teaching of Pandit Pran Nath was the catalyst between ancient and modern that allowed an expanded view of how we and music interact. The book is 580 pages long and weighs three-and-a-half pounds. When I arrived, Guru-ji, quite frail, was sitting upright in his dress whites on a straight back chair, his limp wrists lying on his lap. "Here at last is the book," I said to him. "It is dedicated to you." He turned up his palms and I placed the book upon them. With some effort, he raised and lowered the book slightly, then returned it to his lap. He looked up at me with wet, soulful eyes. "Oh-h-h-h-h," he said in an understanding sort of way, "strong wrists needed." Everyone laughed, even amid such sadness. I have long wanted to use his quote as a blurb, but no, the publisher would have none of it.

Devi and I arrived at Guru-ji's hospital bedside ten minutes after his heart stopped beating. He was surrounded by about twenty family members, students, and friends in various stages of grief and ascension. They said that he had looked into each one's eyes before falling back lifeless. A silver rainbow was streaming from his forehead.

There had often been, in the full swing of his life, light *around* his body. Now his light was arcing out to us and onward to the world.

Terry Riley

I deem Terry Riley one of the best, if not the best, living composer and improviser of concert music, certainly one of the most influential of his time. He also comes as close to a realized human as I've met. He is generous and gracious. The atmosphere around him smiles. Terry and I and Devi and Anne (his wife until her death in 2016) became a quartet of friends well met. At this writing, Terry lives in Japan, stays in touch with his friends around the world, and, at eighty-eight, is happy and productive. Now it's the Japanese air that is smiling.

The surface of Terry's music is mostly ostinatos and obbligatos—repeated patterns over which modal melodies careen like tobogganers. As delightful as these are, I have never been enticed to internalize (i.e., steal) them. The aspect of Terry's music that is most beguiling and mysterious to me is his ability to transition smoothly from texture to texture. The listener, entrained in a certain zone—often a layered, ornate tapestry with lilting or pulsing rhythms—becomes lost in its finery and wakes up an indeterminate amount of time later in another, equally beguiling landscape. How does he *do* that?

I think this mastery comes from years of experimentation with multi-track tape techniques, much of it live and spontaneous—his early performances show this. But then he taught himself to compose such transitions convincingly so that, for instance, the Kronos String

Terry Riley

Quartet could play them. By studying his scores I see how, like Beethoven among others, he telegraphs what is soon to become prominent by concealing it at first until, before you know it, the lesser has become the greater. You could say these are simply intricate crossfades, but it is the skill in execution that is so deeply satisfying. My own music has often sounded chunky to me—some of this, then some of that—which is common enough and quite alright, but not without surcease. Through study of Terry's music, mine has become less sectional, and in musical composition, that's a big deal.

Hamza El Din

What has been additionally instructive to me is how the layers of music do not always line up the way conventional musical layers do—often, each layer does its own thing at its own speed, causing a non-simultaneity that resolves into a lined-up simultaneity: a type of out-of-sync to in-sync polyphonic cadence. So I have learned and continue to learn from my friend and mentor.

Hamza El Din

In the early 1970s, a jet-black singer and oud player appeared in our Sufi Circle. Hamza El Din was from a Nubian village by then flooded over by the Aswan Dam. We embraced him as he embraced us. He taught us the songs and rhythmic cycles particular to his village and region. Hamza and I seemed to recognize each other at sight. We became brothers of the heart until he died over thirty years later.

Hamza was our houseguest over Thanksgiving in 1974. After the feast, Hamza and I went down to our basement studio, where he taught me to sing the Islamic call to prayer, taking care that I tuned the quarter tones convincingly. He played and sang some of the music from his home, explaining the context of each song. I was transported to his vanished village by the Nile, could sense the tribal communion there, and the everyday celebration. To return the favor, I thought to play for him an example of the best in the Western canon.

For a decade I had been learning and re-learning one of Bach's finest fugues, the five-part C-sharp minor Fugue from Book I of *The Well-Tempered Clavier*. It is a stunningly beautiful double fugue with its two subjects in full exposition and a dizzyingly intricate interplay of voices. It is difficult to play, but I had memorized and re-memorized it already several times, and for Hamza's benefit I wanted to make sure all the layers were clear, so I took special care to bring everything forward.

I played the fugue for Hamza. I finished. Silence. I turned to face him.

"What did you hear?"

Carefully finding the right words, he said, "It's as if you didn't want me to hear it."

I was struck mute. Why would he say such a thing? Just then, our four kids came tumbling downstairs to say their long goodnights. The matter was never revisited. Only after quite a few years of knowing Hamza did I recognize the probity of his critique.

Had I asked him to explain his response, he might have said something like, "You were playing to teach me, you weren't playing for Allah. If you were playing for Allah, I would have heard the music." But I didn't have to ask him. The transmission here: The intention behind the music *is* the music. Even with a magically skilled musician who plays with the utmost sincerity, the sincerity is the actual music. An ambitious virtuoso expresses ambition. Bach's C-sharp minor Fugue is as close as we can get to the voice of wholeness reflecting itself, a ray to Source. Had I allowed myself to be in touch with the core of the music as I played it, Hamza would have heard it, and we both would have been in that presence, just as his listeners invariably are when he plays and sings for them. Over our long friendship of walks and talks together, I heard him play hundreds of hours in rehearsals (we had many collaborations) and performances, and not once did he ever not play for Allah. He even practiced for Allah.

I haven't folded much of Hamza's idiosyncratic Middle Eastern style into my own voice; I've just loved his singing voice, his absorption in his playing, and its utter transparency. Millions of listeners across the globe's boundaries have loved him likewise. It is the heart of

Hamza's music, not its anatomy, that I carried with me when he was alive and have carried since. Hamza made a perfect music of place and time, both ours and not ours. He universalized the village. His art unraveled a condition of mortality. When Hamza the mortal man died in Berkeley, California, in 2006, I wrote this for his memorial service:

> Dear Hamza,
> It's your breath that will never stop—the long, slow
> breath of the Nile, the slip-slip of the waves
> Against your boat. You taught this sound,
> and the dark quiet of the bottom water,
> and the desert glare. This stillness
> remains here for us, the joy
> after the fade—after the fade
> when your music—
> when your music is still sounding.

Such have been my living teachers. I know I have been a lucky man but, not to display too false a modesty, I know I was ready for Buddy Hiles to appear, and Stan and Duke, and Viola Spolin; for Bill Russo and Easley and Murshid Lewis and Terry Riley, and Pandit Pran Nath and Hamza to appear, and many another generous souls whom I've met through jazz, theater, schools I've learned and taught in, the Sufis, the Buddhists, and the mere happenstance of walking through the calendar of my days.

Shona Music

They say when the student is ready, the teacher appears, but the teacher does not have to be a person. The teacher can be a body of work, or a living heritage, or a river of consciousness that we dive into. In 1975 I met Paul Berliner, a soulful jazz musician who, after living for years in Zimbabwe studying music with its master teachers, wrote Soul of Mbira. An mbira is a hand-held instrument condescendingly known here as a thumb piano. Through Paul's coaching, and thanks to the transcriptions in his book, I mapped the rhythmic and harmonic patterns of Zimbabwe's Shona people to the piano, which instrument I now refer to as my mbiano.

As is typical in African music, a cycle of twelve fast beats is heard in such a way that any of the twelve will serve as the starting point of the cycle. No downbeat exists, since any stroke can and does serve. The one is everywhere. Mystic alert: Sound familiar?

What makes Shona music so compelling to me is that there is also an ambiguity of harmonic narrative woven into the rhythmic ambiguity; as the rhythmic cycles manifest one way, the harmonic cycles manifest another. It is a transcendent polyphony that lets you somatize different orders of time and space as a single experience. There is nothing else on the planet like it. I set out to learn these mbira patterns on my mbiano. It took me hundreds of hours to be able to navigate the divine turbulence. In the early 1980s, the results are liberally represented on my solo albums. Now, fifty years on, my foreign, wobbly version is fully dissolved in my playing but, of course, I have only the faintest grasp of how the Shona musicians sound so natural and fluent in their own musical language. Is it perhaps that I have never lived in a Shona village surrounded by the forest that feeds us all?

Medieval Music

In the early 1990s, Devi became fascinated by pre-16th-century music, introduced me to Shira Kammen and thus to Project Ars Nova, at that time among the signature interpreters of 14th- and 15th-century music. I was flown aloft by what I heard: polyphonic passages of modal truth. The music was all pre-equal-temperament: that is, no keyboards or fretboards, and everything tuned according to pure fifths and pure thirds. The melodic beauty of the music was similar to the intricate cantillations I was learning from North Indian raga, but in this style it was being heard through the ears of an expanding and awakening Europe.

Also in the early 1990s, Devi discovered the music of Hildegard von Bingen and its primary resuscitator of this era, Barbara Thornton, co-founder with Benjamin Bagby of Sequentia, a group of singers who recorded not only the entire Hildegard oeuvre but also a monumental amount of other medieval music. Ms. Thornton's rigorous scholarship and profound insight into medieval performance guided Sequentia in the recording of sixteen albums of medieval music that had rarely, if ever, been heard by modern ears. Devi and I were both attracted to the early music scene, especially to Barbara herself, who was generous with her attention to Devi as a vocal student and to me as a composer/theorist. The music of Hildegard is monophonic: a single strand of melody sung solo or in unison against a drone that is sounding or inwardly heard. My study of her melodies, married to the Latin texts they set, revealed relationships among the *svaras* of just intonation, the inner knowing of an authentic

Marian mystic, and a once-in-a-century compositional genius. Her music has informed mine as much as any other composer's, and the influence is ongoing. Devi, through the transmission of Barbara Thornton, using the same rote method that Hildegard herself used in her abbey—"through the ear to the heart"—has become a much-trusted teacher of the Hildegard canon. I can't explicate fully here why the work of this composer has so shaped my mind and heart, only this: you can't pack any more feeling, information, and sacred illumination into a single line of text and melody than are in these tropes. Her generation, and she in particular, were the apotheosis of European monophony.

The Balkans

I had long been a devoted listener to Eastern European music, especially the music of the Bulgarian State Choir, so when Devi joined a local group devoted to singing and dancing Balkan music, their community celebrations allowed my imagination to roam the hills and villages of the Balkans. I learned to stop counting compound rhythms and instead to move with the dancers. I learned how, over the distillations of time and the passions of a thousand villages, the wisdom of monophonic melodies could grow so organically into Balkan contemporary music of homophonic chord progressions and polyphonic layers, all with its intricate melodic ornamentation intact. This music, a palpable bridge between Asian Russia and Central Europe, has given me the insight I have needed to allow Guru-ji and Bach to live as old lovers in the same musical being, namely mine.

Common Practice Period

What is called the Common Practice Period stretches from a bit before Bach to somewhat after Brahms. Common to the composers of the time is, primarily, their approach to harmony, especially cadential formulas. In a cadence, the highly affective use of chords expands and contracts the harmonic space much the way lungs expand and contract as we breathe. From before 1700 to well beyond 1900, cadences have been the very metabolism of European music. Much of this music has been my bread and butter since childhood, although I am like a child picky about his food. The French composers, for instance, have had a mysterious influence on me, but even though I have a few favorite pieces, I don't especially listen to them. Their music was well crafted to a fault, and I appreciate that, and I study their scores.

Nevertheless, I find Debussy fascinatingly boring, Ravel a little less so, Fauré hit and miss, Duruflé heavenly when he is. So why does my music always sound French? There is no fighting it—my music has a distinct French accent. I can't find the root cause. Could it possibly be because I am partly French? I've done my obeisance to Bach, Mozart, and Beethoven, so sounding French is just the way it is, perpetually perplexing. Luckily, this condition doesn't seem to want fixing.

Mozart has been a musical father since I was a boy, but truth to tell I'm beginning to know him a little too well now. With such familiarity I listen less, though I still do, now and then, shake my head in awe. His capacity to know what I want to hear next is a wisdom I honor intimately. The rightness of his narrative is my own standard, a standard more difficult to maintain in composition than in improvisation. In the spontaneity of his composition, Mozart is one trustworthy ancestor. He was also a stellar improviser—*as were most of those guys.* Young composers of today, take heed. When composition fuses with real-time wisdom, it becomes authentic. Composition and improvisation nurture one another, and when one is missing, the other longs for its mate.

I've played my share of Beethoven and think, yes, he's right at the top of the heap. By my reckoning, Beethoven was the precursor of Freud in that he presented a musical map of the unconscious. Once again musicians lead the pack. My father expressed his consternation over my desire to be a musician by saying, "Musicians are the ones who come home with bullet holes through their instruments." Beethoven was indeed fearless. I still practice the sonatas I know, and I'm always disturbing a new one. The late string quartets will always call me.

Speaking of picky, I've skipped over most of the Romantics: Mendelssohn, Schubert, Liszt, Bruckner, Mahler, even Brahms. It's not that I haven't studied, I have; it's just that I rarely choose them. Two exceptions: a small selection of Schumann and Chopin. Those two were masters of the short form; Schumann, especially, composed long pieces out of short pieces and, of course, the accompanied tune was Chopin's predominant texture. So there is special delight in their successful long forms, like Schumann's Piano Concerto and Chopin's Fourth Ballade. As many millions know, it is easy to love such pieces. As for me, I've always been attracted to people crazy enough to insist on dwelling in beauty.

Stravinsky, like Mozart, had an eerie sense of what comes next. Even in later life, when his music became ever less accessible and nourishing, the knack of correct next-ness is still there. His life contrasts with that of his contemporary, Picasso. Both were uncompromising explorers, ill content to settle long for any one voice or style no matter how hard-won. The difference? Picasso—like Beethoven most particularly among composers—kept expanding, kept changing for the better; Stravinsky contracted for the worse. This is all opinionated screed, of course, and depends largely on what of each artist I have found illuminating for my own work.

Bartók, undeniably a hero musician full of bullet holes, is a mixed bag for me. As is the case with many composers who lived through the horrors of two world wars, his music was often the music of ruination. But his early music is not that way; it seeks lovingly to perpetuate the village sensibility of Hungarian music specifically and Balkan music generally. Of all composers, he has most convincingly retained and refashioned the modal roots of his homeland. The way he has assimilated the old into the new holds my fascination, and there is always more to learn.

Do I Belong Here?

Do I listen to what most other folks listen to? Yes I do, some share of it, and I am sometimes very moved by what I hear. I love country music when it is acoustic and in tune. In the New York of the '80s, my old student and longtime friend Arthur Russell was one of the musicians who brought downtown and uptown together. I listened as though he were my teacher, that is, carefully. In the '90s, rap caught my ear mostly because it was the oppressed (gangstas) and the greedy masters (capitalism) in bed together *again*, but in a new way, as usual. Rap has developed into a mature American voice thirty years on, and it is my go-to popular music. While it has eviscerated harmony, it has brought African-American rhythm to a new level of complex, urgent joy. Rap has also elevated American English into an intrinsically, compulsively musical language. The vocal sounds of rap have worked themselves into our vernacular, praise God, but not nearly enough— never enough.

As for plain old pop, I am waiting for some kind of newness that, decade upon decade, resists appearing. It is encouraging, however, that I can no longer follow teenage talk, not because teens use words I don't understand but because they talk so fast. Rapid-cut editing became a hallmark of avant-garde films in the 1960s. By the '80s it had become a characteristic of TV advertising, on its way to becoming a generalized cultural mode, and my music often reveled in rapid splicing. The Ghost Opera album of 1971 specializes in it, and as an improviser I took a certain pride in being able to turn corners in jig time. There is a certain kind of high on the cusp between rapid stimulation and death by overdose. So it's little wonder kids talk fast. But gradually I have all but abandoned that aesthetic. As America has sped up, I've slowed down. There is the calm of the inner life. *Don't fill the space,* I tell my students, *let the space fill you.* I seek patience, and my music has gotten more open over the years. We do mellow, some of us. But that doesn't mean I can't be hypnotized by pop videos. Rapid-fire editing has become so masterful that I can say with confidence that The Pop Video is a legitimate American art form waiting to be museumified, if it hasn't been already.

Last Man Standing

I don't have to tell you this, but after seventy-five years of unrelenting foraging in the great music of the world, there has been only one composer whose method I have not been able to *get.* By *get* I mean: comprehend how a composer might have done what he did—which doesn't mean I could do it, except perhaps in maudlin imitation. The music of Johann Sebastian Bach was the apotheosis of the polyphonic style; at the same time, it was a fearless exploration at the vanguard of tonal harmony. He was, in fact, the best and last to merge polyphony and tonal harmony together into a whole musical fabric employing both at their most evolved level, and I simply could not fathom the trick. He was obviously off-the-chart smart, but there must have been some fundamental secret I did not comprehend. As far as getting it goes, Bach was the Last Man Standing. But now, at age eighty-five I've discovered the secret, yes I have, and I'm finding gleeful satisfaction in checking it out through the dozens of pieces I've learned.

Mechanical engineers, people who use materials in novel and useful ways, typically possess an idiosyncratic talent: they can visualize an object in any rotation and in many transformations—it is called mental rotation. What I have intuited is that Bach had a uniquely developed auditory version of this—one could call it audio-rotation, or audio-permutation.

As I've mentioned severally, almost all of the music of tonal harmony consists of two elemental musical processes: sequences and cadences. Sequences spin through the possibilities; cadences expand and contract, ultimately balancing the listener. Spin and balance, spin and balance, that is the game. Since the 1500s, models of sequences and cadences have been internalized by young composers until their ears and fingers are made of them. Bach had the ability, beyond all others, to hear dozens of permutations of these models at will and at once, arranging and rearranging the prescribed tones throughout the octaves rapidly and unexpectedly. My insight: It is through this *harmonic* proclivity that he was able to craft such exquisite *polyphony*.

One thinks *Bach* and so thinks *polyphony*. Not so fast. Bach was a harmonic supergenius, twirling all of its possibilities such that an abundance of polyphonic choices arose. Obviously both processes form at once in any composer, but in this case I *get*, finally, the unique capacity Bach had for instantaneously hearing harmonic permutations, and how that presented the most delicious banquet of (for him) low-hanging polyphonic fruit. For what it's worth, that's my epiphany. It's worth enough for me to not only review Bach's language in a clearer light, but also to incorporate it into my own music year by year, by grace. Of all the miracles in my life, the opportunity to study and play Bach hour upon hour is one of the most clear and present. It is continual, ambrosial transmission.

Advice for Young Composers

Here is my best advice for the up-and-coming composer from (in years remaining) a down-and-going composer. First and foremost, *learn what you love*, the rest will come. It is problematic to spend too much time learning and analyzing music you don't much care for, or even hate, and you will not learn it quickly or deeply anyway. I spent a decade learning and composing atonal music and jettisoned most of it, though not all. Sometimes atonal swatches show up in my music, and I'm glad the texture is available. On the other hand, I am very fond of mid-century jazz and studied it intensively, also for about a decade. That's where the juice went, fermented, and turned to wine. There is nowhere in my music the jazz impulse is not, so jazz has been a fine investment in terms of hours. It is also true that one's tastes change over time; what was once despised might now be embraced. There is always time to learn more when your tastes point you somewhere else. So trust your love, and learn the music that reflects your love back to you.

Second, except for learning to navigate the music you love, *there is no music you must know*, even if you are repeatedly told the opposite. *If* you want a certain thing to happen in your music and don't know how to achieve it, *then* it might be a good thing to investigate music that has in it that certain thing you want to happen. It doesn't pay to be lazy—might as well learn how to achieve the quality you are missing. But if you are not hungry, skip the meal.

Third, *music makes the person as the person makes music*. As you develop as a musician, you will develop as a mindful person, and vice versa.

Hamza and Me

So stay open to new possibilities. Become adroit at getting off the dime—that is, don't hold on to a position because it is your position. Music changes us. So my advice is to be patient about your loves; let them guide you as you guide them.

Finally, and maybe most importantly: The language of music—all of its methods of rhythm and harmony and melody and texture—are *experiences that live inside your body.* The medium of musical wisdom and its potential transmission lives inside of you as surely as blood and bone, artery and neuron, and you *play it out* into the world. The more I know about this process, the less I know. The mystery ever deepens. We are amazing beings with frustrating limits as well as capabilities that seem infinite. So how do the fruits of your probing mind and your tireless practice transform via music into something that illuminates others? Your intention has a lot to do with it, as well as serendipitous circumstances. And enough patience, and time, but enough time just might mean after—long after—you are dead. But so what? Try to live a good life and make a lot of music. The good life will surely benefit those around you, especially those who knew you. The music will be your best autobiography.

19

Teacher, Taught, and the Recognition of Wisdom

You are in a bucket brigade. There is nothing to do except receive a bucket from the left and pass it to the right. There are no conditions, no one to be recognized by name, only your arms swinging from left to right and back again, the feeling of something essential passing through your place in line.

All the musical tones I've combined, and all the written words I've strung together, I consider a kind of teaching, a transmission that palpably flows through me. My life of teaching comes in flavors: making music, writing words, teaching classes or one on one, and simply living life with living others.

Making Music

For me, the most direct way to teach is to play a live concert, either solo or with Devi singing our songs, or with my beloved trio, The Bloom, or with my piano mates Kirk Whipple or Noam Lemish, who might be playing a piece of mine too difficult for me, or sharing an improvised duet. All these versions are joyful; what I am teaching is that joy. For musicians, this is hardly uncommon. Remember how we like to see pictures of performers—Billie Holiday, Jimi Hendrix—in the ecstasy of transport, of total absorption in the flow? In this state, I do not say, *I am playing this* or *I composed this.* There is no claim to anything—the music is simply IZ for now, yes after yes after yes.

And yet: I have a strong impulse to record albums and write books because hard copies—stuff you hold in your hand—could well be around for generations after I am not. From a larger perspective, hard copies protect the dharma, but that assumes that anything I preach, or anyone else preaches, is something needing to be protected. Who can say? Art often burns bright, then dies fast. On the other hand is Bach's B Minor Mass, never performed in its entirety during his lifetime, only to be resurrected by Mendelssohn a century later. Or Beethoven's *Grosse Fugue*—rejected by musicians of his time as being unplayable and crazy besides.

Recorded music is a lavish blessing and a painful necessity of our lives. A blessing because I can listen to whatever I want whenever I want. A pain because recorded music is not real: it is the death of the real, it is against nature, a discontent of civilization.

Obviously most of us accept the absence of live transmission in order to enjoy its all-too-prevalent doppelgänger, the recording. And yet....listening to recorded music is a bit like reading a good story—you forget the reading and enter the story. Especially with high-quality technology, one learns to forget the recording and enter the music. That is the experience I want for the listeners to my thirty-odd CDs out in the world. These albums are transmission in musical form, at the core of my life, and the best teaching I can do.

I love talking about the music I have made and can often be discovered doing so whenever I am not making music. But this book is not the place for that talk. I would rather, Open-Eared Reader, that you listen to it. To give a rough sense of the musical shape of my life, my recordings, listed by category, appear in the back of this book.

Teaching

Little and big transmissions are everywhere always. In a sense, everything that happens, all experiences, all phenomena are potentially useful wisdom. Even though it may be experienced as negative ("Never trust your father"), it might be recognized later as tough love, shrewd and necessary teaching. Conversely, extra little attentions I gave to an attractive student may have seemed mutually positive at the time, but turned out to have been self-serving and negative overall. Someone dispensing high wisdom ("She belongs to all of us") may simply be acting as themselves, and not consciously in touch with any special purpose. Any kindness—a gentle "excuse me," a loving smile to a child—could lodge permanently as guidance. Likewise, a mindless offhand snarl can leave a scar.

What we have been discussing as the transmission of wisdom has morphed into the *recognition* of wisdom, both taken in and given out.

Such recognition might be lightning quick, or it could come only after chewing the inside of your cheek for a week. So how can I ever winnow out what is useful guidance? One answer goes to Intention. If I am quiet, and empty enough of my ego self, I can perceive intention (taken in or given out) operating in my own subtle body. This is not an inner dialogue, God forbid. On the part of both teacher and student, it is a pure feeling of what is transparent and what is not. When I feel compassion arising from transparency, I trust what I am teaching and learning. I am teacher and taught, seeker and sought.

One-on-one teaching has been very kind to me over the years, with or without video. In fact, few of my students are local, the rest are from everywhere. In-person classroom teaching has been relatively arduous for me—all twelve years of it—and I admire teachers who can gain a sense of trust in a classroom of students with a wide range of abilities and interests. Overall, though, it's that bucket brigade again: I have received much from my teachers, and I am teaching students whose teaching will be passed along to their students, and/or their friends, and/or their audiences of millions. I have had some truly illustrious students, many less well-known but profoundly musical ones, and many whose music has developed at a snail's pace but whose presence has been joyful. The occasional students who are drudgery to teach, I let drop themselves, as Duke taught me to do. I like occasional video seminars because I get to be charming, but I really like one-on-one teaching best. It is my living and my pleasure, too. To show folks the beauty of music, tone by chord by sequence by cadence by modulation and by the living life of a well-made composition—that is my home. I teach listeners and readers also, of course, and when I receive good feedback it is heartwarming and often instructive. But I encourage the energy to go forward, not back to me.

Harmonic Experience

Harmonic Experience, my theory book, will not fade soon. My students' students and their students will likely benefit from its pages. It is unique in that it does the obvious thing: it takes ancient musical legacies and couples them with contemporary academic teaching. The book demonstrates how the somatized resonances of singing in tune are beads on the necklaces of modal music. Furthermore, it shows that modal music, broadly considered, is the substrate of our tonal harmony with its sequences, cadences, and modulations as we use them today in our comma-inflected equal-tempered tuning. The

Me At the Piano

crux of the book is what is newly explained in it: what happens when the many tones of just intonation are reduced to the twelve tones of our equal temperament. The text organizes the ambiguities and shows how they are comprehended as a matter of musical context.

In other words, *Harmonic Experience* demonstrates how the twelve tones of equal temperament can do the work of the many more tones of just intonation by supplying a context by which the meanings of the tones are clarified. Think linguistic puns: two like-sounding words change meaning when placed in a different context. Deep understanding of that mechanism in music has been the missing theoretical link, the secret that unlocks the complexity of tonal harmony. The book supplies a lifetime of practices and musical models that internalize and enliven the fundamentals.

I was able to write *Harmonic Experience* only because Buddy Hiles, Easley Blackwood, Murshid Lewis, Pandit Pran Nath, and so many others have been my teachers. Murshid Lewis refers to a teacher as a "condenser and transformer." My understanding of that has been to frame ancient music sensibility in a way that deeply informs contemporary understanding and nurtures a greater union between the experiential and the cognitive.

Harmonic Experience, completed when I was sixty, is the summation of what I knew about musical harmony up to that time. *The Shrine Thief*, completed twenty-five years later, is a summation of what I know about *the single music of life*.

Grand Rivers, Kentucky

It was Devi's idea to find a pleasant spot somewhere in the USA where we two and her sister's family could be in the direct path of The Great American Eclipse (as it was called) of August 21, 2017—a narrow swath curling from the northwest to the southeast of the country. And find it she did: Grand Rivers, Kentucky, population 400. According to Siri, it is part of the Paducah Micropolitan Area, between the Cumberland and Tennessee Rivers, on Lake Barkley.

We stayed in a comfortable old wooden house. The owner was a smallish, wiry, high-spirited lady in her late fifties, fast-moving and secure of foot as a mountain goat. She spoke with a strange accent, partly European-ish and partly Kentucky drawl. As she scurried about the house finding the proper bedding, making sure all the lamps worked, I said I was curious as to her unusual accent—where was she from?

"I lived in Paris for a while, and I've lived here in Grand Rivers since—oh, I don't know, twenty-five years? But I was born in Hungary. We left there when I was a teenager."

So that was it!

"My mom was Hungarian," I replied. "She didn't speak English until she was five. Do you remember your Hungarian?"

"Sure." The lady climbed deftly onto a chair in the middle of the kitchen to replace a light bulb in the ceiling fixture.

"Mom forgot all her Hungarian by the time I was born," I said, "but she remembered one word she had often heard from *her* mother.

I've never been able to find out what it means. Maybe you would know it."

"Maybe," she said, tightening the new bulb.

"Mom used to say, 'A *nyaklevech* I'll give you.'"

In a single motion, the lady leapt from the chair and landed on the floor with the burned-out bulb held high above her head: a drawn sword, a scarred battle-axe. Her face was radiant, ready for any threat. Her neck straight and taut, her pelvis thrust forward, her knees turned out, left leg planted forward, right leg balanced back, she was The Matriarch defending generations of families against the oncoming hordes. Diminutive as she was, from her kitchen floor she looked down upon us all as her children.

"A blow to the neck," she cried out, ready and waiting. Then, after a moment, she broke her pose and tossed the bulb into the trash. "We used to kill chickens that way," she explained, and asked if everyone had enough blankets, it would get chilly tonight.

Everything was fine, we said, thank you very much, we really appreciate your hospitality. Later that night it did get chilly, and everyone did have enough blankets.

Grandma Theresa had six kids at her apron and, no doubt, severely threatened one or more of them with an impending *nyaklevech*. But Mom passed the phrase on to me as a mild, almost humorous warning in the one word of Hungarian she never forgot, and I gave it back to our Kentucky hostess for a blazing moment I'll never forget.

The Recognition of Wisdom

The Kentucky lady was not teaching or preaching; she was changing a light bulb and making small talk with her guests. I doubt she had any religious or spiritual agenda; what I saw was her small self and her Great Self spontaneously merged. Stuff like that happens to us all the time and we have no discernment of anything special. Students tell me that I have said this or done that and changed their lives, and I have no memory of it. These little passings-through occur all around us. *All* experience is transmission of potential wisdom. But the *recognition* of wisdom comes only through the path of refining one's own discernment.

When you decide to look for attunement in yourself, that is a step upon the path. The attunement is in the looking for attunement. When one is listening in order to sing in tune, the listening is the tuning. In this sense, a spiritual person is a person who is tuning their life.

Devi and Me

Does wisdom itself, then, disappear into the mundane, into *mere* experience? I'd say, ideally, yes. Wisdom as a static, fully evolved concept disappears. What does not disappear, but becomes ever more luminous, is one's discernment of experience, one's capacity for recognizing attunement to life's single music while one's experience is passing through it.

Patient Reader, allow one more look at the Inayat Khan quote that seems to have so caught my ear: "The whole of life in all its aspects is one single music; and the real spiritual attainment is to tune oneself to the harmony of this perfect music." These are good words for sure, but just words. They are words intended to give an instant zoom-in/zoom-out view. We know how earthly musical harmony works: a Bach chorale, a Chopin barcarolle, a Balkan song. Such is our musical experience, but it is experience that is highly conditioned (our system of music) and highly selective (the composition itself).

Now what if there were *zero* conditions, if all existence itself were included in *the harmony of this perfect music*, and by everything I mean everything all the way in to quark and all the way out to cosmos. A practice is to close your eyes and *actually* zoom in to quark and *actually* zoom out to cosmos, at least your sense of that. Now come back to your own body, your own singular, conditional, highly selective experience—take inventory, from inside your heart to the horizon of your skin. Now cosmically zoom-in/zoom-out again and then back to your fingers and toes. Does this zooming in and zooming out help clarify the ideal of attunement to the vastness of *one single, perfect music*? Can you simultaneously feel your attunement to your body, and also to IZ?

Sometimes wise words, like those few from Inayat Khan, can jump out of their skins and become part of your life.

Death

A game people play about death: What if you had only *x* amount of time to live? A year? A month? A day? Ten minutes? Ten years? Ninety years? The game makes you think about death, what dying is, what river you are stepping into. I didn't think about it until age six—the cat died; then age eight, the dog died; then age ten, Grandpa Feher died. But these were passing phenomena; they didn't have much to do with my sense of self. Increasingly, as the mourning of friends and relatives came on thicker and faster, the arrow of death began to point at me. Then, in 2021, in the middle of writing this book, several infections depleted my strength to the point that sometimes, between breaths, I could say: I'm out of life, this is what dying is. And I delayed breathing in. For. A. Long. Time. Then I breathed in. Then I got well and am presently projecting my life span into my nineties. On the other hand, maybe I'll be dead before I finish this sentence. Nope.

How 'bout...never mind. At eighty-five I'm thinking about it, wanting to be able to let go. The way I have it in my mind now: The less my death is about me and the more it is about this perfect music and my harmonic presence within it, the easier it is for me to accept the inevitable. No one knows what happens after death, but I have my position: *Poof!* is what happens. I was talking to Coleman Barks last week about this. He asked me plainly, what happens after you die, and I said, "Poof! You are completely atomized. No more pronouns for you. All that remains is the memory of you in those still alive." Unsurprisingly, he agreed. "Atomized," he repeated, "I like that word."

Your being-in-the-memory-of-others doesn't ever disappear, exactly; it morphs continuously until it is no longer identifiable. Eventually, then, the effect of your life has no name left upon it. Your life on Earth has become a part of evolution, and evolution is nameless. *This praising sound* belongs to everyone equally everywhere.

These views are not at all uncommon. I am verbalizing what many folks nod their heads in agreement to, or rephrase their own way. But if you are a person who believes in past lives, reincarnation, or some kind of heaven or hell, please do not disbelieve it. There are as many ways to live and leave this life as there are people to live and leave it.

It is the wisdom of dying that interests me more and more. While living, how can I learn to die a good death? John Cage said that the moment of death is like any other moment, it just comes at a very special place. That helps a little. Studying Zen and Hindu teachings over about sixty years helps, but with lots of mental sifting and shoulder shrugging. Getting old helps a lot. But getting just sick enough to not die has helped the most. When I felt death, I said, "Oh," and realized, and took a deep breath.

Another thing that has helped me, quite unexpectedly, is you, Alive-for-Sure Reader. Especially over the last few months, the work of writing, especially the inner work, has been so exhausting that I kept saying, "This book is killing me." Last week, I was startled to hear myself taking that literally. I grabbed my pad and wrote, "*The Shrine Thief* is killing me because as I tell my life I am losing it." And it was true: I was feeling the vicissitudes of age and mortality and supposing that when I had told my story and said my say, I would be done. But two days later, a good friend died. In my grief, I recognized that he was dead and I was alive. I wrote, "By fixing in print my past, I become empty for a future to fill. Yea!"

As the mystics never tire of reminding us, we learn to die many times before death. First, we are self. Then, we realize as Self. Then Poof! Self atomizes—the sudden leap from phenomena to infinity. Someone asked Jean Cocteau what he would take with him if he discovered his house on fire. "The fire," he replied.

Ashes at Last

It was easy. How wonderfully accommodating to the comfort of the living are the cremated ashes of the dead. They don't fly about in the air. They are so finely homogeneous that the rains will take them deep past the topsoil, past the light. On a drizzly Northern California Christmas Eve, I finally, after twenty-five years of wanting to be ready, took Dad's ashes down from their high shelf, opened the cardboard box, pierced the heavy plastic, and scraped and smoothed them spoonful by spoonful into his favorite salad bowl.

Then Devi and I rescued from the garage the cherrywood headboard that had adorned my parents' bed—I was likely conceived while it looked on—found a tree uphill from my music studio to halfway bury it against, and scattered Dad's ashes in the area of their new, moist bed. Next, we took a few small handfuls of Mom's yellow and lavender and purple potpourri petals and sprinkled them over the misted green grass and the liberated gray ash.

I felt energized, totally awake, and happy, like I felt when I discovered, two-and-a-half years previous, the meticulous demolition work of the blessed shrine thief. Free from shrines, free from ashes, free to live breath by breath, taking in IZ and giving out IZ, being born and dying as IZ in my time. Now, underneath the ashes and the scented petals, dark soil and cool rain make love.

The Catch

A book, if it is a proper book, can't go on forever, and these words are enough words for one book. I have written down a few stories, pointed to what I learned from them, and finally stopped pointing because the pointer and the point are inside. Now I am passing the pointing on to you—Oh! Good catch, Nimble Reader—so you can point until you don't anymore.

Aren't we always pointing until we are the point? When Dad's ashes were scattering onto the glistening ground, I flushed with gratitude toward that *good* man. Over and over again, all of those days and years of waiting to be ready, and then a gust, a zephyr, a sudden fullness arises. It could come from anywhere, happen any time in any form, a crying baby, a smile in the frosted pane, a sigh in the library. So, Reader of My Heart, close this book and look around. Could be any moment now.

Acknowledgments

First of all I'd like to express my gratitude to the publisher of Terra Nova Press, David Rothenberg, for his fine ear and discerning eye.

And deep thanks to the editor of *The Shrine Thief*, Evan Eisenberg, my literary hero-turned-savior, for his openhearted guidance, friendship, and wit beyond words.

Everything I have lived, spoken, composed, and written has been fashioned by the wisdom passed on to me by my teachers, students, guides, and seekers known and unknown, and for these my gratitude is a long sunset in a blazing sky.

Most of all I want to thank my wife Devi for her steadfast patience, loving heart, sweet smile and ruthless editorial pen. May *this praising sound* ring true for all.

જ

W. A. Mathieu Discography

DUET AND ENSEMBLE IMPROVISATIONS

The Ghost Opera (LP 1972; CD 1971) is my San Francisco Conservatory improvisation group, which included The Chicago Improvising Players. The wild novelty of the music is made coherent thanks to copious tape editing. One-of-a-kind, guaranteed.

Game/No Game (1999-2002). Duets with my musician life-friend, percussionist George Marsh.

This Marriage (2002). Improvised duets with Hamza El Din, Joan Jeanrenaud, Shira Kammen, George Marsh, Devi Mathieu, Terry Riley, and the olive-backed thrushes who live by our creek.

The Bloom (2010), *Full Bloom* (2018), and *Garden Being* (2024). Percussionists Jennifer Wilsey, George Marsh, and me, who, like growing things, bring trust and IZ together.

SUFI CHOIR ALBUMS

The Sufi Choir, *Cryin' for Joy*, and *Stone in the Sky* (1971-75). These albums were recorded by the first incarnation of the Sufi Choir. The first (also called "the Blue Album") has the spiritual fervor of new adventure, which it definitely was. The next two successively increase in complexity and musical assurance.

The Dance and Song Album (1973) is a collection of musical practices in the form of rounds, polyphonic chants, and other settings.

The choir dispersed after a 1976 performance run of an opera based on Tarot cards. A second incarnation gathered in 1978, sang together for four years, and made two albums.

The Kabir Album (1980) is a hidden jewel—settings of Robert Bly's versions of Kabir. *Remembrance* (1982) consists of Inayat Khan's prayers, plus adventurous ensemble improvisations.

The Best of The Sufi Choir (2002) is our bona fide hit, recommended as a first listen.

Singing the Sacred (2024) is a complete compendium of music I have composed for the greater spiritual community over a fifty-year span. Scores and explanatory notes are included, as well as several longer pieces that have been recorded but never released. The music is meant for listening, of course, and the scores allow for group practice, or the pleasures of performance.

JAZZ

I think of the mid-century big-band style as a kind of marching army gobbling up territory, a precise display of male aggression. But there is something in the swinging coherence of boys-grown-to-men who are seeking a meaningful world. Great heart is at work here, in a music made by gifted musicians who love excitement. Even the saddest parts turn to beauty, and the transcendent moments turn my body into sounding light whenever I remember what it was like to be inside of them.

Standards in Silhouette (1960), the Stan Kenton band playing my arrangements, plus the other albums from the 1960s that feature cameos of my arranging, are all out of print but searchable variously on the internet. Five of the scores from those Kenton days are for sale and still being purchased by big bands sixty years after the fact, evidence that the big band jazz tradition is still alive and well.

Double Feature (2011) is a two-disc album of Kenton music released by Tantara Records. The first disc contains tracks of the Kenton Band in live performances, including two heretofore unreleased arrangements of mine. The second disc features the Nova Band from St. Paul (directed by Mike Krikava) playing splendidly all my arrangements and compositions for Stan Kenton that the Kenton Band did *not* record.

The Jazz Music of W. A. Mathieu (2013) is a masterful re-do of my Kenton originals by the Nova Band. The album also premieres my composition *Concerto Nova*, featuring the particular abilities of each section of the Nova Band in turn.

SONG CYCLES

Say I Am You (2003), *Rumi and Strings* (2005), and *The Indian Parrot* (2006) contain dozens of Rumi's quatrains and longer poems in English versions by Coleman Barks, and sung by Devi, other soloists, and various choir configurations. These song cycles feel to me like a direct line of wisdom transmission from poet to translator to composer to singer to listener. If there were ever a way to give wings to words, flying in constellation with Rumi via Barks must be the way. My pencil knows its way across the staves, and the words turn tones into restless goddesses.

There are several other poets whose poems I have set to music:

Antiphons Across Time (2013). Medieval settings in the original Latin of Hildegard von Bingen, followed by my contemporary settings in English, sung by Devi and accompanied by Shira Kammenon on vielle, viola, and violin; I am the pianist.

If the Sun Could Sing (2013). Settings of selected poems by Mary Oliver, sung by Devi and accompanied by Shira and me. Released in a private edition.

On Cold Mountain (2010), with the Galax Quartet and contralto Karen Clark, consists of poems by Gary Snyder set to music by Fred Frith, Robert Morris, Roy Wheldon, and me. My cycle, *For All*, sets thirteen poems.

Café Hafez, Twenty-One Songs for Your Serious Entertainment (2014) contains versions of Hafez by Daniel Ladinsky, some settings of small poems by Arnold Weinstein, settings of the botanical descriptions of flowers, and also of Devi's dreams, all sung by Devi and accompanied by the composer/pianist.

In production as of this writing are settings of the love poetry of May Swenson (*The Rest of My Life*) and Robert Macfarlane's *The Lost Words*.

COMPOSITIONS FOR STRINGS

On the album *Rumi and Strings*, sandwiched between the two song cycles, is a suite for cellist Joan Jeanrenaud and violist Hank Dutt called *Harmönika*, an emotive composition they perform with utmost taste and skill.

First String Quartet (2016), performed by the Galax Quartet, and *Second String Quartet* (2022), performed by the Telegraph Quartet, are both music for the sake of music, transmission in a rarefied form. Composing them has been a high teacher for me, a musical Murshid.

Compositions for Guitar (2016) includes a *Guitar Quartet* from 1991 and, for microtonal specialist Tolgahan Cogulu, an elaborate virtuoso piece in just intonation, *Lattice Work* (2008), which he performs with flair. The score is available in lattice notation.

MULTI-TRACK COMPOSITIONS FOR PIANO

Streaming Wisdom (2003) and *Second Nature/In the Wind* (2004). Three original vinyl albums from the early 1980s have been refashioned into two CDs. They are multi-track recordings made when that technology was first commercially available, and they were enormous fun to do—half improvised, half compose-as-you-go, each piece much like painting a mural on a long wall. The music is a combination of playing with a new toy, gratitude for being surrounded by nourishing wildlife, and joy in being very much alive with Devi.

NEW AGE PIANO

Listening to Evening, Lakes and Streams, Available Light (1985-1989). At this time I was deeply in debt, paying child support, teaching my socks off, conducting a local choir, and eyeing, not without envy, New Age pianists who were making tons of money. "I can do that," thought I, supposing that such music was easy to make. Such music was indeed easy to make if you believed in it, which I did not, but I thought I could skim the wealth and almost succeeded. Eventually, however, to my credit and to the credit of New Age listeners, I failed. I did make some beautiful music for the three record labels I recorded for (all of it out of print, much of it still around today on the internet), but ultimately my New Age music was a transmission of false wisdom, adroit yet insincere. "You must never challenge the listener" is the credo of Windham Hill, for whom I recorded *Available Light*. Thus my affair with Lovely Capitalism ended in a merciful parting of the ways.

In the process of failing, however, with the accrued royalties I got myself out of debt, went to Bali with Devi for six weeks, and wrote *The Listening Book*. I don't feel especially wonderful about my New Age experience: my transmission to *myself* was and is: Don't tell half-truths. I learned a lot, though. I learned also to respect the sincerity of pop-folk musicians who play from the heart; their sincerity has become a model for me.

CONCERT PIANO COMPOSITIONS

Twenty-Four (Almost) Easy Pieces (2022). After my New Age adventure, and having set so many poems for choirs and solo singers, I finally trusted myself enough to begin composing *serious* music for my instrument. In 1986 I began by writing simple pieces, during their lessons, for students who could benefit from learning a single thing well. The pieces hinge on a single technical issue, for instance: *Don't Look Down*, or a compositional one, *Thirds/Not Thirds* (pointing out the difference between major thirds and diminished fourths). By 2004 I had composed and recorded a suite of these that become progressively more difficult, and more fun, to play. The album and the scores with instructional commentary are packaged together.

Three Compositions for Piano (2000). In the mid-1980s I began teaching a young piano virtuoso, Kirk Whipple, one of the most talented musicians I have ever taught or met. He is also a theory maven and eventually became a crucial collaborator in assembling *Harmonic Experience.* In the 1990s, Kirk fell in love with his one-and-only, Marilyn Morales, *another* virtuoso, and I wrote *A Wedding Sonata* for them. They premiered it during their marriage ceremony, alternating the three movements with their vows. The album also includes *Gourd Music,* a kind of sonata, as well as *Shiva Weather,* a wild experiment that began as a multi-track improvisation and morphed into a through-composed piece.

5:4 (2015). The collaboration with Kirk and Marilyn was so encouraging that I wrote another piece for them in five movements honoring five of my mentors: Easley Blackwood, Hamza El Din, Pandit Pran Nath, Cecil Taylor, and Terry Riley. This was my way of acknowledging how the voices of my mentors have come through my own experience and spirit. Another mentor is the 19th-century composer Robert Schumann. For Marilyn, who shares my love of Schumann, I wrote *The Poet Variations,* based on one of his well-known pieces, *The Poet Speaks.* During this period I was plumbing the depths of harmony founded on the interval of the major third, the harmonic ratio of which is 5:4, hence the title of the album. The piano playing on *5:4* is simply exquisite, joyful throughout, and perfectly in tune with the intentions of the composer.

The Magic Clavier, Book I (2015) and *Book II* (2018). The underlying premise of my harmony book, *Harmonic Experience,* is that in order to make sense of modern tonal harmony, a musician is best prepared by being able to sing and play a large vocabulary of tones against a given drone, a home note. As you attune to more and more complex modal combinations, the question arises: What are the limits of modality? As a grand pedagogical exercise, I decided to compose a piece in each of twelve keys to demonstrate this. In homage to J. S. Bach, the collection is called *The Magic Clavier Book I.* The next question I would ask as a teacher, especially as a teacher of myself, is: How would modal modulations behave as they move from key to key? This is explored in a series of seven pieces called *The Magic Clavier Book II.* Taken together, both books of *The Magic Clavier* feel like a high watermark for me, the apotheosis of my teaching and music-making. The scores, some in lattice notation, are also available.

In the early 2000s, a radically gifted student, Noam Lemish, magically appeared. He went through the gamut from eager student to virtuosic collaborator to deep friend. Noam plays both books of *The Magic Clavier* to perfection, by which I mean to perfection. These pieces are meant for listening pleasure, but they are also teaching pieces, the conscious transmission of what I have internalized from my own teachers and passed forward in my own fashion.

Seven Affections (2023). Noam and I have collaborated on a suite of pieces composed for the mere joy of composition. Noam plays my pieces, then improvises a set of "Affections" on his own.

And now to bring this list of piano compositions up to date: While writing *The Shrine Thief*, to keep myself sane, I have also composed twenty-four more "almost easy pieces," except that this collection is called *Twenty-Four Pretty Easy, Pretty Hard, and Just Plain Pretty Pieces*, and Noam Lemish will play them; that album, complete with scores, is due in 2024.

During this period I also composed a Piano Sonata for Kirk Whipple; an album including this and some of Kirk's own compositions is due in 2025.

SOLO PIANO IMPROVISATIONS

Narratives (1996-2002), *Songs of Samsara* (2009), and *Transparencies* (2018) are three albums of piano improvisations during three recent periods of my life. It is said that music is the best biography and, for the last twenty-five years or so, these albums are indeed my truth from the inside out. *Transparencies* especially is a summation of my long improvisatory history, a story beyond time.

Please visit coldmountainmusic.com for more detailed information, as well as photos and commentary.

Photo Credits

Cover: *The Shrine*, W.A. Mathieu

Preface: *Murshid Plays Krishna's Flute*, W. A. Mathieu, a still from an 8mm movie taken at Lama Foundation, 1970

Chapter 1:   *The Dew God* and *The Civil War Rifle*, Aron Mathieu

     Mom and Dad Kissing, photographer unknown

Chapter 2:   *Dad the Publisher*, Joe Monroe

     My New Argoflex, Aron Mathieu

     Dad the Friend, Rosella Mathieu

Chapter 3:   *Close Siblings, Mom and the Mail*, and *Clara at Seventy*, Aron Mathieu

     Clara at Twenty, Meins Studio, Cincinnati

     Young Milton Leaps, photographer unknown

     Old Milton Sees, W.A. Mathieu

Chapter 4:   *University of Chicago Friends*, both by W.A. Mathieu

     Dancing at Thirteen and *The Musical Knights*, photographers unknown

     Gigging at Sixteen, Richard Schaefer

     Connie and Me, Sue Mathieu Auerbach

Chapter 5:   *Stan Kenton Conducts "Whistle Walk"* and *Ann Kenton*, W.A. Mathieu

     Fourth Trumpet, photographer unknown

Chapter 6:   *Duke Ellington Listening to Playback, Los Angeles, California, 1960*, photograph by Gordon Parks; courtesy of and copyright by The Gordon Parks Foundation.

     The Duke of Ice Cream (Untitled, 1960), photograph by Gordon Parks; courtesy of and copyright by The Gordon Parks Foundation.

Chapter 7:   *Do Yourself a Favor*, W.A. Mathieu

Chapter 8:   *Webster Street Irregulars* (Carol Sills, Mona and
Dennis Cunningham, me), photographer unknown

Chapter 9:   *At the Steinway*, Todd Cazeaux

Chapter 10:   *The Emotional Symphony* (Rob Reiner, Julie Payne,
David Ogden Stiers, Howard Hesseman, Peter Bonnerz,
Carl Gottleib, Gary Goodrow, Mimi Fariña, and me at
The Committee Theater, 1973), photographer unknown

The Second City Sinfonia (me conducting Howard Alk, Mina Kolb,
Paul Sand, and Eugene Troobnick, Barbara Harris, Andrew
Duncan, and Severn Darden, 1960), Mort Shapiro

All other photographs in this chapter, W.A. Mathieu

Chapter 11:   *Holding the Note While Murshid Leads a Chant* (1968), James Baldocchi
Murshid Sam Lewis and *Conducting the Choir at Murshid's Funeral*
are stills from the film *Sunseed*, courtesy Amertat Cohn;
the cinematographer is Robert Frank

Chapter 12:   *Christmas Day: David at Six* and *David at Fifteen*, W.A. Mathieu

Horsie, Kay Hafiza Mathieu

Chapter 13:   *Rabbi Zalman Schacter-Shalomi*, W.A. Mathieu

Pir Triumphant, photographer unknown

Chapter 14:   *Pointing Out* and *Sister Sue and First Grandchild*, W.A. Mathieu

Me and Poke, photographer unknown

Chapter 15:   *Dad and Mom* and *Mom and Dad*, W.A. Mathieu

Sailor Boy is from a locket Grandmother Clara wore

Chapters 16, 17, and 18: all photos by W.A. Mathieu

Chapter 19: all photos by W.A. Mathieu except for *Me at the Piano*,
photographer unknown

William Allaudin Mathieu, a classically trained pianist, composed and arranged on the staff of the Stan Kenton Orchestra at age twenty-one and was a co-founding member of the Second City Theater at twenty-two. He studied with William Russo, Easley Blackwood, Pandit Pran Nath, and Hamza El Din and taught on the full-time faculties of the San Francisco Conservatory of Music and Mills College. A former columnist for *Downbeat* and *Piano Today*, he is the author of five books, including *The Listening Book* and *Harmonic Experience*, and has released over thirty albums comprising an astonishing range of music. Since the late 1970s he has lived surrounded by woods, pastures, deer, and birds outside of Sebastopol, California, composing, playing the piano, teaching, and being grateful breath by breath for these golden years with Devi.